From Westhoughton Methodist
Church, Bolton for help with
their New church.

THE VICTORIAN
CHRISTIAN
SOCIALISTS

Edward Norman

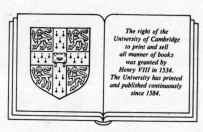

The right of the
University of Cambridge
to print and sell
all manner of books
was granted by
Henry VIII in 1534.
The University has printed
and published continuously
since 1584.

1987 .

Cambridge University Press

Cambridge
London   New York   New Rochelle
Melbourne   Sydney

Published by the Press Syndicate of the University of Cambridge
The Pitt Building, Trumpington Street, Cambridge CB2 1RP
32 East 57th Street, New York, NY 10022, USA
10 Stamford Road, Oakleigh, Melbourne 3166, Australia

First published 1987

British Library cataloguing in publication data

Norman, E.R.
The Victorian Christian Socialists.
1. Christian Socialist Movement – History
I. Title
335'.7'0941   HX51

Library of Congress cataloguing in publication data

Norman, Edward R.
The Victorian Christian Socialists.
Bibliography.
Includes index.
1. Socialism – Great Britain – History.   2. Socialism,
Christian – Great Britain – History.   I. Title.
HX243.N67 1987   335'.1   86–21550

ISBN 0 521 32515 3

VN

CONTENTS

I

INTRODUCTION

There are usually a few men and women in each generation who succeed in transcending the common assumptions or intellectual orthodoxies of their contemporaries, or who stand outside the social prejudice of their times, and achieve insights of lasting value. Sometimes, it is true, their appearance of originality is enhanced by the sacralizing tendencies of later beliefs: they are represented as more accurately anticipating the preoccupations of succeeding generations than they probably did; and sometimes, also, their novelties of view or opinion express only a single level of their understanding, while other dimensions of their outlook remain faithfully suffused with contemporaneous pieties. Both conditions have affected the Christian Socialists of Victorian England. Yet what must most impress the student of their beliefs – and largely constitutes the substance of this work – is the importance and authenticity of their social vision. Much will be pointed out to suggest that their 'Socialism' was not, by most available tests, either 'political' or 'Socialist', and that the surviving references to traditional social attitudes were thickly distributed within their thought. But for all that, the Victorian Christian Socialists produced a radical departure from the received attitudes of the Church, both in their religious and in their social contentions, and their contribution to what Frederick Denison Maurice, their greatest thinker, called the 'humanizing' of society[1] disclosed qualities of nobility and unusual discernment. Many others in their day sought the alleviation of social suffering, and most, beneath the prevailing orthodoxy of Political Economy and the strength of surviving social paternalism, looked to the application of Christian works of charity, and to the (it was hoped) elevating consequences of popular education. There was a growing sense that political society would be more effectively stabilized if its basis was reinforced from below. 'At no time within the history of our country have the working class been more talked of than at present',[2] observed two of

[1] *Politics for the People*, No. 15 (29 July 1848), 'Is there any hope for Education in England?', 246.
[2] J. M. Ludlow and Lloyd Jones, *Progress of the Working Class, 1832–1867* (London, 1867), 1.

I

the leading Christian Socialists in 1867, when one of the accessions of fresh blood to the body politic was being accomplished. The Christian Socialists, however, in their different ways and with varying degrees of consistency, went far beyond these palliatives and dared to contemplate, if not a transformed political structure, at any rate the vision of a humanity emancipated from the thrall of custom and the existing ties of social deference. The craving of the working men, Charles Kingsley noticed in 1849, was 'for some idea which shall give equal hopes, claims, and deliverances, to all mankind alike'.[3]

What follows is not a collection of essays about individual Christian Socialists; nor is it a series of abridged biographical studies. It is an attempt to describe the history of the Christian Socialists' ideas, and to show their development through the century. The emphasis on personalities, rather than a chronological account of events, is deliberate: although contemporaries came to speak of a Christian Socialist 'movement' or 'tradition' – and those words, for convenience of expression, are sometimes used in the present study – there was in fact nothing so coherent or durable. Very little agreement was reached between individuals that went much further than a rejection of existing social evils. In 1852 Maurice concluded that the 'ideas of Christian Socialism were so divergent that only confusion was created when they spoke up'.[4] Two years later John Malcolm Ludlow, the founder of the 'movement', registered a similar opinion. 'Now he understood that their many controversies had been caused by the fact that Maurice all the time had had something quite different in mind', he wrote about their understanding of Christian Socialism; 'they had meant different things by the words they used'.[5] Organizations were short-lived. In 1848 Maurice, Ludlow, Kingsley and some others, excited by the Revolution in France, fearful of the wrong priorities (as it seemed to them) of Chartism, and anxious to promote co-operative enterprises as a means of releasing at least some working men from the baneful effects of the competitive system, promoted the first 'movement'. It was marked by experiment in associationism, attempts at a popular literature, and adult education. It collapsed, in 1854, because Maurice was anxious to avoid political or economic action, and because some of the others, notably Edward Neale, distrusted the diversion of energies and resources into educational work. Co-operative enterprise had preceded the Christian Socialists – there were the experiments of Owen in the 1830s, and the Rochdale Pioneers in 1844 – and distinct Christian involvement survived the collapse of coherent Christian Socialism in 1854. Neale, Ludlow and Thomas Hughes persisted, often very effectively, in this work, and in 1869 took a leading part in the organization of the first Co-

[3] Charles Kingsley, *Alton Locke, Tailor and Poet. An Autobiography* (Oxford (World's Classics edn.), 1983), 12.
[4] Torben Christensen, *Origin and History of Christian Socialism, 1848–54* (Aarhus, 1962), 291.
[5] Ibid., 364.

operative Congress. But the co-operative movement was not, by then, in any sense an expression of 'Christian Socialism'. The next phase, indeed, like the first one, came from a group of Anglican clergymen whose primary purpose was educative and propagandist. The Guild of St Matthew, founded in 1877 and dominated by Stewart Headlam, was much more characteristically Socialist than the first phase had been, and it was, accordingly, as internally divided over issues of political doctrine, in just the same kinds of proportion, as was the secular Socialism to which it was drawn. The result was a series of defections and the eventual establishment, in 1889, of a moderate body, the Christian Social Union, which in some sense restored the social critique of the Maurician circle of the 1850s. While this development had the advantage of attracting liberals of good-will within the higher levels of the Church – men like Gore, Scott Holland and Westcott – it left those with greater attachment to more genuine Socialism with only the ailing Guild of St Matthew as the vehicle of their moral seriousness. By then, too, religious Socialism was spreading beyond the academic and Anglican places of its genesis. The *Christian Socialist* journal had begun in 1883, and in the same decade Nonconformist organizations for social radicalism first appeared. Christian Socialism developed along 'Sacramental' lines inside the Church of England, and separately in a sequence of Free Church bodies. The latter produced some of the most telling propagandist literature: the Congregationalist *Bitter Cry of Outcast London* in 1883, and William Booth's *In Darkest England* in 1890. The Christian Socialist League of 1894 was almost entirely a Nonconformist society, and it contained men who had clear commitment to collectivist Socialism. By then, also, the ideals had distributed beyond the main centres, and few large cities were without a Christian Socialist organization of some kind.[6] The Church Socialist League of 1906 was distinctly Anglican and political in flavour, but in 1912, with its conversion to Guild Socialism, the Christian Socialist spearhead of the time returned to a version of associationism. It was a discontinuous and fragmented history, with few connecting links except those provided by particular individuals. That is why it is difficult to speak of a 'movement' and why an account centred around the various social and political analyses of the leading figures has much to commend it.

The particular men chosen for this study are not a sample collection. They were the effective leaders of Christian Socialist opinion. All but one were involved in attempts at organization. By temperament, thought and achievement they were very different, and the list comprises a University professor (Maurice), a country vicar (Kingsley), a lawyer (Ludlow), a Liberal politician (Hughes), an unemployed priest (Headlam), a professional art critic (Ruskin), a

---

[6] Peter d'A. Jones, *The Christian Socialist Revival, 1877–1914. Religion, Class and Social Conscience in Late-Victorian England* (Princeton, 1968), 5.

Methodist minister (Price Hughes), and an Anglican bishop (Westcott). Some omissions require explanation. Edward Neale financed a lot of the early co-operatives and continued to work for them long after Maurice had pulled out: but he was not a Christian, and wavered between Positivist moralism and a kind of Pantheistic ethicism. Charles Gore and Henry Scott Holland were arguably better social analysts than Westcott, yet their coincidence of views, especially in the Christian Social Union, was sufficiently close to enable the least accomplished of them, nevertheless, to speak for their particular contribution: Westcott was unquestionably the one who adhered large numbers of moderate Anglicans to the cause. John Clifford was certainly a more convinced Socialist than Price Hughes, but as a representative of the Free Church involvement in Christian Socialism Hughes had, again, the great advantage of an especially articulate platform and a large following. Although the thoughts of all these men are dealt with individually, the themes are arranged to draw the reader on from one to another, and so to create a unified history, not of any 'movement' as such, but of Christian Socialist ideas. Where the conclusions of particular leaders underwent change this is indicated; in general, however, they did tend to show a remarkable consistency and it is often possible to describe their ideas without chronological qualification. One theme is so common to them all that it would be tedious to reiterate it in reference to each man. They were all critics of the application of what they took to be the main tenets of classical Political Economy. With earlier figures some attempt has been made to show how they treated this matter; in later ones, however, only variations are shown.

Previous assessments of nineteenth-century Christian Socialism have tended to depend upon the interpretation of one or two important texts in relation to the (better known) theological writings of particular men. While this has yielded much information of value, the present study is based also upon an examination of the lesser-known and occasional writings of the leaders, in the belief that their social and political ideas have a greater clarity than has sometimes been assumed, and that the relationship of their political to their theological ideas is much less straightforward than general surveys have suggested. Specialist writers on Christian Socialism have always noticed this, and even Charles Raven, who was particularly drawn in sympathy to the subject, concluded that the leaders were 'lacking in clear and constructive policy'.[7] Some observers have sought to find sophisticated variants of scientific Socialism in the writings of the Christian Socialists, or novel adaptations of utopian or co-operative ideals. These are not, in general, to be found. There has always been a recognition of how difficult it is to define exactly what 'Christian Socialism' meant to its own practitioners,[8] and this in some measure derived

---

[7] Charles E. Raven, *Christian Socialism, 1848–1854* (London, 1920), 136.
[8] Geoffrey Best, *Bishop Westcott and the Miners* (Cambridge, 1966), 2.

from the Christian Socialists' own lack of acquaintance with the Socialist thought current in their times. It would clearly be unhelpful to define Christian Socialism by exclusive reference to one only of the very incoherent collection of socialist doctrines, attitudes, and practices available in the middle and later years of the nineteenth century. But nor would there be any virtue in producing a careful analysis of Owenite, associationist, utopian, Fourierist, Fabian, collectivist or Marxist versions of socialism only to show that Christian Socialism was not particularly aware of any of them. This was true even of associationism – the co-operative ideal – to which all Christian Socialists attached themselves in some degree. Ludlow and Jules Lechevalier were well acquainted with the ideas of Buchez and Louis Blanc, and so was Charles Sully, the paid secretary of the Promoters of the Christian Socialists' Co-operatives in 1850; but the practice of co-operation, as envisaged and actually carried out by Maurice and his colleagues, was much more indebted to English pragmatic experiments in association than it was to French theory. Even the English experiences were not that familiar: it has been correctly noted by one historian of Christian Socialism that 'Maurice and his friends were only dimly aware of their existence'.[9] Throughout the 1860s, furthermore, English Socialism 'counted its support merely in terms of a few scattered individuals',[10] and even had the Christian Socialists themselves been more organized at that time, and more ideologically conscious, they would anyway have lacked a vibrant tradition of ideas to which to relate themselves.

The more their extensive writings on social issues are probed, the more it becomes clear that the social and political ideas of the Christian Socialists were derived from reformist currents of opinion within the educated classes rather than from their own theological learning. Their very starting point – the critique of competitive economic practice – was, by the 1840s, already becoming quite widespread within sections of opinion, sometimes stimulated by Carlyle's writings, and sometimes, probably more commonly, through reaction to the revelations about social misery being made by the accumulating data of the parliamentary Blue Books, and the growing seriousness with which social enquiry was treated by journalists. The one literary offering which really moved the first Christian Socialists to action, in 1849, for example, was the publication in the *Morning Chronicle* of Henry Mayhew's articles on 'London Labour and the London Poor'. In Thomas Hughes's recollection, it was these 'which startled the well-to-do classes', and made 'all fair-minded people wonder'.[11] The problem with the Christian Socialists is not really to determine

[9] P. N. Backstrom, *Christian Socialism and Co-Operation in Victorian England. Edward Vansittart Neale and the Co-operative Movement* (London, 1974), 33.

[10] Royden Harrison, *Before the Socialists. Studies in Labour and Politics, 1861–1881* (London, 1965), 2.

[11] Thomas Hughes, 'Prefatory Memoir' to the 1881 edition of Kingsley's *Alton Locke*, 7.

the source of their outrage at social evils, but in what kind of ways their response disclosed peculiarly theological or religious characteristics.

It is at least very clear that their response was religious rather than political; most historians of Christian Socialism are agreed about that. The whole point of Maurice's involvement at all was a self-conscious attempt to 'Christianize' Socialism. Of his attitude to the working classes Christensen has written: 'their economic and social conditions, often desperate, their slums with unhealthy and overcrowded dwellings, the problems at their place of work – all this does not seem to have entered his mind'. There is some exaggeration here, but Christensen's general point is true enough. Maurice, he continued, regarded the real problem as how 'to make the workers understand themselves as spiritual beings belonging to the Divine Order'.[12] The priorities of Christian Socialism, through most of its expressions, were moral and religious rather than economic or political; 'far from aspiring to independent thought', Harrison has noticed, 'they conceived their task to be the revival of Christian influence through a re-statement of Christian principles in terms relevant to contemporary social relations and problems'.[13] The later Christian Socialists, of the era of the Guild of St Matthew and the Christian Social Union, Jones concluded, paid their respects not to the economic ideas of Ludlow 'but to the religious thinking of Maurice'.[14] It was, indeed, this very emphasis upon the spiritual condition of men which made secular Socialists sceptical of the political seriousness of the Christian Socialists. Their failures, it could be supposed, were due to 'a misconception of the real economic conditions of the time, an exaggerated belief in the spirit of brotherhood, and the absence of a thorough knowledge of the market'.[15] This was a harsh judgment, but it indicates the difference of priorities. Neale said that the 'Christian' part of Christian Socialism was 'rather a something floating over it than definitely embodied in it'.[16] The implication was that the theological arguments adduced to support the Christian Socialists' schemes, and actual Socialist experiment, had no necessary connexion, and Neale himself discarded, for a time, a religious basis. Christian Socialism was essentially moral rather than political, and emphasized voluntary solutions to social ills rather than collectivist ones. The Christian Socialists, Jones concluded, were 'naive in matters of theory', they made 'no startling advance or breakthrough in the evolution of socialist thought'.[17]

If the Christian Socialists learned so little from authentic political Socialism, and gave so little to it, why then are they to be regarded – as they should be – as having made an important contribution to the evolution of social radicalism?

[12] Christensen, *Origin and History*, 345.   [13] Harrison, *Before the Socialists*, 15.
[14] Jones, *The Christian Socialist Revival*, 10.
[15] Colwyn E. Vulliamy, *Charles Kingsley and Christian Socialism* (Fabian Tract No. 174, London, 1914), 12.
[16] Backstrom, *Christian Socialism and Co-operation*, 31.
[17] Jones, *The Christian Socialist Revival*, 6.

The answer, of course, is partly that Socialism was only one of many forces making for social change in the nineteenth century – and it was a very minor force at that in England. But as far as Christian Socialism is concerned, the answer really lies in their view of humanity. Here theological learning was important, and the great prophet of the new attitudes was Maurice.[18] 'The truth is', Maurice observed, in what was surely his most famous sentiment, 'that every man is in Christ; the condemnation of every man is, that he will not own the truth'.[19] He believed this with such consistency that by early in the 1850s he had even come to dislike the word 'Christian' itself, as 'something limiting, sectarian'.[20] At times he was thought to border on the theological impropriety of universalism, and it was this, as much as his association with Socialism (and especially with Kingsley), which led to dismissal from his chair at King's College London in 1853. Maurice's 'Platonism', or rather his debt to some of the intellectual methods of the Idealists, also had some practical consequences. It induced him to suppose that the universal and spiritual Kingdom of Christ was already in existence, and that men needed only to realize the fact to be free. The implication seemed to some of his colleagues to be that political measures and social or economic transformation were not actually necessary, and Maurice's own reluctance, which at times amounted to a phobia, to take part in organizations for any purpose on the grounds that they were sectarian or partial, added to the impression that his influence inhibited action. About Maurice's doctrine of humanity, however, there were no reservations. It unified all the Christian Socialists of the century behind a liberating appraisal of the possibility for a betterment of mankind. It was the essential inspiration for social reform, and its results were felt within the Church rather than within political society. That, indeed, was the very nature of Christian Socialism: a new impetus for social reform (not Socialism) which had lasting and dynamic qualities. Maurice's theological learning provided the basis, and although it is difficult to show precise connexions between his view of humanity and all later Christian Socialism, later Christian Socialists themselves all expressed their indebtedness to Maurice's vision. In this sense the phenomenon of Christian Socialism was an example – of which both the Broad Church and the Oxford movements were others – of the liberating effects in the minds of some individuals of the rejection of Evangelicalism. It was the Evangelicals' insistence on the dead-weight of human depravity which Maurice had removed: men were no longer to be divided between the elect and the damned, for the Kingdom of Christ

[18] See Kenneth Leech, 'Stewart Headlam', in *For Christ and the People. Studies of Four Socialist Priests and Prophets of the Church of England between 1870 and 1930*, ed. Maurice Reckitt (London 1968), 138.

[19] Frederick Maurice, *The Life of Frederick Denison Maurice. Chiefly told in his own Letters* (second edn., London, 1884), I, 155.

[20] John Ludlow, *The Autobiography of a Christian Socialist*, ed. A. D. Murray (London, 1981), 116.

encompassed the whole human race, and although the reality of sin divided men from the purposes of the creation the mercy of God yet raised them to a fellowship of dignity of which society itself – existing society – was evidence. For Maurice and his disciples the evil conditions of living and labour into which competitive economic practice had allowed the large majority of their brothers to fall was not only in itself disgraceful: it was a blasphemy, a denial of the intentions of God for his creatures. To this vision Maurice added the notion that 'the spiritual is also the practical'.[21] Christianity was about the physical state of society. 'If the foundation of this kingdom were the end of all the purposes of God', he wrote, 'if it were the kingdom of God among men, the human condition of it could be no more passed over than the divine; it was as needful to prove that the ladder had its foot upon the earth, as that it had come down from heaven'.[22] What they called 'Christian Socialism' was the application of this teaching to the society of their day.

That they called themselves 'Socialists' at all requires some comment; indeed they questioned the title themselves fairly often. It earned them unnecessary execration. 'Our opponents called us Utopians and Socialists', Thomas Hughes observed, 'and we retorted that at any rate we were Christians'.[23] There was a rhetorical element in the use of the word – a deliberate association with extremism in order to demonstrate solidarity with those whom respectable opinion despised. For the same kind of reason Kingsley once called himself a Chartist. Maurice believed that the title 'Socialist' would 'commit us at once to the conflict we must engage in sooner or later with the unsocial Christians and the unChristian socialists'.[24] The truth is that not until later in the century did Christian Socialists come to regard Socialism, at least in their understanding of it, as political. Before that the concept was moral and educative, having essentially to do with generous human impulses to further the physical lot of working men and to elevate their lives through acquaintance with higher culture. What most shocked them about the revelations of working class life – in Mayhew's articles, for example – was not the low wages or the dreadful slums but the debased leisure activities of the poor. They were shocked, too, at further evidence of the extent to which rural as well as urban working-class people had 'broken with the Church'.[25]

It was their very innocence of Socialist thought which probably, in the longest perspective, made for the effectiveness of the Christian Socialists. They were not, it is true, a large body of opinion within the Church until the first two decades of the twentieth century, but their influence on behalf of religious

[21] F. D. Maurice, *The Prayer Book, Considered Especially in Reference to the Romish Systems* (London, 1849), 13.

[22] F. D. Maurice, *The Kingdom of Christ* [1838, 1842] (London, 1958 edn.), I, 252.

[23] Thomas Hughes, *Memoir of a Brother* (second edn., London, 1873), 112.

[24] Jones, *The Christian Socialist Revival*, 27.

[25] Frederick Engels, *The Condition of the Working Class in England*, ed. W. O. Henderson and W.M. Chaloner (Oxford, 1958), 303.

involvement with social reform was nevertheless considerable. Hostility attached to their Socialist identification rather than to the kind of changes they sought: there was, indeed, in their educational and moral emphases, much that echoed the traditionalist paternalism of the Tory Church of the first half of the nineteenth century. Their aim of social fellowship, also, was not dissimilar to (and in some cases was actually related to) the old Tory desire to restore the benevolent relationships of the past. Their loathing of Political Economy was not greater than that of the backwoods exponents of pre-industrial social values. The absence of a systematic political scheme within the Christian Socialists' thought placed them near to the pragmatism of English political experience; it gave their advocacy of social reform an acceptable basis. Yet it was not only hostility to their self-adopted label that got the Christian Socialists a bad name. There hung about them a certain oddity, which Hughes, who was above all things a social conformist, found particularly distressing. 'I am bound to admit', he wrote, 'that a strong vein of fanaticism and eccentricity ran through our ranks, which the marvellous patience, gentleness, and wisdom of our beloved president [Maurice] were not enough to counteract or control'.[26] Some, he pointed out, were 'vegetarians, bearded, wore wide-awake hats'; Kingsley and Ludlow went in for mesmerism; Charles Mansfield wore cloth shoes (because of a surely rather laudable reverence for animal life) and supposed himself haunted by the ghost of a seal. Hughes exaggerated the significance of all this. East, it must be remembered, in *Tom Brown's School Days*, Hughes's most celebrated literary achievement, had advised that 'a great deal depends on how a fellow cuts up at first'. If he has 'got nothing odd about him' then 'he gets on'.[27] Another condition which limited the influence of the Christian Socialists, at least until the establishment of the Church Socialist League in 1906 (with its northern orientation and leadership) was the London bias of the various organizations.[28] This seemed to reinforce the middle-class nature of the Christian Socialists, and gave their social protest, for all their efforts to the contrary, an indelible respectability.

Two events precipitated the first appearance of Christian Socialism in 1848. First, the Revolution in France seemed to show that there was no inherent hostility to religion within 'Socialism': there was no assault upon the Church by the French radicals. In the *associations ouvrières*, furthermore, the Paris working men showed that they were capable of self-help organization. Secondly, the great Chartist demonstration planned to take place at Kennington Common shocked the ruling classes: 'Chartism was gaining force every day, and rising into a huge threatening giant'.[29] It also made Kingsley, Maurice and Ludlow recognize the justice of the working men's case. They rejected the Chartists'

[26] Hughes, *Memoir of a Brother*, 114.
[27] Thomas Hughes, *Tom Brown's School Days, (by An Old Boy)* (London, [1857] 1889 edn.), 74.
[28] Raven, *Christian Socialism*, 333.
[29] Thomas Hughes, *Tom Brown at Oxford* (Cambridge, 1861), III, 113.

own solution – for being merely political – and sought, instead, to inspire them with the ideals of education and moral improvement. Chartism, in fact, contained a strong religious element; the Chartist Church movement was not an attack upon religion but an attempt to recover Christ, who was represented in popular Chartist literature as 'the first Chartist', from the existing Churches, which were seen, not incorrectly, as class institutions.[30] It was, perhaps, the last occasion in English social development when protest from below associated itself with Christianity: the Labour Church of Trevor and Wicksteed, begun in 1891, was intended as a replacement for religion. The first Christian Socialists actually failed to discern the Christian elements within Chartism; their purpose was to re-introduce the unchurched masses to the conventional Anglicanism of the times, through educational and social reforms. Chartism was a social and religious movement with a political programme. Christian Socialism was a religious and moral movement intended to make political activity unnecessary. The two never came near to a meeting point, despite the mutual exploration of opinions at the Cranbourne Tavern meetings in 1849, but at least the Christian Socialists learned something of the passion of the working-class protest. They also sensed, as did other men, the apocalyptic atmosphere of the times. Society seemed near to dissolution. Action to elevate the poor was urgently needed, or the poor would themselves destroy existing institutions. 'Expect nothing but from your own actions', Ernest Jones told the Chartists: 'God aids those who aid themselves!'[31] The Christian Socialists reached out for a solution, and found it in co-operative practice.

They had three immediate intellectual sources. Coleridge, whose influence on Maurice's thought was enormous and acknowledged, provided an organic view of the state and of society, and an Idealist theory about the relationship of Church and State. Coleridge's influence was not reserved for the Maurician circle; others in the 1830s and 1840s who contemplated the philosophical bases of English society were attracted to the Coleridgean formulations. They were at the core of Gladstone's book of 1838, *The State in its Relations with the Church*. Carlyle was the first source of the Christian Socialists' critique of competitive economic relationships and of the conditions of industrial society. The great assailant of the 'Dismal Science' of Political Economy was their first prophet. Although Carlyle did not himself contribute 'new ideas to political and social reform',[32] he successfully undermined confidence in existing reliance on the moral character of *laissez-faire* practice. 'There is a deep-lying struggle in the whole fabric of society', Carlyle declared in 1829; 'a boundless grinding collision of the New with the Old'.[33] The Christian Socialists took over the

---

[30] *Chartism and Society: An Anthology of Documents*, ed. F. C. Mather (London, 1980), 272–3.
[31] *An Anthology of Chartist Literature* (Foreign Languages Publishing House: Moscow, 1956), 357.
[32] B. E. Lippincott, *Victorian Critics of Democracy* (Minneapolis, 1938), 6.
[33] F. W. Roe, *The Social Philosophy of Carlyle and Ruskin* (Port Washington, 1921), 42.

diagnosis complete. A whole range of their interests, if not always directly derived from Carlyle, were moulded by his attitudes. Here they found scorn for the rich and sympathy for the working classes; hatred of materialism and the machinery of the industrial age; opposition to democracy and egalitarianism as destructive of the social fabric; encouragement of emigration as a social panacea; exultation of leadership by men of prophetic discernment; an enhanced rôle for the state in social and educational reform – this last was not to find uncritical acceptance among the Christian Socialists. It was Carlyle, too, who in his pamphlet *Chartism*, in 1839, had recognized that the cry of the poor for change was not the consequence of disordered priorities or false expectations but a genuine and important sign that something was radically wrong in the condition of England. The Christian Socialists inherited that vision as well. Their third major intellectual source was Thomas Arnold. He does not at first seem a likely candidate, being known, to modern readers, through the screen of interpretation provided by Arthur Penrhyn Stanley and Thomas Hughes, as merely a great headmaster and, perhaps also, as a liberal advocate of radical ecclesiastical reform. Arnold died when he was only forty-seven; Stanley produced his *Life* in 1844 and revealed (or created, according to interpretation), through Arnold's letters, a man of quite extraordinary social vision. The more the writings of the Christian Socialist leaders are examined, the more clear it becomes that Arnold's ideas had a major importance for them,[34] even though, as Westcott lamented years later, 'the true portrait of Arnold has yet to be drawn'.[35] Arnold was a liberal, impatient to see a progressive and rational arrangement of society. His objective of '*Christianizing* men's notions and feelings on political matters'[36] declared in 1831, was an obvious anticipation of Maurice's desire to 'Christianize' Socialism. His endorsement of the co-operative principle, if in a rather vague fashion and intended primarily as an ecclesiastical device, must also have inspired the Christian Socialists. 'The direct object of Christian co-operation was to bring Christ into every part of common life', Arnold wrote; 'to make human society one living body'.[37] The Christian Socialists, too, sought co-operative methods to foster social harmony. Arnold also believed, as they did, that the real evils of society were 'neither physical nor political, in the common sense of the word, but moral'.[38] In 1839, furthermore, Arnold aspired (vainly, as it turned out) to organize a society 'for drawing public attention to the state of the labouring classes'.[39] Ten years later the Christian Socialists fulfilled his desire. Above all, however, Arnold projected a

---

[34] See Eugene L. Williamson, *The Liberalism of Thomas Arnold. A Study of his Religious and Political Writings* (Alabama, 1964), 210–11.

[35] Arthur Westcott, *Life and Letters of Brooke Foss Westcott* (London, 1903), I, 288.

[36] Arthur Penrhyn Stanley, *The Life and Correspondence of Thomas Arnold, D.D.* (fifteenth edn., London, 1892), I, 258.

[37] Thomas Arnold, *Fragment on The Church* (second edn., London, 1845), 8.

[38] Ibid., 146.

[39] T. W. Bamford, *Thomas Arnold* (London, 1960), 152.

view of humanity not unlike Maurice's; his Broad Church theology accepted the value of progressive developments in society and in men. 'There is nothing so revolutionary, because there is nothing so unnatural and so convulsive to society', he wrote, 'as the strain to keep things fixed, when all the world is by the very law of its creation in eternal progress'.[40]

It is often necessary to show how much of the old world remained lodged in Christian Socialist minds. Those who detach themselves from the prejudices of their age in some things do not usually manage, or even wish, to separate themselves from all of them. 'No man, I think, will ever be of much use to his generation', Maurice wrote, 'who does not apply himself mainly to the questions which are occupying those who belong to it'.[41] Yet the areas in which the Christian Socialists pioneered new Christian perspectives were very considerable, and although it would be an exaggeration to see their influence behind all Church involvement with social questions in the later decades of the nineteenth century,[42] they nevertheless furnished a social critique which achieved increasing acceptance. As primarily concerned with the education of opinion, and through actual work of lasting importance for the adult education of the working classes,[43] the Christian Socialists made a notable contribution to the advance of education in England. They furthered the social emancipation of women. In the novels of Kingsley and Hughes their opinions reached into some of the most popular of Victorian popular literature – although it cannot be said that their journals and tracts, intended to reach the working men themselves, really did so on any significant scale. *Politics for the People*, the most important as well as the first of the Christian Socialists' attempts at a popular press, never sold more than two thousand copies. There was, anyway, resistance to this kind of product. 'Of all things they hate tracts', Mayhew noticed of the London costermongers: 'They hate them because the people leaving them never give them anything'.[44] The Christian Socialists did much to encourage co-operative economic enterprise, and in the process forged an enduring link with at least one aspect of the emergent labour movement. Through the work of Kingsley, especially, they promoted sanitary and public health reforms. Although most of them were opposed to democracy – or at least to democratic political practices until the masses had been educated to the point at which they could exercise a responsible voice in public life – the Christian Socialists plainly stimulated the idea that popular political aspirations had to be treated with respect. Above all, they were insistent on the accountability of the economic order to moral law.

[40] Stanley, *Life of Arnold*, I, 249.
[41] Maurice, *The Kingdom of Christ*, II, 359.
[42] D. O. Wagner, *The Church of England and Social Reform since 1854* (New York, 1930), 60.
[43] See J. F. C. Harrison, *A History of the Working Men's College, 1854–1954* (London, 1954).
[44] *Mayhew's London. Being Selections from 'London Labour and the London Poor' by Henry Mayhew*, ed. Peter Quennell (London, 1969), 58.

Their respect for humanity, the great Maurician legacy, infused political consciousness with a broad and serious dimension, tempered, however, by a measured realism. 'We dare not forget', Ludlow observed in *Politics for the People*, 'that the laws of politics have to be applied by the spirit of man'.[45]

[45] *Politics for the People*, No. 3 (28 May 1848), 'Politics', 33.

2

F. D. MAURICE

It was the Christian Socialist revivalists in the generation of Westcott, Scott Holland and Gore, during the 1870s and 1880s, and their successors in the 1920s, and especially Temple, who established F. D. Maurice as the great progenitor of their ideals. The attribution has endured to the present time, despite Alec Vidler's careful correctives. Maurice's Christian Socialism, Vidler wrote in 1948, was 'no more than an incidental aspect of his thought'.[1] It covered, he added on a later occasion, 'only a small segment of his interests'.[2] How Maurice came to be involved in the first place is clear: a disposition to favour social action derived from his inherent interest in the current affairs of his day – to which there were references throughout the whole body of his writings – and from some of his theological presuppositions. 'It is the great struggle of every time to realize the union of the spiritual and eternal with the manifestations of it in time', Maurice wrote to Mrs Williams Wynn[3] in the August of 1855. At a certain moment, and in the peculiarly heightened context of the radical atmosphere of the 'Hungry Forties', he thought he found one of those manifestations attainable in the ideals of Co-operative Socialism. In 1848 he felt the time had come to act. But the prospect closed up again, and by 1854 Maurice had abandoned the vision and expended his energies, instead, in the work of popular adult education. While the enthusiasm for co-operative enterprises had lasted, however, it had demonstrated with helpful clarity a feature of Maurice's general thought which was expressed in the grander strategies of his theology. This was his desire to purge the Christian world of wrong attitudes through the construction of a screen of analytical interpretation that did not itself become a theoretical system. The intellectual result was a pointing of the way; the practical result was insufficiently pure to retain Maurice's own interest, and he

---

[1] A. R. Vidler, *The Theology of F.D. Maurice* (London, 1948), 11.

[2] A. R. Vidler, *F.D. Maurice and Company. Nineteenth Century Studies* (London, 1966), 18.

[3] Frederick Maurice, *The Life of Frederick Denison Maurice. Chiefly told in his own Letters* (second edn., London, 1884), II, 264.

passed on to other things. As his contemporary Christian Socialist, Jules Lechevalier, put it: 'Mr Maurice's system is a very good one for bringing men in, but it is all door'.[4]

Between Maurice's early political radicalism and his later Christian Socialism there was no thread of continuity. The home background had been faintly radical: his sisters were admirers of Sir Francis Burdett, and Maurice's own youthful pantheon had also included Lord Brougham and Joseph Hume.[5] As a Cambridge undergraduate, and in the London Debating Society, which he attended with Sterling, his sympathies lay with the Philosophical Radicals. But there were already idiosyncrasies, for unlike most of that school, Maurice defined a strong distaste for Benthamism. It became a lasting characteristic of his political outlook. The principle of Utility, and the Greatest Happiness principle, allied with what seemed to Maurice, as to many of his contemporaries, to be the soulless mechanisms of statistical science, were completely rejected. The enormously long, and in parts autobiographical novel which Maurice published in two volumes in 1834, called *Eustace Conway*, has several hostile descriptions of the Benthamites. Theirs was a system of negative denunciation, an 'intellectual all-in-all'.[6] As Maurice's horror of systems of ideas grew, so did his opposition to Benthamism, and his later writings return, from time to time, to the assault. *The Kingdom of Christ*, in 1838, took Bentham as the archetype of those materialists who believed that 'men had no rights except those derived from civil society';[7] that Bentham envisaged a society 'upon the hypothesis that mankind is an aggregate of individual atoms'.[8] The Benthamites, he later wrote, were 'indifferent to the traditions of the past'; they were 'incredulous of anything but statistics'.[9] 'The old English belief that the life of a people is a continuous life – the dream of a nation as anything but the sum of its inhabitants at any given time', he observed, 'was also scattered to the winds'.[10] Even in his Cambridge lectures, towards the end of his life, and at a time when most men had long since given up bothering with Benthamism, Maurice returned to gnaw away again at the poisoned meat.[11] These opinions, as encountered in the 1830s, were typical enough of Tory opponents of Political Economy. But Maurice, despite his loathing of the principles of competition, was not an

---

[4] John Ludlow, *The Autobiography of a Christian Socialist*, ed. A. D. Murray (London, 1981), 116.

[5] Frederick Maurice, *Life*, I, 16, 39.

[6] [F. D. Maurice], *Eustace Conway: or, The Brother and Sister. A Novel* (London, 1834), I, 228. See also: I, 88, 250; II, 28.

[7] F. D. Maurice, *The Kingdom of Christ or Hints to a Quaker Respecting the Principles, Constitution and Ordinances of the Catholic Church* (revised edn. based on the second edn. of 1842, London, 1958), I, 195.

[8] Ibid., I, 197. For an amplification of this view, see F. D. Maurice, *Subscription No Bondage* (Oxford, 1835), 60.

[9] F. D. Maurice, *The Workman and the Franchise. Chapters from English History on the Representation and Education of the People* (London, 1866), 193.   [10] Ibid., 194.

[11] F. D. Maurice, *The Conscience. Lectures on Casuistry* (London, 1868), 45, 49, 58.

opponent of Political Economy as such. Indeed, it became central in his defence (when he was attacked for supposedly supporting Revolutionary politics in the few years after 1848) that he had upheld the new science of society. 'We are not setting at naught the principles of political economy', he then expostulated, 'but are vindicating them from a mean and dishonourable perversion of them'.[12] Kingsley sprang to Maurice's defence on precisely this ground: 'Professor Maurice has never, for the last twenty years', he wrote, 'spoken a word in disparagement of political economy, or of any who have contributed to the elucidation of its principles'. What he had done, Kingsley maintained, was to point out 'the gross injustice of identifying political economy with the idolatry of competition'.[13]

Maurice's declared separation of the principles of Political Economy from competitive economic practice was not a paradox of dazzling intellectual inventiveness. He simply performed the severance and innocently ignored the theoretical difficulties. Competition, he argued, was 'a disease';[14] a 'monstrous and anarchical condition';[15] a 'struggle to get for oneself and to prevent any one else from getting'.[16] It was 'the selfish principle'.[17] He could not tolerate, he said, 'the blasphemous thought that this destructive principle is a divine law'.[18] Yet a distinguished succession of divines had maintained just that very position, and for theoretical reasons, for the preceding half-century. Maurice's objections, like those of other critics of *laissez-faire* practice in the mid-century, were largely based upon observation of the social effects of the competitive principle, as they were thought to be, on the conditions of working-class society. He did not disapprove of capitalism itself, however. The capitalists, he argued, must be the judges of technical issues relating to the market and to the procedures of manufacture – even though the more enlightened would in time admit the workers to a greater share in the profits.[19] At the Cranbourne Tavern conferences with working men, first begun in 1849 and resumed in 1852, Maurice actively disallowed discussion of capital and labour, urging the men to direct themselves to the ethical issues of social duty and social relations.[20] Capital, he told the working men in 1850, 'could benefit those who had regarded it as an enemy'.[21] The mechanism to achieve this, of course, was association. Maurice's understanding of co-operative enterprise was essentially educative and ethical. It distinctly lacked a socialist economic base. Properly ordered co-operatives, he argued, were 'schools for learning obedience and government'.[22] An accumulating network of co-operative workshops would

[12] F. D. Maurice, *Reasons for Co-operation. A Lecture Delivered at the Office for Promoting Working Men's Associations* (London, 1851), 22.   [13] Ibid., Appended Letter, 26.

[14] F. D. Maurice, *The Lord's Prayer. Nine Sermons Preached in the Chapel of Lincoln's Inn* (third edn. revised, London, 1851), 71 (Sermon V).   [15] Maurice, *Reasons for Co-operation*, 12.

[16] F. D. Maurice, *The Reformation of Society, and How all Classes may Contribute to it* (London, 1851), 13.   [17] Ibid., 15.   [18] Ibid., 26.   [19] Frederick Maurice, *Life*, II, 48.

[20] Ibid., II, 113.   [21] Maurice, *Reasons for Co-operation*, 14.   [22] Ibid., 18.

eliminate class attrition, not by social transformation, but by good-will. The working classes themselves would become 'fellow-workers instead of rivals',[23] the 'old feeling that trades are brotherhoods' would be cultivated,[24] and property would be protected,[25] so preventing what he called 'an accursed and hateful communism'.[26] The co-operatives would also produce 'a new sense of fellowship between all classes'.[27] There would be mutual understanding between the professional and working classes.[28] Even before he had refined his commitment to the co-operative ideal, through his meeting with John Ludlow in 1846 – in *The Kingdom of Christ* in 1838, in fact – Maurice had outlined a vision of class harmony. He describes how 'each portion of the community may preserve its proper position to the rest, and may be fused together by the spiritual power which exists for each'.[29] There were to be no fundamental alterations to the structure of society, and it was precisely because he came to suspect that Ludlow and some of the other promoters of co-operation envisaged some kind of social change that Maurice withdrew from Christian Socialism in 1854 and 1855. The social classes, he believed, were mutually dependent. 'Property is holy, distinction of ranks is holy', he declared in 1848, the very year of his adhesion to Socialism.[30] 'Men cannot be merely joined together in support of certain plans', he wrote in 1848; 'They must learn to act and feel together as men'.[31]

There were, of course, obligations attached to rank, and like the old Tory churchmen he was at pains to stress their existence: they were 'primary, eternal bonds', not 'vague abstractions'.[32] But social levelling was, he supposed, positively harmful to the organic inheritance of the nation. 'Reverence for ancestry' he declared, was not emphasized enough in the progressive atmosphere of the nineteenth century: the aristocracy should abandon 'low, degrading habits' in order to fulfil their essential social rôle.[33] He repudiated the notion that Socialism implied a changed relationship between master and servant – 'a relation', he declared, 'which forms a distinct part of the order of the world'. Co-operative enterprise, he added, made this relation 'a reality and not a fiction'.[34] Towards the end of his life, in the Lectures entitled *Social Morality*, Maurice persisted, despite the social changes he had by then witnessed, in calling for a 'profounder reverence' for the ideal of service in the relationship of master and servant. Conscious, however, of the altered social climate, he added: 'I am

[23] Maurice, *The Reformation of Society*, 32.   [24] Ibid., 36.
[25] Maurice, *Reasons for Co-operation*, 13.   [26] Ibid., 19.
[27] Maurice, *The Lord's Prayer*, 67.   [28] Frederick Maurice, *Life*, II, 550.
[29] Maurice, *The Kingdom of Christ*, II, 337.   [30] Maurice, *The Lord's Prayer*, 65 (Sermon V).
[31] *Politics for the People*, No. 1 (6 May 1848), 'Fraternity', 3.
[32] Maurice, *The Lord's Prayer*, 65.
[33] F. D. Maurice, *Administrative Reform and its connexion with Working Men's Colleges. An Address* (Cambridge, 1855), 6.   [34] Maurice, *Reasons for Co-operation*, 17–18.

uttering no paradox'.[35] His social conservatism, and his adherence to the principles of Political Economy, also appeared in his opposition to trades unions.[36] Maurice regarded strike action as contemptuous of the proper authority of employers, and as giving the workers a 'dangerous sense of their own power'.[37] At the time of the engineering and iron trades strike in 1852, he advised the men to go back to work and so demonstrate their nobility of character.[38] 'Human relations', he contended, should come above the impersonal categories which those people employed who provoked disputes between capital and labour: such agents, he believed, 'destroy our English life and English constitution'.[39] The proper course was to 'Christianize' the co-operative movement, to foster social harmony and spread respect for capitalism by widening the social basis of those engaged in its transactions.

Maurice's adhesion to co-operative enterprise, in fact, demonstrated the kind of social paternalism that was widespread among the ruling classes of his day. In *The Kingdom of Christ*, he urged the clergy to call upon the wealthy inhabitants of their parishes to undertake good works for the poor – although he confessed that his own 'practical ignorance' made him unwilling to enlarge upon the subject.[40] Even in familiar and accepted exhortations to social duty, therefore, he was hesitant to advance concrete courses of action. After giving his support to associationism, he still advocated emigration overseas for the poor, as a solution to social ills: it was preferable to tinkering with the structure of society at home. Ludlow and the Christian Socialist activists were very disappointed.[41] He did eventually come to see associationism as superior to personal charity, because of the morally elevating effect that self-help action produced upon the working classes.[42] But his opposition to state intervention for social reform, in some of the most elementary areas of concern where there were respectable lobbies for action, was immovable. When, in November 1849, the other leaders of Christian Socialism tried to found a Health League, to urge government action for public health reform, Maurice's opposition forced the abandonment of the project.[43] He spoke of the hazards of collective action, and pointed to the example of the Anti-Corn Law League: 'They laid their sacrifices on the altars of the evil spirit called Public Opinion, and they have or have had their reward'.[44] Instead, he sought to inspire private philanthropic work. As a result

[35] F. D. Maurice, *Social Morality. Twenty-one Lectures Delivered in the University of Cambridge* (London, 1869), 96.

[36] Peter d'A. Jones, *The Christian Socialist Revival, 1877–1914. Religion, Class, and Social Conscience in Late-Victorian England* (Princeton, 1968), 23. On one or two occasions, however, Maurice was open to the educative side of unions: see Ludlow, *Autobiography*, 241.

[37] Frederick Maurice, *Life*, II, 48.

[38] Ibid., II, 107.   [39] Ibid., II, 114.   [40] Maurice, *The Kingdom of Christ*, II, 337.

[41] Frederick Maurice, *Life*, II, 30.   [42] Maurice, *Reasons for Co-operation*, 15.

[43] Frank M. McClain, *Maurice, Man and Moralist* (London, 1972), 65; Ludlow, *Autobiography*, 155.   [44] Frederick Maurice, *Life*, II, 25.

of local social contact between the classes, Maurice supposed, there would eventually arise a 'universal organization' which would do much better work than leagues or societies or state action.[45] He had a similar confidence in the universalizing of local enterprise, without the need for state intervention, in his policy for allotments. Like the authors of the Chartist Land Plan, he believed that small unit cultivation elicited moral virtues which fostered political independence. He said of the working class: 'Their English feelings, their domestic feelings, their power of watching natural processes, their sympathies with nature itself, are called forth when they are working upon ground attached to their homes, upon which they are not hirelings, to which they can escape from the smoke of the towns and the narrowness of the workshop'.[46] The object, he went on, was to devise means for these benefits to be 'secured upon a large scale to our civic as well as our rural population'.[47] It was, in the end, like the Chartist Land Plan itself, a reactionary programme, for it continued to assume a social and economic structure which was rapidly passing away – that there was a necessary link between landholding and political power. Maurice was attracted to the smallholding ideal partly because it coincided, anyway, with his old-fashioned Tory paternalism, and partly because it side-stepped the need for state intervention.[48] Release the traditional springs of Englishmen's virtue, he believed, and society would disclose self-correcting mechanisms.

His rural romanticism also, to some extent, explains Maurice's dislike of the Manchester Radicals. In 1852 he wrote of what he called the 'horrible catastrophe of a Manchester ascendency', which would be 'fatal to intellect, morality, and freedom, and will be more likely to move a rebellion among the working men than any Tory rule which can be conceived'.[49] To avoid the disaster he urged the Conservative government of Lord Derby to 'throw themselves into social measures'. But he plainly did not mean the advancement of collectivism. It is not clear what he meant: in these years he had already ruled out state education, state involvement with slum clearance, and state direction of economic relationships. The Manchester Radicals were the great enemies of aristocratic influence on public life; they were also the operators of the competitive system. That is why they earned Maurice's obloquy. To make things worse, they were, above all, the enemies of the Establishment of the Church, of that union of Church and State which lay at the centre of Maurice's vision of the Kingdom of Christ. Yet he did not feel that repulsion for the infrastructure of the 'steam-age mentality' which other romantics of his era did. 'I believe we are born among factories and railways, and that it is good for us

[45] Ibid., II, 27.
[46] Maurice, *The Reformation of Society*, 29.   [47] Ibid., 30.
[48] For general comment on the smallholding ideal of social reform, see G. Kitson Clark, *Churchmen and the Condition of England, 1832–1885* (London, 1973), 169.
[49] Prefatory memoir by Thomas Hughes to the 1881 edition of Charles Kingsley's *Alton Locke* (London, 1881), 51.

that we are', he said in 1854, in addressing an audience at the Working Men's College in Red Lion Square. 'I believe that they are gifts of God, and reasons for thankfulness, just as beautiful cathedrals and beautiful paintings are'.[50]

What emerges so far from Maurice's political attitudes amounts to a deep distrust for actual programmes. In 1850, indeed, he praised Kingsley's tract denouncing the sweat-shops, *Cheap Clothes and Nasty*, precisely because it lacked political content. 'I like your method of dealing with the subject', he wrote to Kingsley, 'because you do not commit yourself to any specific plan'.[51] It was Kingsley who, in the same year, defended Maurice on the ground that the Christian Socialists did not seek to 'remodel' society, that they 'had no faith in great schemes, and only invite individuals to take part in the humblest and most cautious efforts on the very smallest scale'.[52] On more than one occasion, Ludlow records Maurice as saying to him, 'I am not a builder, but one who uncovers foundations for building on'.[53] Maurice himself explicitly declared his scepticism about building. 'I fear all economics, politics, physics, are in danger of becoming Atheistic', he predicted, because they were in danger 'of making a system which shall absolutely exclude God'.[54] In *The Kingdom of Christ* he had warned that without a recognition of the true religious foundation of the social order the state would begin to assume the appearance and perform the duties of a universal spiritual society – and then there would be real 'danger to individual liberty'.[55]

Whatever Maurice's distrust of actual politics, therefore, there was in him a fundamental belief in the close and essential relationship between the religious and the political. The evils of the day derived from their separation. 'Religious men have supposed that their only business was with the world to come; political men have declared that the present world is governed on entirely different principles from that', he observed.[56] A close relationship of the religious and the political was to be realized, however, in the consciousness of the governors; through their sense of their trusteeship of those family and national identities and virtues which were the building materials, not of mere political schemes, but of the very substance of human association – of the Kingdom of Christ. Maurice condemned the 'artificial, visionary state of feeling' which left the oppression of men unattended, which did not address itself to the alleviation of social suffering.[57] But the means of overcoming evil was 'through a larger and wider sympathy in civil governors, through a deeper knowledge of the ends for which the Church exists', and, finally, 'from the manifesting of Him to whom state-rulers and Church-rulers alike owe

---

[50] F. D. Maurice, *Learning and Working* (Cambridge, 1855), 100 (Lecture IV).
[51] F. D. Maurice, *Life*, II, 32.
[52] Maurice, *Reasons for Co-operation* (Appended Letter by Kingsley), 28.
[53] Ludlow, *Autobiography*, 117.
[54] Maurice, *Life*, II, 136.   [55] Maurice, *Kingdom of Christ*, I, 207–8.
[56] *Politics for the People*, No. 1 (6 May 1848), 'Prospectus', 1.
[57] Maurice, *The Lord's Prayer*, 30 (Sermon III).

homage'.[58] This was the substance of Maurice's indebtedness to the politics of Idealism: the structure of the political fabric, like the structure of society, is to remain unaltered. It is the way men look for its identity and purpose that is to change, so that the true nature of the Kingdom may be realized.

Christian Socialism, for Maurice, was educative and ethical: it was hardly in any sense political. It certainly did not imply any party organization – Maurice's extreme distrust of parties and organizations for any purpose saw to that. Reference to his *Reasons for Not Joining a Party in the Church*, a tract of 1841, will reveal his conviction that all parties, for whatever laudable purpose, degenerate into agencies 'to rob other men of their principles'.[59] Parties were by nature exclusive: they each emphasized a particular aspect of truth whilst denying the reality of the whole. The result was a species of sectarianism – 'a disease of the heart'.[60] Maurice readily translated the diagnosis to the political sphere. 'How the dread of societies, clubs, leagues, has grown up in me', he wrote to Ludlow in November 1849.[61] 'While they belong to parties', Maurice wrote of politics in 1848, 'they have no connexion with what is human and universal'.[62] The 'mutual reverence' of the classes, he also noted, 'it is the object of our party writers, religious and political, to destroy'.[63] He opposed the development of any sort of centralized administration of the co-operatives because of this same horror of organizations.[64] The ideological equivalent of this feeling was Maurice's rejection of what he called 'systems'; the intellectual and theoretical constructions made to provide universal explanations, in political as in religious phenomena. *The Kingdom of Christ* was itself, as Thomas Hughes pointed out, an attack on 'attempts to squeeze Christianity into any system',[65] and the *Kingdom* actually closes with an exhortation to the readers not to form a school 'to oppose all schools'.[66] Intellectual systems, he wrote in the book, were a 'miserable, partial, human substitute' for the divine order.[67] They were particularly inappropriate to the English, for whom 'system-building' was 'not natural'.[68] There are other appraisals in Maurice's writings of the empirical and pragmatic style of English political discourse; an amplification of the observation, made in *The Kingdom of Christ*, that the English were 'by constitution', as he put it, 'politicians and not systematizers'.[69] Many years later,

[58] Ibid., 32 (Sermon III).
[59] F. G. Maurice, *Reasons for Not Joining a Party in the Church. A Letter to the Ven. Samuel Wilberforce* (London, 1841), 22. See also Maurice's 'Explanatory Letter' of 1870 about this tract, in *Life*, I, 235–6.
[60] F. D. Maurice, *National Education* (London, 1853), 8.
[61] Frederick Maurice, *Life*, II, 23.
[62] *Politics for the People*, No. 1 (6 May 1848), 'Prospectus', 1.
[63] Ibid., No. 9 (24 June 1848), 'A Dialogue in the Penny Boats', No. III, 157.
[64] Ludlow, *Autobiography*, 162.
[65] F. D. Maurice, *The Friendship of Books and Other Lectures* (London, 1880), *Preface* by Thomas Hughes, xiv.
[66] Maurice, *The Kingdom of Christ*, II, 346–7.
[67] Ibid., II, 328.   [68] Ibid., II, 329.   [69] Ibid., II, 331.

in 1868, he wrote: 'It seems to me that Englishmen are more likely to be led back into faith by the political road than by the German metaphysical road';[70] but by 'politics', in this sort of context, he did not mean parties, or even the conduct and theoretical basis of public life. He meant only the pursuit of existing public order and the eschewing of theoretical explanations of the political process: it was a worldly counterpart to his religious belief that the Kingdom of Christ was already in existence, and not something for which a theoretical blueprint or an actual transformation of society was necessary.

Comparable to his distrust of parties and systems was Maurice's loathing of public opinion. This characteristic, too, limited his capacity for political involvement. According to his son and biographer, General Sir John Frederick Maurice, he was the antagonist of 'the great idolatry of the day, the worship of Public Opinion'.[71] Maurice himself wrote: 'it is the worship of opinions which is enslaving both theology and science'.[72] There were, for him, direct political implications. 'The sovereignty of the people, in any sense or form', he wrote in December 1848 – just nine months after the start of the Christian Socialist movement – was to be repudiated 'as at once the silliest and most blasphemous of all contradictions'.[73] The monarch and the aristocracy, he maintained, were 'intended to rule and guide the land' since they held their authority from God.[74] That was written in 1852; in the same year he suppressed a pamphlet by Lord Goderich, called *Duty of the Age* – and which had already been printed by the Christian Socialists – precisely because it advocated democracy.[75] Like most mid-nineteenth century liberals, Maurice believed that admission to political society should be related to educational achievement. Thus he was in favour of teaching political history in the working men's colleges, for it prepared them 'to learn the lessons of the past' and so eventually to become qualified for a public voice in the affairs of the present.[76] He also believed that 'politics must be taught in schools'. It was to be instruction in 'politics which shall not be merely against popular systems, but which shall explain the meaning and secret of their power'.[77]

The whole tenor and argument of his 1866 book, *The Workman and the Franchise*, spells out Maurice's rejection of popular sovereignty in the circumstances not only of the day, but of all conceivable days. 'So help me

[70] Frederick Maurice, *Life*, II, 579.

[71] Ibid., II, 70.

[72] F. D. Maurice, 'The Mote and the Beam: A Clergyman's Lessons from the Present Panic', in *Tracts for Priests and People* (London, 1860–1), I, 15.

[73] Frederick Maurice, *Life*, I, 485.   [74] Ibid.. II. 129.

[75] Ibid., II, 126. See also, Claude Jenkins, *Frederick Denison Maurice and the New Reformation* (London, 1938), 55; and McClain, *Maurice, Man and Moralist*, 66.

[76] Maurice, *Learning and Working*, 138 (Lecture V).

[77] *Politics for the People*, No. 12 (8 July 1848), 'Is there any hope for Education in England?', No. I, 196.

God', he wrote there – against the background of the franchise reform proposals then before Parliament – 'I do not mean to follow the will of a majority, I hope never to follow it, always to set it at nought'. The popular choice, he added, would always be 'something profoundly low and swinish'.[78] He railed against 'the miserable theory of numbers',[79] 'the slavish reverence for numbers',[80] and the opinions of 'a mere multitude'.[81] The people were not just an aggregate. Looked at atomistically, as the reformers tended to do, they lacked a sense of their continuity with the past of the nation. They lacked an organic sense. They lacked religious unifying wholeness. 'All faith in a living God had', he told the working men, 'been bound up with faith in this national freedom'.[82] It was a freedom which was not guaranteed by numbers, but by individual conscious-ness of the organic life of the people as a people.[83] Maurice's doctrine of nationality became a repudiation of popular sovereignty. The nation, he wrote the year following these reflexions on democracy, was not 'a secular thing'.[84] This theme descended directly from the essential thesis of The Kingdom of Christ, that the nation, like the family, was a basic unit of the spiritual and universal society in which all men exist. The work of 'social reformation' in England, he said in 1851, as he opened a new co-operative workshop in Southampton, would come when working men themselves 'became a living, organic part of our English nation'. The 'masses', in contrast, he said, 'form a rude chaos'.[85] The virtue of association and self-help, the whole point of the co-operatives, in fact, was to transform this 'wild floating mass of atoms';[86] it was to cultivate an atmosphere in which the participants on a mass scale would 'feel that they have a common life and a common object'. Then men will recover their 'manliness',[87] and society will recover that organic identity and those personal freedoms which Maurice, in classic nineteenth-century radical style, supposed were a feature of Saxon England – when institutions had been 'for freedom' and when the family had become 'the root of the state'.[88] In considering the whole matter of the franchise, Maurice wrote, he was guided by his concern for 'the moral, as superior to the material interests of the community'.[89] The working classes should certainly be admitted to the Constitution, but only when they had been educated into the means of making proper choice. Needless to say, Maurice endorsed the contemporary schemes for 'fancy' franchises, of giving electoral weight according to a graded scale of educational attainment, and of excluding

---

[78] F. D. Maurice, The Workman and the Franchise, Chapters from English History on the Representation and Education of the People (London, 1866), 203.

[79] Ibid., 207.   [80] Ibid., 211.   [81] Ibid., 217.   [82] Ibid., 174.   [83] Ibid., 204.

[84] F. D. Maurice, The Ground and Object of Hope for Mankind (London, 1868), 45.

[85] Maurice, The Reformation of Society, 35.

[86] Ibid., 36.   [87] Ibid., 37.

[88] Maurice, The Workman and the Franchise, 22.

[89] F. D. Maurice, The Suffrage, Considered in Reference to the Working Class, and to the Professional Class, in Macmillan's Magazine, II, No. 8 (June 1860), 97.

the uneducated altogether. Voters must be 'independent and intelligent'.[90] It was a cry very much at the centre of the general debate about the Second Reform Bill. The whole issue of the suffrage, however, did not, for Maurice, 'touch the core of what is wrong among us'. Neither universal nor household suffrage 'can remove the evils, moral and political, under which England groans'.[91]

The more the assessments made of Maurice's thought by his disciples in the Christian Socialist movement are examined, the more it becomes clear that what they valued in him was not a social or political principle but his sympathy for humanity. They were attracted by his sense that all of mankind constitutes the living material of the spiritual and universal kingdom, and that social behaviour which recognized Christ in a brother creature was a form of reverence to God himself. Maurice's Platonic method was another important legacy – at least in the way in which it emphasized the unitary nature of truth, including social truth. One of the reasons why Maurice and the Christian Socialists were reluctant to endorse particular social panaceas, or single political parties or ideas, was the paramount necessity of recognizing the need for the reconciliation of opposites. Men's perception of social wrong, like their grasp of other phenomena of human life, was linear and partial: the way forward lay not in the forceful imposition of one dimension, as political parties sought to do, in Maurice's judgment, but in the progressive education of men until they recognized the universal brotherhood of human imperfection. Then would the partial understandings find some centre, though each would continue to develop his own contribution to the rich mixture of separate purchases upon social reality. To elevate the part as if it was the whole was, for Maurice, the most common and the most heinous mistake of contemporary politics.

To this view of the necessary totality which grows out of the partial appropriations of social truth, Maurice added an organic doctrine of the state taken directly from Coleridge. Because society was an organism – the supposition which had inspired Maurice's critique of the Benthamites – and because the State had a moral identity, it followed that the universal and spiritual kingdom was resident within the institutions whose development described the growing consciousness of a people. The Kingdom was not reserved for some ethereal existence: it was to be recognized in the social arrangements of men. Hence, again, the enormous moral seriousness with which Maurice approached the question of social relationships. It accounts, also, for his concern with the structures of government. The nature of God himself and his knowable will for mankind, was disclosed, for those with eyes to see, in the self-consciousness of peoples, in their national development. God was, in this crucial sense, immanent in the world: the material habitations of social

[90] Ibid., 96.
[91] *Politics for the People*, No. 6 (3 June 1848), 'Mr. Lovatt's Address to the Middle Classes', 110.

principles – social structures and institutions – were, for all their partiality and imperfection, fragments of the divine purpose. To treat collected human wisdom and experience, as embodied in social structures, as if they were to be determined by mere majorities, or by atomistic tests of social utility, was, for Maurice, a kind of blasphemy. Perhaps no English writer of the nineteenth century gave such an ultimate pedigree to social arrangements. The consequent Coleridgean application was the union of Church and State, about which Maurice wrote a great deal, and principally in *The Kingdom of Christ*. Another result, which Maurice developed in the 1860s, was an exaltation of military virtues as a necessary defence of the organic centre of the nation state. There were obvious affinities here with a more general drift of European opinion, and Maurice was, indeed, a declared admirer of Bismarck.[92] 'Every Nation should be an armed Nation', Maurice told his Cambridge students in 1869, 'because its own soil, its own language, its own laws, its own government are given to it, and are beyond all measure precious to it'. He added: 'Courage or Valour has been deemed in old times the characteristic of a man', and nothing had changed – 'I cannot hold that opinion to be obsolete'.[93]

Opposition to democracy, extreme distrust of collective action for any social purpose apart from local co-operative enterprise, and antipathy to enemies of the established governing classes: these were not the sort of attitudes which easily combined with Socialism, 'Christian' or otherwise. How did Maurice get involved with the events of 1848 to 1854? The answer is that he was moved by the condition of the urban working classes as disclosed by two episodes. First was the 1848 Revolution in France, which occurred at a time when Maurice was anyway – as seen in his sermons on *The Lord's Prayer*, delivered between February and April of that year – concerning himself with the need for more charitable work to be undertaken by the privileged classes. He had, since early in the 1840s, been interesting himself with social issues, and had begun to send young men into the slums of a parish adjacent to Lincoln's Inn. It was Ludlow whose first-hand accounts of the French Co-operative experiments, and of the Revolution itself, inspired Maurice with the idea of 'Christianizing' Socialism. 'God himself is speaking to us', Maurice declared on learning of the events in Paris.[94] In April, the Chartist convention at Kennington Common persuaded him of the urgency of the task of educating the working classes before they became a real revolutionary threat to order and property. But he had come to see that the wretched material conditions of life and work, which gave birth to Chartism, were unjust and required some sort of attention. The second decisive event was the publication during 1849 of the articles on 'London Labour and the London Poor' by Henry Mayhew, in the *Morning Chronicle*. These, now well-established classic descriptions of working-class life in the metropolis, appeared

[92] McClain, *Maurice, Man and Moralist*, 119.   [93] Maurice, *Social Morality*, 222–3.
[94] Frederick Maurice, *Life*, I, 458.

while Maurice was holding his conferences with working men, and while the cholera epidemic was simultaneously at its height. To the articles Maurice attributed 'the full and clear discovery that a system which is undermining the honesty of the seller, which is promoting and promoted by the dishonesty of the consumer, is also a main cause of the demoralization and misery of the producer'. Maurice particularly liked the fact, as he supposed it to be, that the revelations came 'from a perfectly impartial witness who is entirely indifferent to theories'.[95] Mayhew had used the London costermongers as the centre of his descriptions, and Maurice, who was largely unacquainted with industrial society, even after a tour of the Lancashire manufacturing districts in 1851, seems to have taken the small-trade world of the costers as typical. Co-operative workshops were the appropriate means of raising such a class to moral respectability. Mayhew's writings had also persuaded Maurice of the need for more suitable recreational activities for the poor.[96] They had convinced him of the need for some sort of new departure. 'Given a moral state, and it seems to me the *Morning Chronicle* revelations are rather in favour of the conclusion that the old position of master and labourer might be a healthy one', Maurice wrote. But his new realization was that the old condition had been replaced by 'an accursed new one' – the 'devilish theory' of competition, with its consequent depression of working-class life.[97] In *The Kingdom of Christ* Maurice had castigated the Church in 'our awful manufacturing districts' for failing to see 'that it existed to testify that man as man is the object of his Creator's sympathy'.[98] The whole body of Maurice's theological writing could be cited to show that his views of humanity, so full of respect and universal compassion, impelled an urgent desire to alleviate suffering. 'Christ is in every man', he reflected in a famous passage: it was a sentiment that offended those for whom it implied a kind of universalism. But, Maurice later affirmed, 'I am more than ever convinced that it was necessary' to make the declaration.[99] Maurice's sense of human need, of the presence of Christ in all men, and of the reality of Christ's Kingdom as the end and purpose of human association, was the noble and sacrificial vision which underlay his involvement with Christian Socialism. 'To speak of these questions calmly', he said of current agitations in 1848, 'is a duty; to speak of them coldly is a sin; for they cannot be separated from the condition of men who are suffering intensely'.[100] In the prescient and resonant words of Montagu Butler, spoken at the time of Maurice's death in 1872: 'Wherever rich and poor are brought closer together, wherever men learn to think more

---

[95] Maurice, *Reasons for Co-operation*, 11.
[96] Maurice, *Learning and Working*, 160 (Lecture VI).
[97] Frederick Maurice, *Life*, II, 32.
[98] Maurice, *The Kingdom of Christ*, II, 325.
[99] Frederick Maurice, *Life*, II, 168. The original quotation came from his *Theological Essays* (1853), the work that precipitated his difficulties with the authorities of King's College, London.
[100] *Politics for the People*, No. 1 (6 May 1848), 'Prospectus', 1.

worthily of God in Christ, the great work that he has laboured at for nearly fifty years shall be spoken of as a memorial of him'.[101]

That great work, however, was not systematically pursued. Worried by the political radicalism of some of his associates, disillusioned by a series of dishonest appropriations of funds by some of the working men who became officials of the Co-operatives, and nagged by his wife, Maurice had, by the end of 1854, more or less withdrawn from the co-operative movement, and he concentrated, instead, on the work of adult education. Ludlow, and the other co-operative leaders, believed that it was this which effectively undermined the whole enterprise. Maurice, Ludlow recorded, seemed unaware of 'the crushing nature of the blow' his defection administered.[102] Maurice, as Vidler accurately observed, was 'a man of thought rather than a man of action'.[103] It was inevitable that he would depart from any enterprise that became truly activist. An examination of his understanding of what 'Christian Socialism' actually implied will show how slight was the prospect that he could ever have remained within it for long.

Maurice's theological writings are innocent of political implications. *The Kingdom of Christ*, which some later interpreters regarded as an ideological blueprint for his later adoption of Socialist attitudes, contains no social or political schemes. The critiques of St Simon[104] and of Owen[105] are intended to illustrate the evil effects of arranging social reality around one-dimensional theoretical propositions. Maurice was, anyway, broadly hostile to the ideas of both men because of their disregard of transcendence. The high doctrine of man laid out in *The Kingdom of Christ* certainly encouraged Maurice in his desire to see the emancipation of the working classes from the thrall of material deprivation. But that did not especially distinguish him from the Tory paternalists whose comparable sense of the dignity of humanity had inspired numerous philanthropic exercises and the awakening of a public conscience on the question of 'Spiritual Destitution' in the first three decades of the nineteenth century. In *The Kingdom of Christ* Maurice explicitly blames the rise of Socialism and Chartism on the failure of the Church to speak of anything but the expiation of individual sin. What he recommended, as the means of eliminating the situation in which Socialism achieved an appeal, was 'active Charity' – not a structured or political rearrangement of society.[106] This was indeed central to his purpose of 'Christianizing Socialism': 'We wish to begin on a small scale, but also to explain what we mean by a series of tracts', he wrote in 1850, in outlining the idea behind the publication of the *Tracts on Christian Socialism*.[107] The 'small scale' referred to was the co-operative workshops; the

101 Frederick Maurice, *Life*, II, 648.
102 Ludlow, *Autobiography*, 260.
103 Vidler, *F.D. Maurice and Company*, 177.
104 Maurice, *The Kingdom of Christ*, I, 197–8.
105 Ibid., I, 199–200.
106 Ibid., II, 336.
107 Frederick Maurice, *Life*, II, 36.

tracts were explanatory literature intended to show the working classes that their hope lay in associationism and education – not in politics. Maurice's contributions to that other series of publications, the more famous *Politics for the People*, were also bereft of political matter. 'The greatest anomaly about the paper', Ludlow later observed, 'was that, springing as it did out of the conviction that Socialism must be Christianized, it never dealt with the subject of Socialism'.[108] For Ludlow's own paper, *Christian Socialist*, Maurice wrote very little.[109] It was distinctly Socialist in flavour.

Maurice's actual understanding of Socialism was probably rather imprecise. He also gave a peculiar definition to 'Communism', which he seems to have associated almost exclusively with the monastic life.[110] Applied to contemporary society, the limited economic egalitarianism of the medieval cloister was, he imagined, re-created in co-operative enterprises. Hence his reference to 'the duty of helping all I can to give the Communist principle a fair trial'.[111] But there was no question of applying the same values to the state or to the political area in general. The purpose of the state, Maurice argued, was to preserve individual rights and property. He approved some limited state action in social issues – explicitly endorsing legislation to protect factory children – but in such instances it had to be acknowledged that the state was 'going out of its own sphere'.[112] He also held that although the title to property was sacred, it was held as 'dependent upon certain services'.[113] These were conceived traditionally, however. 'We are not opposed to the old English doctrine of property', he wrote, 'but are asserting it'.[114] Property, he wrote in *The Commandments, Considered as Instruments of National Reformation* (1866) was protected by the injunction 'Thou shalt not steal': it was 'holy, established by the Most High'.[115] It was the Church, in its proper condition, which embodied the principle of Communism, he believed, and the State which protected the principle of property. The union of Church and State, 'of bodies existing for opposite ends', held the principles in balance. 'A Church without a State must proclaim Proudhon's doctrine if it is consistent with itself', Maurice wrote; 'a State without a Church is merely supported by Jew brokers and must ultimately become only a stock exchange'.[116]

To the extent that the Christian Socialism of the late 1840s had a genuinely socialist content, it came largely from the French thinkers whose ideas were transmitted through Lechevalier and Ludlow. Maurice was fully aware of their ideas, but not, evidently, in any real depth. This was earliest revealed in his knowledge of Lamennais. In 1836 Maurice read *Affaires de Rome*, Lamennais's

[108] Ludlow, *Autobiography*, 130.   [109] Frederick Maurice, *Life*, II, 55.

[110] Ibid., II, 7.   [111] Ibid., II, 8.

[112] Ibid., II, 8.   [113] Maurice, *Reasons for Co-operation*, 21.

[114] Ibid., 22. See also Maurice's *The Reformation of Society*, 34.

[115] F. D. Maurice, *The Commandments, Considered as Instruments of National Reformation* (London, 1866), 117.   [116] Frederick Maurice, *Life*, II, 9.

account of his appeal to the Holy See over the question of his orthodoxy. He was 'impressed and disturbed' by the book.[117] Yet it was what the Lamennais episode revealed to him about the nature of Catholicism, not the author's social radicalism, that attracted his attention. In the *Paroles d'un Croyant*, of 1834, Lamennais had unfolded an almost apocalyptic design of the proximity of the Kingdom of God; he had elevated humanity and sympathized with the sufferings of the people; and he had depicted the solution of social ills as resident in economic self-help. In his *Le Livre du Peuple* (1837), he had argued for co-operative enterprise.[118] These are all ideas to be found in Maurice's thinking in the 1840s. What is remarkable is that Maurice seemed unaware of the intellectual affinity with at least these aspects in the development of Lamennais's thought.[119] Of the French Socialists proper, it is equally difficult to show any real influence. 'I do not know enough of Fourier to be aware what his affinity between him and us is', Maurice wrote in 1842.[120] Ludlow, however, described himself as 'more of a Fourierist than anything else'.[121] In 1850, after the launch of the co-operatives, Maurice was still able to remark that he 'knew nothing of the French systems, very little indeed of the French Associations',[122] although he did confess that the French had produced 'the ablest books upon the subject' because 'they have immeasurably greater talents for systematizing than we have'.[123] When it is recalled how little taste Maurice had for 'systems', it will be seen why he left the French authors alone. In 1855 he excluded Talandier and Jourdain, two of the leaders of French Socialism, from participating in the Working Men's College. He could not allow, he said, their 'mad and wicked doctrines'.[124] Maurice appeared to owe no intellectual debts to Buchez or to Louis Blanc, doubtless because both intended the eventual displacement of capitalism, and both had evolved critiques of society which gave prominence to the existence of a class struggle.

In seeking to judge Maurice's understanding of Christian Socialism it is also essential to recognize the incompatibility, as he saw it, of the Kingdom of Christ with radical worldly transformation. It has long been realized that the apocalyptic, messianic strain in Maurice's writings, which he owed to the early influence of Stephenson of Lympsham, was a deep and at times decisive one.[125] Christ, Maurice came to believe, was the Redeemer of the world as it is: he is seen in actual historical events: the Millenarians, he argued, have shifted our location of heaven to the present.[126] 'We cannot reverence heaven or know

---

[117] W. G. Roe, *Lamennais and England. The Reception of Lamennais's Religious Ideas in England in the Nineteenth Century* (Oxford, 1966), 38. [118] Ibid., 13, 17, 19. [119] Ibid., 156.
[120] Frederick Maurice, *Life*, I, 334. [121] Ludlow, *Autobiography*, 153.
[122] Maurice, *Reasons for Co-operation*, 6. [123] Ibid., 5.
[124] Frederick Maurice, *Life*, II, 268.
[125] F. D. Maurice, *Letters on the Apocalypse, or Book of the Revelation of St. John the Divine* (second edn., London, 1885), vii. See also McClain, *Maurice, Man and Moralist*, 3, 54–6.
[126] Frederick Maurice, *Life*, II, 243.

what it is', Maurice observed, 'if we do not reverence the earth on which Christ walked and which he redeemed'.[127] The Kingdom is a present reality, 'which men have been trying to set at nought and deny, but under which they have been living notwithstanding'.[128] Maurice's purpose was to show that 'society is not to be made anew by arrangements of ours, but is to be regenerated by finding the law and ground of its order and harmony, the only secret of its existence, in God'.[129] Society and humanity are divine realities, '*as they stand*, not as they may become'.[130] The 'Spiritual and universal society' is not 'the beginning of a new order and constitution of things'.[131] Even in his Lincoln's Inn sermons of 1848, entitled *The Lord's Prayer*, which were among Maurice's more radical offerings, the Kingdom was described as a present reality which knit society together, and not as a plan for future reform on earth or future bliss in heaven. 'We are bound to affirm', he said in the ninth address, 'that a Fatherly Kingdom is established in the world; that to be members of it is our highest title, and that the beggars of the land share it with us; that in it the chief of all is the servant of all; that under Him all may in their respective spheres reign according to this law; that all ranks and orders stand upon this tenure, and are preserved or overturned by their honour or contempt for it . . .'.[132] But Ludlow, Neale and most of the other leaders of the Christian Socialist movement did not want 'all ranks and orders' preserved at all. They had come to believe that existing society had to be reconstructed as the essential prerequisite for the realization of Christ's Kingdom. They envisaged a blueprint for a new order. Real political power would eventually need to be employed: the co-operatives were merely an educative preliminary. Maurice's doctrine of an existing kingdom, which they inherited who adjusted their social consciousness and heightened their religious convictions, was of a quite different – and deeply conservative – genus.

Charles Kingsley was probably nearer to Maurice's understanding of the purpose of the movement than Ludlow. To some quite large extent, Maurice was drawn into Christian Socialism by Kingsley's enthusiasm. The two first met in 1844, and Kingsley rapidly fell under Maurice's influence. He called him, as is well known, his 'Master', and even named his first son after Maurice.[133] What is less appreciated in subsequent commentary is the extent to which Maurice was influenced by Kingsley, despite the clear intellectual disparity that existed between them. Mrs Maurice, indeed, came to suppose that there was 'something quite peculiar' in Maurice's affection for Kingsley.[134] It was the tone of Kingsley's writings which sometimes got Maurice into trouble: the works of

[127] F. D. Maurice, *The Ground and Object of Hope for Mankind* (London, 1867), 49 (Sermon II).
[128] Maurice, *The Kingdom of Christ*, II, 283.   [129] Frederick Maurice, *Life*, II, 137.
[130] Ibid., II, 138.   [131] Maurice, *The Kingdom of Christ*, II, 283.
[132] Maurice, *The Lord's Prayer*, 122 (Sermon IX).
[133] R. B. Martin, *The Dust of Combat. A Life of Charles Kingsley* (London, 1859), 70. *Charles Kingsley: His Letters and Memories of His Life*, edited by his wife (thirteenth edn., London, 1878), I, 127.
[134] Ludlow, *Autobiography*, 127.

the two men were often bracketed together in hostile press commentary, as in the notorious *Quarterly Review* attack of September 1851. In the King's College controversy over Maurice's continued tenure of his Chair, in November 1851, the authorities cited Kingsley's 'inflammatory language' and blamed Maurice for appearing to condone it.[135] In his defence, Maurice pointed out that their object had been to demonstrate to the working men that Christianity was 'the only means of promoting their well-being and counteracting the moral evils which lie at the root of their physical evils'.[136] It was a cause which virtually any Christian philanthropist of the first half of the nineteenth century would have recognized. 'God's order seems to me more than ever the antagonist of man's systems; Christian Socialism is in my mind the assertion of God's order', Maurice wrote on another occasion; 'Every attempt, however small and feeble, to bring it forth I honour and desire to assist'. He added: 'Every attempt to hide it under a great machinery, call it Organization of Labour, Central Board, or what you like, I must protest against as hindering the gradual development of what I regard as a divine purpose, as an attempt to create a new constitution of society, when what we want is that the old constitution should exhibit its true function and energies'.[137] This was to return, again, to his central theme: that the Kingdom already existed, that the present structure of society contained organic elements which could not be obliterated without damage to the moral entity of the state itself – an idea explicitly derived from Coleridge, to whom Maurice admitted his enormous indebtedness[138] – and that political action was inappropriate since the work of raising consciousness was educative. Kingsley shared Maurice's social conservatism, and was, in fact, even more noted for his respect for aristocratic principles of government. His enthusiasm for Christian Socialism proved slightly more tenacious than Maurice's, however, and did not burn off until several years later than his.

The adoption of the title 'Christian Socialist', in 1848, had actually caused Maurice some anxiety. His son and biographer believed the label was chosen in order to avoid using the word 'Co-operative' – to which, he supposed, some odium was attached at the time. He added, however, that Socialism 'conveyed a number of ideas with which my father had no sympathy'.[139] Maurice himself was less given to understatement. He was out to wage a campaign of moral attrition against the 'unsocial Christians' and the 'unChristian Socialists', he said.[140] The task was one of diverting Socialism from its radical and materialistic purposes. As he looked back from the perspective of 1866, he persisted in believing that the almost paradoxical use of the title was justified. 'The phrase "Christian Socialism"', he then wrote, 'I still think was worth all

---

[135] Frederick Maurice, *Life*, II, 79.   [136] Ibid., II, 83.   [137] Ibid., II, 44 (March 1850).
[138] Maurice, *The Kingdom of Christ*, II, 349 (Dedication from the second edition of 1842).
[139] Frederick Maurice, *Life*, II, 34.   [140] Jones, *The Christian Socialist Revival*, 27.

the obloquy and ridicule which it incurred'.[141] What in fact he had done, to the disquiet of Ludlow in particular, was to have emptied 'Socialism' of its political content. In Maurice's understanding it had become a matter of adult education, self-help economic enterprise and general exhortation to mutual respect between the social classes. When it became clear to him that his colleagues in the movement had other ideals – and actually sought to change society – Maurice began his disengagement. More and more of his time went into the scheme for a working men's college.[142] References to Christian Socialism, and to Socialism of any sort, began to disappear from his correspondence and his writings. Increasingly, his concern was for the interior dignity of men, for discovering the means by which the working classes could achieve some insight into the great truths of Christianity. 'I was sent into the world that I might persuade men to recognize Christ as the centre of their fellowship with each other', he reflected in later years; 'that so they might be united with their families, their countries, and as men, not in schools and factions'.[143] And not, he might have added, in those factions which political action produced.

If Maurice's real adhesion to Christian Socialism was slight, then, what can be his claim to be remembered as a social reformer at all? The answer lies in his co-operative work, in his elevated view of humanity, and in the examples he gave of involving the Church with the aspirations of working men. The co-operative movement, at the time when the Christian Socialists of 1848 began their practical involvement with it, was already in existence, in the north of England, and in less structured self-help enterprises got up by local philanthropists, on a very small scale, elsewhere. It was largely un-political. To Maurice and his collaborators belongs the credit of having stamped the movement with moral seriousness. It cannot be said that they gave it respectability: rather the reverse, in fact, in view of the notoriety with which they were themselves suffused because of their declared adhesion to Socialism. Maurice's attacks upon the competitive aspects of contemporary economic practice were not original. His most telling criticisms were made at a time, in the 1840s, when Tory paternalists, and well-meaning clergymen of no distinct political label, were opposing *laissez-faire* policies because of the insensitivity of those policies to traditional social relationships. Maurice's writings form an interesting commentary on the rejection of the competitive principle but they added little to the existing deposit, and are mostly remarkable for the fact that he was at greater pains than most men were to show that he continued to subscribe to the broad outlines of Political Economy. The example Maurice gave of Church concern for the fate of the working classes was in itself noble, and doubtless held some potential activists back from precipitate action. After a meeting with a group of Chartists in 1849 he wrote to Kingsley: 'They seem to think it a very wonderful

---

[141] Frederick Maurice, *Life*, II, 550.   [142] Ibid., II, 233.
[143] Ibid., I, 237 ('Explanatory Letter' of 1870).

thing that a clergyman should be willing to come among them'.[144] Maurice
sought to regularize the contacts, and to make the Church, as it had once been,
the traditional agent of social harmony. 'We ought to feel that we are in a
transition state', he wrote in 1848; 'that we may come out of it into a state of real
fellowship and co-operation'.[145] It was a vision which returned to inspire
Christian social reformers in the later decades of the nineteenth century.

There is one other, completely neglected aspect of Maurice's social interests
which deserves notice. He became concerned, at an early point in his writings,
with the social and material conditions which affect the adoption of religious
ideas by individuals and by nations. His own progression, from a Unitarian
background to Church of England minister, probably helped in this, for he was
constantly aware of the worldly considerations which produced sectarianism in
the sort of religious bodies he had abandoned. *The Kingdom of Christ* contained
some almost classic descriptions of the movement of religious organizations
from sect to church type. These especially occurred when he was writing about
the early history of the Quakers.[146] He showed how man fell away from the
churches, once formed, to found new spiritual kingdoms elsewhere: the
flowering of new sects.[147] 'It is the common complaint of all sects', he observed,
'that wherever the hereditary habit has begun to prevail, the religion becomes a
matter of course, its power is exhausted; some violent efforts must be made to
revive it'.[148] The rise of denominations, he noticed – taking Methodism as his
marker – had more to do with 'human policy' than with 'any spiritual
principle'.[149] He also noticed the non-Christian elements which Christianity
had incorporated, as part of its institutional adaptation to the world.[150] In
recording the different styles of religious observance, pagan and Christian, he
laid emphasis on 'the influence of locality and of periods'. He stressed the effects
of 'nationality' and of 'changes in society upon religious opinion' – remarking
their high incidence in Christianity, and their slight influence on Hinduism and
the traditional religions of China.[151] In his Boyle Lectures, *The Religions of the
World and their Relations to Christianity,* published in 1847, Maurice examined
these material causes of religious phenomena in some detail. He was
contending, it is true, for the priority of Revelation in each religious system: but
first he analysed the 'non-theological elements' which had, as he put it,
'corrupted' the world religions – the 'drapery' which men's social circumstances had thrown around the universal presence of God.[152] 'Most important is it
then to ascertain whether we are holding a faith which addresses us as members

---

[144] Ibid., I, 538.
[145] *Politics for the People*, No. 13 (15 July 1848), 'Is there any hope for Education in England?',
No. II, 211.   [146] Maurice, *The Kingdom of Christ*, I, 66.   [147] Ibid., I, 70.
[148] Ibid., II, 266.   [149] Ibid., I, 144.   [150] Ibid., I, 83.   [151] Ibid., II, 35.
[152] F. D. Maurice, *The Religions of the World and their Relations to Christianity* (London, 1847),
54–5.

of a class', he wrote, 'or one which addresses us as men, which explains the problems of our human life'.[153] Had Maurice not had such distaste for statistical methods of enquiry, these interests might have anticipated some later intellectual advances. For in seeking the non-religious reasons for which men hold religious ideas, and in observing the effect of the structures of society upon ecclesiastical organizations, Maurice was a precursor of the sociology of religion.

[153] Ibid., 256.

3

CHARLES KINGSLEY

Christian Socialism was one among a number of enthusiasms which lodged in Kingsley's mind – mesmerism, and sea shell collecting were others – and it was rather characteristic of his impulsive and passionate nature that it did not remain there for more than a few years. He was, according to John Ludlow, his colleague in the Christian Socialist movement, a man of 'rugged strength and headlong dash'.[1] According to another colleague, Thomas Hughes, he was 'born a fighting man and believed in bold attack'.[2] Recent writers have tended to agree in noting the significance of Kingsley's impulsiveness. His actions have been described as 'so unco-ordinated' that 'each faded into oblivion when succeeded by another';[3] he had 'no staying power'.[4] His enthusiasms were 'inconsistent or even flatly contradictory'.[5] He had, another has remarked, great energy 'in seizing upon the ideas of men more original than he'.[6] His mind was certainly innocent of great intellectual insight: his theological learning at the time of his ordination in 1842 amounted to the gleanings and scraps picked up from a collection of books he had taken with him on a fishing trip to South Devon.[7] It was subsequently enriched by his wife, who was steeped in the writings of the Tractarians. Charles Mansfield, who had known him from undergraduate days in Cambridge, used to say 'that Kingsley knew all that was in a book by looking at the outside of it'.[8] He became an eclectic reader, moving from subject to subject as successive moods of interest and impulse directed, acquiring sufficient knowledge of each to be able to offer firm and definitive

---

[1] John Ludlow, 'Some of the Christian Socialists of 1848 and the following Years', in *Economic Review*, III (1893), 495.
[2] Thomas Hughes, 'Prefatory Memoir' to *Alton Locke*, by Charles Kingsley (London, 1881 edn.), I, 21.
[3] Una Pope-Hennessy, *Canon Charles Kingsley. A Biography* (London, 1948), 4.
[4] Ibid., 9.
[5] Susan Chitty, *The Beast and the Monk. A Life of Charles Kingsley* (London, 1974), 16.
[6] R. B. Martin, *The Dust of Combat. A Life of Charles Kingsley* (London, 1959), 15.
[7] Chitty, *The Beast and the Monk*, 65.   [8] Ludlow, in *Economic Review*, 498.

opinions. 'Had he lived a century later', Elspeth Huxley has concluded, 'he would no doubt have become a famous radio and television personality, called upon to take part in every controversial discussion on the issue of the day'.[9] His parish life at Eversley was just the same: he was a devoted pastor and guardian of the bodily as well as of the spiritual welfare of his villagers, but he also became bored when he was there for too long.[10] Kingsley himself admitted his leading characteristic: 'I fear sometimes that I shall end by a desperate lunge into one extreme or the other'.[11] But the spread of his interests, and the seemingly indiscriminate seriousness he allocated to each, ought not to obscure his very great achievement as a publicist for social reform. He was the disseminator of the ideals of the Christian Socialists; and if, at first, those ideals attracted odium and suspicion, it was through Kingsley's novels and occasional writings that they came to have, in later years, a greater acceptability. His generosity of spirit, and the outrage to his sensibilities and spiritual consciousness that the conditions of working people provoked, have deservedly given Kingsley an honoured place in the history of the Christian Socialist movement.

His involvement with all the social reform issues derived from his embodiment of that great Victorian virtue: moral seriousness. He had an early start. At the age of four he was already writing poems and composing sermons.[12] There was then something of a recession, for his student years were marked by a careless exuberance and by a loss of orthodox religious belief. The recovery of his faith was closely associated with the cultivation of his love for Fanny Grenfell – who later, after some family dislocations, became his wife. It was, indeed, Mrs Kingsley's extravagant editing of his letters, for publication in 1877, which makes him appear even more serious than he actually was. She contrived, as one interpreter has noticed, to omit 'every phrase and sentiment which he would not have uttered in the pulpit'.[13] Fanny was seven years older than Charles Kingsley, and when she met him she found, like Argemone in Kingsley's novel *Yeast* (with whom she may be identified in many particulars),[14] 'a human soul to whose regeneration she could devote her energies'.[15] As recreated, Kingsley emerged apparently as the archetypal Victorian man, and that is the way he has gone down in the record. 'He was a true representative of his age', one of his many biographers has concluded; 'he gathered to himself those influences and modes of thought that chiefly characterized the Victorian period'.[16] It has become the conventional view, but

---

[9] Elspeth Huxley, *The Kingsleys. A Biographical Anthology* (London, 1973), 7.

[10] Martin, *The Dust of Combat*, 112.

[11] *Charles Kingsley: His Letters and Memories of his Life, edited by his wife* (thirteenth edn., London, 1878). II, 19.   [12] Ibid., I, 8.

[13] Margaret Ferrand Thorp, *Charles Kingsley, 1819–1875* (Princeton, 1937), 25.

[14] Pope-Hennessy, *Canon Charles Kingsley*, 66.

[15] Charles Kingsley, *Yeast. A Problem* (London, 1888 edn.), 132.

[16] S. E. Baldwin, *Charles Kingsley* (Ithaca, 1934), v.

it requires considerable modification. The process of reconstruction was never uniform enough, nor sufficiently destructive of Kingsley's old self, for the resulting product to be what it appeared to be. Kingsley's sermons and novels seem to disclose an extrovert, showing the prejudices of landed society, yet decently open to the obligation of attending to the welfare of the poor, a man of common sense and practicality, a 'muscular Christian' and an English nationalist, a Broad Churchman of liberal judgments. He was certainly all these things, but he was the opposite of most of them also, as the layers of his being ruptured in his moulded personality and burst out in patches over his life. The sporting parson – who declared that 'hunting and fishing' had 'unutterable and almost spiritual charm' – was also given to regular nervous collapses and neurotic illnesses, sometimes having to spend months each year away from his parish in order to recover. The stalwart anti-Catholic propagandist was at the same time plainly fascinated and attracted by the Roman practices he so vehemently denounced: he wore a hair-shirt, slept on thorns, and practised self-flagellation, as mortification of the flesh.[17] The great advocate of masculinity was noticed, by some, to have 'a deep vein of woman in him'.[18] The Christian minister whose practical religious sense attracted the eye of the Court was actually given to periodic losses of faith. Most important of all, however – for the purpose of the present analysis – his enthusiasm for improving the conditions of the working classes was held in balance with a profound belief in the general unsuitability of these classes for government or for social influence.

On the face of it, Kingsley's political utterances show him to have been 'an old-fashioned Radical Tory'[19] – in the tradition of so many paternalist Tories, like Ashley and Oastler, Parson Bull of Byerley or F. D. Maurice. But the reality, again, was not quite so simple. In October 1831, while a boy at a Clifton preparatory school, he had witnessed the Reform Bill riots and, as he put it years later, 'received my first lesson in what is now called "social science"'.[20] At first it made him into a convinced supporter of existing social authority; later in life he discerned in those terrifying events the first stirrings of a sense that ordinary people should not be brutalized like the rioters, and that reform in the worldly conditions of their lives would prepare them for higher ideals. As a student and a young cleric he does not seem to have been particularly moved by political questions. His career did not bring him into a working relationship with the great institutions which were the bastions of traditional Toryism. He took no part in ecclesiastical administration until, towards the end of his life, he was successively a canon of Chester and of Westminster: for most of his

---

[17] Chitty, *The Beast and the Monk*, 75, 80.

[18] *Letters and Memories*, I, 299; Chitty, *The Beast and the Monk*, 53, 124; Pope-Hennessy, *Canon Charles Kingsley*, 3.

[19] Brenda Colloms, *Charles Kingsley. The Lion of Eversley* (London, 1975), 19.

[20] *Letters and Memories*, I, 21.

ministry, at Eversley, he was staunchly opposed to the intervention of episcopal
authority in parochial concerns. As a professor in Cambridge, after 1860, he was
again unconcerned with the wider life of the institution he served, and had little
intercourse with the other dons. His only connexion with the guilded
corporations came when the Haberdashers' Company appointed him to the
Golden Lectureship. During the crucial decade of his life, the 1840s, such social
instincts as he had appear to have directed him towards a kind of liberal
progressivism, and it was this which suddenly flowered in the Christian
Socialist movement. But neither the movement itself, nor his social reformism,
suggested political action.

The progressive impulses pointed to the sort of liberalism expressed by
Thomas Arnold – with whom Kingsley also shared Broad Church principles
and a horror of Tractarianism. 'It is the new commercial aristocracy; it is the
scientific go-a-headism of the day which must save us, and which we must
save', he wrote in 1846 to Cowley Powles, a friend since schooldays at Helston.
The clergy, he continued, must 'Arnold-ise'. He would 'devote soul and body
to get together an Arnoldite party of young men', whose purpose would be 'to
show how all this progress of society in the present day is really of God'.[21]
Throughout his life Kingsley associated himself with scientific thought,
sometimes in the pursuit of evolutionary theory, sometimes in the categoriz-
ation of rock-pool specimens from the seashore. In 1851 he believed that 'it was
God who taught us to conceive, build, and arrange that Great Exhibition'.[22]
Later he began to emphasize the importance of self-help as the chief
characteristic of authentic progress. 'Railroads? Electric telegraphs? All honour
to them in their place', he declared in 1867, 'but they are not progress; they are
only the fruits of progress'. Progress, he then believed, was inward, 'of the soul':
'The self-help and self-determination of the independent soul – that is the root
of progress'.[23] It was a quality independent of social class. 'Give me a man who,
though he can neither read nor write, yet dares to think for himself, and do the
thing he believes', he said: 'that man will help forward the human race more
than any thousand men who have read, or written, either a thousand books
apiece, but have not dared to think for themselves'.[24]

This was the way he came to see Chartism. However mistakenly its leaders
might pursue political objectives, its essential importance, for Kingsley, lay in
its ability to direct the attention of the working men themselves towards self-
help and self-improvement. It was, therefore, properly redirected, a progressive
force. Hence his declaration to the meeting of working men called in London

---

[21] Ibid., I, 143–4.
[22] Charles Kingsley, *Sermons on National Subjects* (London, 1852), Sermon XII, 'The Fount of
Science', 144.
[23] Charles Kingsley, *Three Lectures on the Ancien Régime* (London, 1867), 129.
[24] Ibid., 130.

by the Christian Socialists in June 1849: 'I am a parson and a Chartist'.[25] The paradox was evident at the time, and was intended to be. At the very end of Kingsley's novel *Alton Locke* (published in 1849) the hero explains his final position, and it is clearly Kingsley's own. 'If by a Chartist you mean one who fancies that a change in mere political circumstances will bring about a millennium, I am no longer one,' he says; 'But if to be a Chartist is to love my brothers with every faculty of my soul – to wish to live and die struggling for their rights, endeavouring to make them, not electors merely, but fit to be electors, senators, kings and priests to God and His Christ – if that be the Chartism of the future, then am I seven-fold a Chartist'.[26] Kingsley believed in self-help, education, and social mobility. The last goal made for a 'more homogeneous' society,[27] but it was a society which was still stratified in class terms, and in which each knew his place. Many provincial Chartists were Tories in the 1840s, and it would be tempting to conclude that Kingsley was like them. That cannot have been the case, however, both because of the peculiarity of his definition of Chartism itself and because, whilst not defining himself in other party terms, he distanced himself from Toryism. It was the party of the Tractarians, he stressed in 1840; 'they are inseparably connected; they are the same principle, the one applied to the political, the other to the religious constitution of mankind'.[28] His progressivism placed him outside the Whig interest, with which there was anyway no family link. Between 1848 and 1852 he called himself a 'Socialist'[29] but there are reasons, later to become evident, why that cannot have been intended as a description of his *political* opinions.

Despite his enthusiasm for the forces of social progress, Kingsley was a great opponent of one of the most dynamic elements in English public life which represented them: the Manchester Radicals. As with Maurice, this derived from a rejection of the principles of competition in economic relationships; yet Kingsley seems also to have had some distaste for the urban bourgeois nature of the manufacturers themselves, and for their assault upon the position of the aristocracy and aristocratic institutions. He admired the landed classes and the working people. That is why he could ostensibly be categorized alongside the Tory paternalist, and why the Manchester Radicals actually did so categorize him. Kingsley ruefully noted: 'The present dodge of the Manchester School is to cry out against us . . . "These Christian Socialists are a set of medieval parsons, who want to hinder the independence and self-help of the men, and bring them back to absolute feudal maxims"'.[30] Manchester Radicalism,

---

[25] Chitty, *The Beast and the Monk*, 123.
[26] Charles Kingsley, *Alton Locke, Tailor and Poet. An Autobiography* (Oxford, World's Classics edn., 1983), 383.
[27] Kingsley, *Three Lectures on the Ancien Régime*, x.
[28] *Letters and Memories*, I, 50.
[29] For example, in the *Morning Chronicle* (28 January 1851).
[30] Thomas Hughes, 'Prefatory Memoir' to *Alton Locke*, 47.

Kingsley exploded, was 'narrow, conceited, hypocritical, and anarchic and atheistic'. He added 'I have no language to express my contempt for it'.[31] The 'Lancashire system' of organizing labour and resources was 'exceptional' and 'transitional',[32] and would last only so long as true principles of humanity were suppressed by those who treated their work-force like machines. It stirred another of Kingsley's preoccupations. 'Mill-labour effeminates the men', he contended; the workers should emigrate rather than put up with that, and 'the life of a colonist would, by calling out the whole man, raise them in body and mind'.[33] During the depression of the cotton industry, early in the 1860s, he wrote to the papers complaining that the capitalists did little to attend to the social and educational needs of those whom they employed.[34] In 1852, at the time of Slaney's proposals for legislation to give legal protection to co-operative enterprises, he had denounced 'the competitive enslavement of the masses', and called for an alliance of 'the Church, the gentleman, and the workmen, against the shopkeepers and the Manchester School'.[35] This, again, exhaled an authentic expression of traditional Tory paternalism. So did Kingsley's opposition to governmental centralization – 'because it is founded on an error'. It 'treats men as that which they are not, as things, and not as that which they are, as persons'.[36] Centralization, that is to say, was destructive of the organic relationships of traditional society. Most squires and landowning magnates shared the same opinions.

Like Maurice, Kingsley accepted the main structure of Political Economy, whilst rejecting the principle of competition and Malthusian population ideas. Political Economy, he declared in 1857, 'forms the subject matter of all future social science, and he who is ignorant of it builds on air'.[37] The danger implicit in its tendency to materialism, however, was to regard men as mere creatures of circumstance; its 'error' was to say to men 'you are the puppets of certain natural laws', and liable to 'drift whithersoever they carry you'. He blamed the French Socialist writers, and especially Fourier, for the same species of materialism.[38] Both erred, he supposed, through ignoring 'that self-arbitrating power of man, by which he can, for good or for evil, rebel against and conquer circumstances'.[39] This brought Kingsley near to his heroic view of men of destiny – a notion picked up from Carlyle – of men who were capable of creating their own means of manipulating or surmounting the conditioning of their social circumstances. 'But for the majority, who are neither brave, self-originating, nor earnest, but the mere puppets of circumstance, safety and comfort may, and actually do, merely make their lives mean and petty, effeminate and dull'.[40]

[31] Ibid., 51. See *Letters and Memories*, I, 314.   [32] Ibid., I, 148–9.
[33] Ibid., I, 149.   [34] Chitty, *The Beast and the Monk*, 215.
[35] Colloms, *The Lion of Eversley*, 148.   [36] *Three Lectures on the Ancien Régime*, 49.
[37] *Letters and Memories*, II, 35.
[38] Charles Kingsley, *The Limits of Exact Science as Applied to History. An Inaugural Lecture delivered before the University of Cambridge* (Cambridge and London, 1860), 38.   [39] Ibid., 39.
[40] Charles Kingsley, *Health and Education* (London, 1874), 'Heroism', 201.

Loyal to one of the central tenets of Political Economy, Kingsley was opposed to the indiscriminate giving of alms. The proper course was for the rich to deploy their resources in improving social conditions, and especially conditions of housing and sanitation, so that the labouring classes could exercise the capacities of self-help. The most lucid articulation of this conviction came with Tregarva, the game-keeper who is the central exponent of social doctrine in Kingsley's novel *Yeast* (serialized in 1848). Charity, he declaimed, stopped a little misery, but did nothing for 'the oppression that goes on all the year round'.[41] Charities 'are keeping the people down'.[42] Kingsley stressed the providence of God in his rejection of Malthusianism, and, in practical terms, pointed to the option of emigration for those who could most effectively express self-help by removing themselves from society altogether. The novel *Westward Ho!* (1855) suggested that this would also help to people the globe with Protestant Christians, and so defeat the dark forces of 'Popery'. Like his views on individual social transcendence, Kingsley's attitudes to Malthusian doctrines were originally derived from Carlyle. His clearest repudiation of Malthus came in *Alton Locke*.[43]

It was characteristic of Kingsley that the intellectual foundation of his openness to social reform, and to Christian Socialism, should have been provided by the pursuit of what Maurice would have called 'system'. Kingsley was looking, early in the 1840s, for a guiding intellectual theme. Having renounced the lazy life of sports and casual study at Cambridge, in order to be tutored in moral seriousness by Fanny Grenfell, he wanted a clearly defined order of ideas. First, he thought he had found what he was looking for in the writings of Richard Whately: 'his is the greatest mind of the present day',[44] he declared in 1842. Then, in the following year, Fanny sent him a copy of Maurice's *Kingdom of Christ*. The effect was instantaneous, and as Fanny herself recorded, 'it proved a turning point in his life'.[45] Kingsley converted the work into exactly the sort of universal explanation of things that Maurice had written it to discourage. 'To your works', Kingsley told Maurice after their first meeting, in 1844, 'I am indebted for the foundation of any coherent view of the word of God, the meaning of the Church of England, and the spiritual phenomena of the past and present ages'.[46] Thus to the basis of moral seriousness established in him by Fanny, Kingsley now added a structure of ideas culled from Maurice. He saw it as his duty to interpret Maurice – whose literary style was, to say the least, difficult at times to follow – for a wider readership. He became, as Ludlow remarked, the 'popularizer' of Maurice's ideas.[47] 'I do not

---

[41] Charles Kingsley, *Yeast. A Problem* (London, 1888 edn.), 39.
[42] Ibid., 171.
[43] Kingsley, *Alton Locke*, 112.
[44] *Letters and Memories*, I, 70.
[45] Ibid., I, 53. Chitty, *The Beast and the Monk*, 70.
[46] *Letters and Memories*, I, 127.
[47] Ludlow, in *Economic Review*, 499.

think there is a true thought in Kingsley which has not its root in Maurice's teaching', Ludlow also declared.[48] Kingsley took the spiritual message of 'The Master' to the agricultural labourers and to the slum-dwellers of the industrial cities: it was a self-conscious missionary enterprise.[49] In the process he used the fiery language of his passionate enthusiasm, and the result was to make Maurice appear more militant than he had intended. Influence also operated the other way. Maurice seems to have been attracted to Kingsley's youthful zest, so that it sometimes seemed 'as if Kingsley were the real leader'.[50] How else could Maurice have said what he did about 'the tendency of the non-sporting man in all ages to be a liar and a sneak'?[51] But there was no sense in which it may be said that Kingsley got his *social* and *political* ideas from Maurice: both men got their shared attitudes from a common source – from the social journalism of the 1840s and from their understanding of Ludlow's Christian Socialism.

Fanny Grenfell had also sent Maurice works by Carlyle, and these, too, became 'the foundation' of his thought.[52] Kingsley disapproved of Carlyle's theology, but adopted most of his social attitudes.[53] Sandy Mackaye, in *Alton Locke*, is a portrait of Carlyle.[54] A confidence in the benefits of emigration and a distaste for Malthusianism have already been noticed as among Carlyle's contributions to Kingsley's outlook; he also provided some of Kingsley's distrust of democracy, his belief in the destiny of the individual, and his conviction that social reform was the necessary prerequisite for spiritual improvement.[55] Kingsley's advocacy of social reform was often expressed, indeed, 'in language that he borrowed from the greater social prophet'.[56] A more immediate inspiration to concrete social action came from Sydney Osborne, a clergyman who, as a result of Kingsley's eventual marriage to Fanny Grenfell, became his brother-in-law. For nearly forty years, Osborne addressed letters to *The Times* on the need for social reform, and particularly the need to improve the dwellings and wages of agricultural labourers. In most things he shared the assumptions of Tory paternalists, and he kept clear of party politics. Although Kingsley felt no great personal liking for Osborne, he learned much from him about the prospects for reform.[57] Kingsley met Ludlow for the first time on the day of the great Chartist demonstration in 1848, and for a few years thereafter, until their relations cooled as a result of Ludlow's discovery of some

---

[48] John Ludlow, *The Autobiography of a Christian Socialist*, ed. A. D. Murray (London, 1981), 126.

[49] A. J. Hartley, *The Novels of Charles Kingsley. A Christian Social Interpretation* (Folkestone, 1977), 169.

[50] Baldwin, *Charles Kingsley*, 72. [51] Pope-Hennessy, *Canon Charles Kingsley*, 73.

[52] *Letters and Memories*, I, 84. [53] Ibid., II, 22.

[54] Kingsley, *Alton Locke*, Chapter III, 34ff. [55] Baldwin, *Charles Kingsley*, 52–8.

[56] Ibid., 66.

[57] Chitty, *The Beast and the Monk*, 91; Colloms, *The Lion of Eversley*, 70–1; Pope-Hennessy, *Canon Charles Kingsley*, 40.

of Kingsley's ideas about race and warfare, they were frequent correspondents. It was almost certainly through Ludlow that Kingsley read the French Socialist writers. There are references to them, and especially to Fourier, in Kingsley's novels and articles,[58] but he does not seem to disclose any really deep knowledge of their ideological intentions or analyses, and appears to have grasped them to himself with the same sort of enthusiastic acclaim that he gave to other apparently sympathetic influences. Alton Locke, in fact, is made to say that, having read Fourier and Proudhon, and some other writers, 'I made them all fit into that idol-temple of self which I was rearing'.[59] The French Socialists were clearly, therefore, to be used circumspectly. By 1860, Kingsley had come to attack them for their materialism: they fell into 'the extraordinary paradox of supposing that though man was the creature of circumstances, he was to become happy by creating the very circumstances which were afterwards to create him'. This, he declared, was the great error of the Socialists, 'with Fourier at their head'.[60]

Kingsley traced his own concern with social reform to his clerical background – to his father's attention to social duties, especially during his period as incumbent of St Luke's, Chelsea, in the later 1830s. 'I have been brought up in the most familiar intercourse with the poor', Kingsley noted; 'I speak what I know, and testify that which I have seen'.[61] He did not, in fact, enjoy the experience. He thought the life of the Chelsea rectory 'a prison',[62] and the social workers who gathered around his father 'ugly splay-footed beings'.[63] His own ministry of Eversley, however, was from the start an education in social misery, and he learned the lessons rapidly. He was, as Ludlow truly remarked, 'an admirable parish priest'.[64] He built up just that popular confidence in the clergy which seemed to be so markedly lacking: they were regarded by the ordinary people, he observed in *Alton Locke*, as 'chosen exclusively from the classes who crush us down'; they were merely 'the advocates of Toryism'.[65] The people fell into infidelity because 'the cream and pith of working intellect is almost exclusively self-educated': a result of 'the neglect of the Church'.[66] Especially through regular house-to-house visiting, Kingsley saw the conditions of the agricultural labourers in all their vivid squalor. The times – the later 1840s – were particularly hard for rural society, and the tenants of his neglectful patron, Sir John Cope of Bramshill Park, must have been among the most depressed. Mrs Kingsley had little taste for parish work, and it was therefore Kingsley himself who organized the various charitable clubs which sought to induce thrift, self-help, and godliness among

[58] In *Yeast*, for example, 219.
[59] *Alton Locke*, 374.
[60] Kingsley, *The Limits of Exact Science as Applied to History*, 39.
[61] *Letters and Memories*, I, 249; Hughes 'Prefatory Memoir', 32.
[62] *Letters and Memories*, I, 37.
[63] Chitty, *The Beast and the Monk*, 48.
[64] Ludlow, in *Economic Review*, 496.
[65] Kingsley, *Alton Locke*, 194.
[66] Hughes, 'Prefatory Memoir', 30.

the poor of Eversley. Benefit societies, in particular, he regarded as 'patterns of Christ's Church',[67] the very foundations of social, and therefore, in due course, of spiritual enlightenment.

With this background, it was not surprising that Kingsley should have reacted vehemently to the great Chartist demonstration of 10 April 1848. He was moved, indeed, to a pitch of excited enthusiasm which, according to his wife's recollection, 'seemed for a time to give him a supernatural strength'.[68] Together with John Parker, son of the publisher, who had been staying with him at Eversley, Kingsley set off for London with the intention of going to the Chartist meeting at Kennington Common and making a speech which he hoped would deter bloodshed. He had already persuaded himself that the Chartists' immediate objectives only encompassed 'futility after futility',[69] and that – as he explained to Parker on the way to London – the Church needed to work with 'Socialism' and not against it. Maurice, who remained indoors with a cold, had given him a letter of introduction to Ludlow, and, after a meeting in the latter's chambers, they set off for the demonstration. It had, in fact, been called off, and just as they were about to cross Waterloo Bridge they encountered the first dispirited bands of Chartists returning from Kennington Common.[70] But the stirring events had, in effect, launched Christian Socialism, and it was Kingsley who now composed their placard *Workmen of England!* (by 'a working parson'), which rejected the idea of universal suffrage and called, instead, for education which would make the people 'fit to be free'.[71] For Kingsley personally, something like a rebirth took place. 'A glorious future is opening', he wrote to Fanny, 'and both Maurice and Ludlow seem to have driven away all my doubts and sorrows'.[72]

There then began a serious attempt to understand both Chartism and the true nature of working-class discontents. This had the great advantage that it added a knowledge of the urban poor to Kingsley's existing, and first-hand, store of information about rural social misery. From Walter Cooper, who became manager of the tailors' co-operative set up by the Christian Socialists in Castle Street in 1849, he learned about the horrors of the sweat-shops. Walter Cooper eventually appropriated the funds and disappeared. A more durable source of information was provided in Thomas Cooper, the model for Crossthwaite, the Chartist tailor in *Alton Locke*,[73] whom Kingsley plainly depicted as the ideal 'moral force' Chartist. Not that Cooper was entirely typical: he had become a Chartist in 1840, after being a journalist and a Methodist Preacher, and could understand Latin, Greek and Hebrew. He spent two years in Stafford Gaol for

---

[67] Charles Kingsley, *Village Sermons* (London, 1849), Sermon XX, 'Association', 214.
[68] *Letters and Memories*, I, 154.   [69] Kingsley, *Alton Locke*, 342.
[70] Ludlow, in *Economic Review*, 496.   [71] Text in *Letters and Memories*, I, 156–7.
[72] Ibid., I, 155 (Letter of 11 April 1848).
[73] Kingsley, *Alton Locke*, 29ff., for an account of Crossthwaite's thought.

incitement (just like Alton Locke), and it was there that he wrote the poem *The Purgatory of Suicides* which attracted Kingsley's admiration. They met in 1848, conducted a close correspondence for some years; and eventually Cooper was converted to religious faith through Kingsley's influence. In his letters, Kingsley's language was characteristically dramatic. 'I would shed the last drop of my life blood for the social and political emancipation of the people of England', he told Cooper in June 1848; 'I want someone like yourself, intimately acquainted with the mind of the working classes, to give me such an insight into their life and thought, as may enable me to consecrate my powers effectually to their service'.[74] Kingsley was equally ardent in his acclamation of the *Morning Chronicle* revelations about the London poor made by Henry Mayhew in 1849. Some of the factual details about the sweat-shops in his tract *Cheap Clothes and Nasty* came from the *Chronicle* articles,[75] and so, evidently, did some of the background for *Alton Locke*.[76] But he had already written *Yeast*, and there is actually a note in the book, declaring that the social details were not 'copied out of the Morning Chronicle'. Kingsley acknowledged, however, those 'invaluable investigations' and commended them for study.[77] 'If you wish to get a clear view of the real state of the working classes', he told a country clergyman who had written to him in 1851, then the *Chronicle* articles were the place. He assured his correspondent, however, that he did not himself 'speak from hearsay' or from 'second-hand picking and stealing' from the Chronicle articles – but from a real knowledge of the poor beloved of Christ and 'for whom He died'.[78] It may, in fact, be fairly concluded that Kingsley's social knowledge of rural conditions was direct, and that most of what he knew about urban society was derived from the journalism of the later 1840s and the enquiries he undertook after reading it. It was as a result of the *Morning Chronicle* revelations that he went down to Jacob's Island in Bermondsey to see for himself the slum conditions which allowed the cholera epidemic of 1849 to spread so rapidly.[79]

Kingsley was deeply and permanently moved by the social misery that had been opened up to him; his finest sensibilities were outraged that human life could be so stunted and deprived of higher things by the crippling effect of poor housing and bad sanitation. His solutions – and they form the content of his understanding of Christian Socialism – were co-operative associations, education, sanitary reform, recreation, and religion. What did not appear in this list was political reform. Kingsley was opposed to democracy; not until the 1860s

[74] *Letters and Memories*, I, 184.
[75] [Charles Kingsley] Parson Lot, *Cheap Clothes and Nasty* [London, 1850], reprinted in the 1880 edn. of *Alton Locke*, 76.
[76] Kingsley, *Alton Locke*, 443: 'Facts still worse than those which Mr. Locke's story contains' can be found in the *Morning Chronicle* articles.   [77] Kingsley, *Yeast*, 97.
[78] *Letters and Memories*, I, 249.
[79] Ibid., I, 216; Pope-Hennessy, *Canon Charles Kingsley*, 431.

did he begin to contemplate parliamentary reform, and eventually he abandoned the idea – remarking in 1866 that even a system of plural voting for the established classes was 'practically hopeless just now'.[80] He favoured minor legislative changes to help the rural poor (an adjustment in the game laws, for example), but no assault upon the chief legislative protections to the landowning class. He also declared for a range of laws to help the urban proletariat – to assist slum clearance and public health. But his limited view of the competence of the state, his reverence for the operation of the existing constitution, and his belief in the 'natural' authority of aristocracy, until almost the end of his life, inhibited his advance into anything like collectivist solutions to social ills.

In Kingsley's earliest work, *The Saint's Tragedy* – the drama about Queen Elizabeth of Hungary, originally composed in honour of Fanny – there were anticipations of the social outpourings to come. Elizabeth herself laments the housing conditions of the poor of medieval Hungary: the 'inky pools, where reeked and curdled the offal of a life'.[81] Count Walter, another character, condemns the landlords, 'in a fools' paradise of luxury', who left 'the poor man in the slough', and who were shamefully maintained in power by corrupt clerics, 'the hired stalking-horses of the rich'.[82] It was a short step from this position to Kingsley's sermon in St John's Church, Charlotte Street, of June 1851, with its condemnation of 'all systems of society which favour the accumulation of capital in a few hands', and which, citing the exhortations of Moses, denounced the accumulation of large estates. Such things were 'contrary to the Kingdom of God'.[83] A considerable sensation, much discussed in the press, was caused when the sermon was itself publicly condemned, at its conclusion, by the vicar of the church. The Bishop of London went so far as to ban Kingsley from further preaching in the diocese.[84] The theme of landlord neglect was central to the plot of *Yeast*: 'Are men likely to be healthy when they are worse housed than a pig?' asked the righteous gamekeeper.[85] It was also Tregarva who composed a bitter set of verses about the condition of rural society:

> A labourer in Christian England,
>   Where they cant of a Saviour's name,
> And yet waste men's lives like the vermin's,
>   For a few more brace of game.[86]

The novel was sufficiently offensive to the landowners themselves that they began to cancel their subscriptions to *Fraser's Magazine*, in which it had been

[80] *Letters and Memories*, II, 243.
[81] Charles Kingsley, *The Saint's Tragedy; or, The True Story of Elizabeth of Hungary* (London, 1848), 91 (Act II, Scene iii).   [82] Ibid., 117 (Act II, Scene ix).
[83] Colloms, *The Lion of Eversley*, 136; Chitty, *The Beast and the Monk*, 144.
[84] *Letters and Memories*, I, 291.   [85] Kingsley, *Yeast*, 36.   [86] Ibid., 147.

serialized from July 1848 (so obliging the editor, Parker, to ask Kingsley to bring it to a rapid end. Hence the rather hurried and unsatisfactory structure of the novel as it finally appeared, in 1851, in book form). But *Yeast* does reveal the mind of Kingsley as it was, in his most militant phase, in the months following the Chartist demonstration and the foundation of the Christian Socialist movement.

In turning attention to urban squalor, Kingsley's analysis follows very closely the style of the *Morning Chronicle* articles. 'We have, thank God, emancipated the black slaves', he wrote in *Cheap Clothes and Nasty*, the tract of 1850; 'it would seem a not inconsistent sequel to that act to set about emancipating the white ones'.[87] This was very much the language used by factory reformers like Ashley, many of the Tories, and by the propagandists of the Ten Hours' Day Movement. It was addressed to the affluent classes: 'men ought to know the condition of those by whose labour they live'.[88] It was, Kingsley said in a sermon of 1847, these conditions, of 'tyranny' and 'carelessness', which forced the poor 'to lodge in undrained stifling hovels', the very breeding ground of all diseases, 'and worse and last of all, the cholera'.[89] The emphasis on environmentalism showed how well Kingsley had already absorbed the attitudes of the advocates of Public Health reform. He applied it generally. Writing in another of the journals of the movement, on the 'Frimley Murder' – a sensation of 1850, when a landowner was shot dead by a burglar – he argued that a more enlightened social organization (and one suffused with Christianity) would eliminate the conditions which gave rise to such an atrocity.[90] Most commentators had merely expressed outrage at the crime and condemned the violators of property rights. There was also a strong sense of the importance of environment in Kingsley's advocacy of improved recreational facilities for the working classes. It was the accounts of the crudities of proletarian fun made by Mayhew in his articles which had most shocked Maurice, too, and they seem to have moved Kingsley to a comparable attempt to prescribe approved and morally serious pastimes for the poor. In *Politics for the People* he wrote essays to show that 'picture-galleries should be the workman's paradise',[91] and that museums were 'where the poor and the rich may meet together'. He wanted cathedrals to be turned into 'winter gardens', where 'people might take their Sunday walks'.[92] It was not surprising that the High Church party found Kingsley's understanding of Anglicanism rather wanting in some particulars.

A sense of the unnecessary estrangement of the working classes, which comes so powerfully through Kingsley's writings, lay at the heart of his desire to promote what he understood as Christian Socialism. He saw, essentially, the

---

[87] [Kingsley] *Cheap Clothes and Nasty*, 92.   [88] Ibid., 97.

[89] Charles Kingsley, *Sermons on National Subjects* (London, 1852), XIII, 'first Sermon on the Cholera' [27 September 1849], 176.

[90] *The Christian Socialist* (November 1850). See Colloms, *The Lion of Eversley*, 125.

[91] *Politics for the People*, No. 1 (6 May 1848), 5; No. 2 (13 May 1848), 39.

[92] Ibid., No. 11 (1 July 1848), 183.

need for a work of restoration: the landowning systems were right and should be beneficial – provided the old relationships of the past, before capitalist acquisitiveness, could be recovered; the progress of industrial society was desirable and productive – but the new classes who ran the various enterprises needed to be schooled in the sort of social paternalism which their aristocratic predecessors once operated so effectively; the people were potentially noble and sensible – if only they were given a chance, through education, good housing, and religion, to live like men. The craving of the working class, Kingsley declared in *Alton Locke*, 'is only for some idea which shall give equal hopes, claims, and deliverance, to all mankind alike'.[93] Like Maurice, Kingsley gave very little *political* content to Christian Socialism; it was an educational and moral programme achieved through periodic measures of reform, but lacking a systematic, party, or collective basis. 'Of modern Socialism there is little trace', Colwyn Vulliamy observed in the *Fabian Tract* on Kingsley.[94] That had been clear even in the placard Kingsley had composed to the *Workmen of England!* in 1848: the workmen were actually told to direct themselves to education rather than franchise reform – what they needed was 'something nobler than charters and dozens of Acts of Parliament'.[95] Kingsley's view of social equality was just as elevated, and just as removed from the political sphere. In 1851 he told a correspondent that 'true socialism, true liberty, brotherhood, and true equality (not the carnal dead level equality of the Communist, but the spiritual equality of the Church idea, which gives every man an equal chance of developing and using God's gifts, and rewards every man according to his work, without respect of persons) is only to be found in loyalty and obedience to Christ'.[96] In 1852 Parker wrote a sympathetic and critical piece in *Fraser's Magazine* which raised the question of whether the doctrines of the Christian Socialists were not 'dangerous to the repose of society'. In his reply, published as a pamphlet, Kingsley gave an extremely limited definition of the purposes of the movement. 'We are not a party, and do not wish to become one', he declared, in authentic Maurician style: 'we do not wish to convert everyone to our own notions'. Indeed (though he acknowledged that it was 'paradoxical'), the truth was that 'any upright and kindly Christian man, doing his duty where God has put him, even though he shudder with horror at the name of Socialism, is in our eyes, a Christian Socialist'.[97] The movement, he declared, was 'most eminently conservative of order, property, and all else which makes human life pleasant to its possessor'.[98]

---

[93] Kingsley, *Alton Locke*, 12.

[94] Colwyn E. Vulliamy, *Charles Kingsley and Christian Socialism* (Fabian Tract No. 174, London, 1914), 24.

[95] *Letters and Memories*, I, 156.

[96] Ibid., I, 248; Hughes, 'Prefatory Memoir', 31.

[97] Charles Kingsley, *Who are the Friends of Order? A Reply to certain observations in a late number of Fraser's Magazine on the so-called 'Christian Socialists'* (London, 1852), 3.

[98] Ibid., 6. See also Martin, *The Dust of Combat*, 145.

It is in this sort of context that Kingsley's remarks on Chartism, made in 1848, need to be reassessed. 'My only quarrel with the Charter is that it does not go far enough in reform', he said – and the words were later used against him, to show he was the friend of revolutionary ideas. But the point he made was that 'men's hearts' could not be 'changed by Act of Parliament'.[99] He went on to tell the Chartists that 'too many of you are trying to do God's work with the devil's tools'.[100] The theme was repeated in *Alton Locke*: 'The Charter will no more make men good, than political economy, or the observance of the Church Calendar'.[101] The future of the working classes lay with spiritual regeneration, and this was first prepared by reforms in their living conditions and by education. 'The people cannot be prosperous whilst it is made up of suffering men and suffering classes', he declared in his *Letters to the Chartists*.[102] The admission of those classes to the political life of the nation must wait upon their advancement. It was laid up in some distant time. The Bible, Kingsley contended, was 'the true Reformer's Guide'. The clergy, he believed, had not realized this truth themselves. 'We have used the Bible as if it were the special constable's handbook – an opium dose for keeping beasts of burden patient while they were being overloaded – a mere book to keep the poor in order'.[103] The simile was not an especially original one, and there was little likelihood that Marx borrowed it from Kingsley; both men used a common enough expression of the 1840s to show that life was made tolerable but inactive by palliatives which did nothing to correct essential ills. The Bible, Kingsley claimed, shows the 'dawn of a glorious future', better than any 'universal suffrage, free trade, communism, organisation, or any other Morison's-pill measure can give'.[104] 'You say that the poor man has his rights, as well as the rich', Kingsley noted in his third *Letter*: 'so says the Bible; it says more – it says that God inspires the poor with the desire of liberty; that He helps them to their rights'.[105] There is, in the same genre, a sentence in *Alton Locke* which would give great comfort to contemporary advocates of 'Liberation Theology'. The 'great idea', Kingsley wrote, was that 'the Bible is the history of mankind's deliverance from all tyranny, outward as well as inward'. All that was needed was for the working men to realize it. 'Who is there now to go forth and tell it to the millions who have suffered?'[106]

In the same way, Kingsley argued that Christianity was the creed of democracy. Part of the purpose behind the writing of *Hypatia* (1853) was to illustrate the point from the lives of 'simple' Alexandrians of the fifth century, 'who had conquered temptation and shame, torture and death, to live for ever

[99] *Letters and Memories*, I, 163.   [100] Ibid., I, 164.   [101] *Alton Locke*, 111.
[102] *Politics for the People*, No. 2 (13 May 1848), 'Letters to the Chartists', i, 17.
[103] Ibid., No. 4 (27 May), 'Letters to the Chartists', ii, 58.
[104] Ibid., 'Letters to the Chartists', ii, 59.
[105] Ibid., No. 8 (17 June 1848), 'Letters to the Chartists', iii, 136.
[106] *Alton Locke*, 290.

on the lips of men, and take their seats among the patricians of the heavenly court'.[107] The theme was clear: the exaltation of the poor through belief in Christian hope. The novel was a favourite with Queen Victoria.[108] By 'democracy', however, Kingsley did not mean a political arrangement to secure the representation of the people's voice in government. For him the word was used to suggest a kind of comradeship and 'fellowship' between the social classes – it existed where landowners were friendly to their tenants; it was a quality of paternalistic relationships. To Cowley Powles he wrote, in 1846, that by democracy he did 'not mean foul licence, or pedantic constitution-mongering, but the rights of man as man'.[109] Kingsley was fully aware of the existence of only formal freedoms for working people, and saw it as one of his tasks to awaken the ruling classes to the need for education to raise the consciousness of the masses. 'True, they are free men, in name, not free though from the iron necessity of crushing toil'.[110] With the achievement of 'democracy', as Kingsley understood it, mutual esteem and a diffused sense of fairness would guarantee just dealings between the various social sections. As a first step, he advocated co-operative associations: in *Cheap Clothes and Nasty* he combined the need for these enterprises with the ideal of 'self-sacrifice for the sake of one another'.[111] He was a member of the Council of Promoters of the Associations set up by the Christian Socialists under Ludlow's guidance, and seems to have been consulted about its business, despite the fact that he was in Eversley, or away recovering from his bouts of nervous exhaustion, for much of the time.[112] Edward Neale's interest in agricultural co-operatives was stimulated by the 'long discussions'[113] he had with Kingsley on the question in 1849. In a lecture for the Society of Promoters, in May 1851, Kingsley not only favoured agricultural association-ism but even sketched two systems of ideal rural communities.[114] Kingsley was less involved with Maurice's Working Men's College, set up in 1854, and although he acknowledged it as 'a noble plan',[115] and gave a few lectures, he was by that date more concerned with the issue of sanitary reform. Beneath all these motives and ideas, Kingsley's Christian Socialism actually rested on a bedrock fear of social cataclysm. His sense of some apocalyptic event was less developed than Maurice's, but Kingsley nevertheless looked to the real possibility of general disruption. 'A crisis, political and social, seems approach-

---

[107] Charles Kingsley, *Hypatia, or, New Foes with an Old Force* (London, 1881 edn.), I, 156.

[108] Pope-Hennessy, *Canon Charles Kingsley*, 123; Chitty, *The Beast and the Monk*, 203.

[109] *Letters and Memories*, I, 141.

[110] Charles Kingsley, *Sermons on National Subjects* (London, 1852), XII, 'The Fount of Science', 167.

[111] Kingsley, *Cheap Clothes and Nasty*, 104.

[112] Hughes, 'Prefatory Memoir', 18, 33.

[113] P. N. Backstrom, *Christian Socialism and Co-operation in Victorian England* (London, 1974), 80.

[114] Charles Raven, *Christian Socialism, 1848–1854* (London, 1920), 180–1.

[115] *Letters and Memories*, I, 433.

ing', he noted in 1846, 'and religion, like a rootless plant, may be brushed away in the struggle'.[116] Hence the urgent need, perceived at last in the Chartist demonstration of April 1848, to 'Christianize' socialism. Without some attempt of this sort, he supposed, 'the boiler will be strained to bursting pitch', as the working men claim their rights. 'What then?' he asked: 'Look at France and see'.[117]

By the mid-1850s Kingsley's enthusiasm for Christian Socialism was diminishing, and by 1859, when he first achieved royal favour, it had virtually disappeared altogether. He never, it is true, renounced his earlier opinions, and his continued advocacy of such measures as sanitary, educational, and even limited franchise reforms, kept him in a number of progressive camps. 'If I have held back from the Socialist movement', he told Hughes in 1855, 'it has been because I have seen that the world was not going to be set right in any such rose-pink way, excellent as it is, and that there are heavy arrears of destruction to be made up before construction can even begin'.[118] It was also around this time that he said 'I am getting more of a Government man every day'.[119] In the summer of 1856, as he prepared for a fishing trip with Hughes, he declared: 'The long and short of it is, I am becoming an optimist'. He now felt that 'the world is going right'.[120] Following this aspect of Kingsley's development, some modern writers have attributed his declining interest in Socialism to the changed social scene – they have supposed that the achievement of social reforms had rendered much of his earlier diagnosis obsolete, that Kingsley was 'overtaken by the changes which he had laboured to produce, so that his criticisms became less outspoken as social conditions improved'.[121] Kingsley certainly seems to have felt this himself. *Two Years Ago*, published in 1857, was markedly lacking in the radical criticism of the earlier social novels. Since the closing years of the 1840s, he now wrote, 'a spirit of self-reform has been awakened', there was greater social mobility – 'rich and poor meeting together more and more' – and the labourers were 'better off than they have been for fifty years'.[122] The preface to the 1859 edition of *Yeast* is also full of social optimism: 'I believe that things are improved', he observed, with the working classes acquiring 'greater self-help and independence'.[123] In 1862, at the time when he held the Regius Chair of History at Cambridge, he revised *Alton Locke*, reducing the hostility he had shown to the authorities of the University – represented, originally, as gross beneficiaries of a corrupt and unreformed institution. 'It's a system of humbug, from one end to the other', he had written in the first edition.[124] By 1867 he felt

[116] Ibid., I, 142.   [117] Kingsley, *Cheap Clothes and Nasty*, 109.

[118] *Letters and Memories*, I, 440; Guy Kendall, *Charles Kingsley and his Ideas* (London, 1947), 73.

[119] Hughes, 'Prefatory Memoir', 55; *Letters and Memories*, I, 434 (Letter of December 1854).

[120] Hughes, 'Prefatory Memoir', 70.   [121] Colloms, *The Lion of Eversley*, 20.

[122] Charles Kingsley, *Two Years Ago* (London, 1881 edn.), I, 8.

[123] Charles Kingsley, *Yeast. A Problem*, Preface to the fourth edn. (1859); in the 1888 edn., v.

[124] Charles Kingsley, *Alton Locke* (World's Classics edn., 1983), 134.

able to affirm that 'there is no widespread misery, and therefore no widespread discontent, among the classes who live by hand-labour'.[125] Doubtless the opposition of his wife, who feared for his preferment prospects, also contributed to Kingsley's evaporating enthusiasm for Christian Socialism.[126] The sad death of Charles Mansfield ('He was my first love'[127]), in 1855, the victim of an accident in the laboratory when he was preparing benzol, must also have helped to seal off the past and the heady political passions of 1848. It must also be said that Kingsley's dislike of the sort of people who attached themselves to progressive causes must have contributed to his falling away from his earlier zeal. They were 'restless and eccentric persons', 'bearded young men and vegetarians'.[128] Later in life, he was to lose enthusiasm for women's rights because of what he called the 'suppressed sexual excitement' of the activists.[129] Above all, however, it was Kingsley's essential conservatism which dictated the decline of his social radicalism.

In 1850, under the title 'My political Creed', Kingsley explained the essentials of his position. He was, he declared, a monarchist. The Crown, in fact, had too little real power in the political constitution of the day, and 'the ancient balance between King, Lords and Commons is destroyed'. Instead, the power of 'capital' was increasing: all his antipathy to Manchester Radicalism breathes through this part of his analysis. Popular sovereignty, he believed, was 'atheistic in theory and impossible in practice'.[130] Hughes recorded him as remarking that a 'true democracy' was impossible 'without a gentry'.[131] This all approximated to a kind of 'Young England' social romanticism, without the high Tory politics. Those who sensed it, especially within the Chartist movement, accused him of seeking to restore 'medieval tyranny'.[132] The charge was not entirely without substance. Kingsley had a growing regard for the feudal order – whilst at the same time despising the historical middle ages because of the Catholicism and the lack of progressive ideals which characterized it. He disliked the Pre-Raphaelites, since they were the great admirers of gothicism in taste, and in *The Saint's Tragedy* he represented the medieval world as given over to barbarism, and to a false religiosity typified by 'whimpering meagre second-hand praises of celibacy'.[133] Only the concept of chivalry, from among the deposits of medieval Christendom, seemed to him to have a lasting – indeed an almost crucial – importance. He believed it was the 'higher ideal' of chivalry which 'contained the first germ of that Protestantism which conquered at the Reformation'.[134] From Carlyle he acquired the idea of a sort of chivalry

[125] Kingsley, *Three Lectures on the Ancien Régime*, vi.
[126] Pope-Hennessy, *Canon Charles Kingsley*, 78.
[127] Chitty, *The Beast and the Monk*, 52.   [128] Hughes, 'Prefatory Memoir', 23.
[129] Chitty, *The Beast and the Monk*, 254.
[130] *The Christian Socialist* (14 December 1850). See Kendall, *Charles Kingsley and his Ideas*, 69.
[131] Hughes, 'Prefatory Memoir', 52.   [132] Colloms, *The Lion of Eversley*, 101.
[133] Kingsley, *The Saint's Tragedy*, xxiii.   [134] *Letters and Memories*, II, 213.

of labour, and his conviction that the Manchester Radicals were destroying all that was 'time-honoured refined, and chivalrous in English society' became a part of his assault upon their general position. One of the chapters in *Two Years Ago* is actually called 'The Broad Stone of Honour',[135] clearly after Kenelm Digby's celebrated book of chivalry, published in 1823. Kingsley wrote an elegy in 1849 in which he called himself a 'knight-errant of God';[136] his pupils remembered him for his 'chivalrous teaching' at Cambridge,[137] and when he died, in 1875, Arthur Penrhyn Stanley, in a memorial panegyric, described his defence of the poor as 'chivalrous'.[138]

This was not all empty romanticism. Kingsley had a serious belief in the virtues of feudal society, and in 1871 he wrote, 'I would, if I could, restore the feudal system, the highest form of civilization – in ideal, not in practice – which Europe has ever seen'.[139] The 'practice' was what he had condemned in *The Saint's Tragedy* as 'the tyranny of the feudal caste';[140] the 'ideal' was a species of paternalism. In 1843 he remarked that the relationship of master and servant had been corrupted by modern commercialism, and that what society needed was a return 'to the patriarchal and feudal spirit' in which masters and servants enjoyed a natural interdependence.[141] To his parishioners at Eversley – where he retained the old system of pew-renting, so contriving a practical segregation of the social classes at worship – he preached sermons which eulogized traditional relationships. 'If the rich help and defend the poor, and the poor respect and love the rich, and are ready to serve them as far as they can', he told them in 1849, at the height of his Christian Socialist period, 'that parish is a happy one'. A nation, he added, is just the same.[142] Kingsley's love of social stability and order was also expressed in his defence of an Established Church. There is little of the Coleridgean and Maurician in Kingsley's attitude to the union of Church and State, but a great deal of English Protestant Nationalism and a desire to preserve the Church of England from sectarianism. He disliked Dissent. The Baptist ministers were 'muck enthroned on their respective dung hills'.[143] In 1872 he said, 'I dread all exaggerated language. It should be left for non-conformists'.[144]

Kingsley's conviction that the aristocracy were the natural rulers of English society, and should remain so, was plainly at variance with Christian Socialism

[135] Kingsley, *Two Years Ago*, II, 271ff.

[136] Mark Girouard, *The Return to Camelot. Chivalry and the English Gentleman* (Yale, 1981), 132.

[137] C. W. Stubbs, *Charles Kingsley and the Christian Social Movement* (London, 1899), vii.

[138] A. P. Stanley, *Charles Kingsley. A Sermon Preached in Westminster Abbey* (London, 1875), 10. On this theme in Kingsley's writings, see Norman Vance, *The Sinews of the Spirit. The Ideal of Christian Manliness in Victorian Literature and Religious Thought* (Cambridge, 1985), 94.

[139] Baldwin, *Charles Kingsley*, 65.

[140] Kingsley, *The Saint's Tragedy*, xxiii.   [141] *Letters and Memories*, I, 109.

[142] Charles Kingsley, *Village Sermons* (London, 1849), Sermon XX, 'Association', 212–13.

[143] Chitty, *The Beast and the Monk*, 95.   [144] *Letters and Memories*, II, 383.

– at least as it was understood conventionally. The great object of reform, he said, was 'to reconcile the workmen with the real aristocracy'.[145] All nations, he believed, were striving for 'a true aristocracy'; for a society, that is to say, which was 'democratic' as Kingsley defined that concept: a matter of inter-class *camaraderie*. Democracy was 'bringing to the surface and utilizing the talents and virtues of all classes'. France had erred during the ancien régime because its aristocracy, like the feudal barons of the middle ages, had become 'a caste'.[146] A 'true aristocracy', however, was recognized in 'a governing body of the really most worthy', and was 'perpetually recruited from below'.[147] It seemed to him that the English aristocracy of his day were reforming their manners, and so were especially qualified for the rôle he was anxious to justify. In the preface to the fourth edition of *Yeast* (1859) he noticed that, as evidence of this, 'one finds, more and more, swearing banished from the hunting field'.[148] There was a 'growing moral earnestness' in the 'landlord class'.[149] He thought the House of Lords were authentically the voice of the people: 'a person or body may be truly representative without being elected by those whom they represent'. The House of Commons, on the other hand, could 'only represent the temporary wants and opinions of the many'; it could not 'represent the hereditary instinct which binds man and the state to the past and future generations'.[150] These views were not, it should be noticed, the conservative reversions of old age. Kingsley articulated them when he was forty-seven years old. His belief in aristocracy went well with his conviction – clearly influenced by Carlyle – that history was created by men of destiny and not by economic, social or cultural influences. 'History is the history of men and women, and of nothing else', he declared in his Inaugural Lecture at Cambridge, in 1860; 'in proportion as you understand the man, and only so, will you begin to understand the elements in which he worked'.[151] The dons were not impressed.

Kingsley's belief that aristocracy should be 'perpetually recruited from below' was ostensibly well-matched with his exhortation to the working men to engage in co-operative enterprises and other devices for self-help and education. In practice, however, he came to doubt the ability of associationism to perform the task he had allocated to it. In 1856 he observed that the associations had failed because of 'their democratic constitution'. Successful ones owed their achievements to 'the presence of some one master-mind'.[152] In the following year, he claimed that the associations were a 'failure' because 'the working men are not fit for them'.[153] The educative process had a long way

[145] Colloms, *The Lion of Eversley*, 147.
[146] Kingsley, *Three Lectures on the Ancien Régime*, 9.   [147] Ibid., 10.
[148] Kingsley, *Yeast* (1888 edn.), vi.   [149] Ibid., x.
[150] *Letters and Memories*, II, 243.
[151] Charles Kingsley, *The Limits of Exact Science as Applied to History*, 4, 6.
[152] *Letters and Memories*, I, 474.   [153] Ibid., II, 35.

further to go. He also became sceptical of trades unions. Originally he defended the right of workers to combine for mutual protection.[154] That was early in the 1850s; by 1862 he was condemning the unions for 'outrages'. He wrote, 'I have seen enough of trade unions to suspect that the biggest rogues and the loudest charlatans are the men who lead or mislead the honest working man'.[155] He did defend the right of the Iron Workers to strike in 1852, though he thought it was not suitable for the Christian Socialists to get involved with the technical details of the dispute.[156] By 1856 he had come to advise the workers to 'emigrate, but never strike'. The trades unions, he then said, were 'interfering with the natural accidents of trade'.[157]

There was a certain unease in Kingsley's mind about the actual social mobility he advocated. He declared that 'the moral' of *Alton Locke* was 'that the working man who tried to desert his class and rise above it enters into a lie'.[158] His real ideal was a kind of stratified social fellowship. His dislike of party politics was because they divided men unnaturally: 'Class legislation is selfish legislation. Party politics are selfish politics'.[159] Social reform would assist social stability: 'When you put workmen into human dwellings, and give them a Christian education, so far from wishing discontentedly to rise out of their class, or to level others to it, exactly the opposite takes place'.[160] Social harmony was to be achieved, he suggested, by the cultivation of personal fellowship. Class distinctions, he claimed, were 'but a paper prison of our own making, which we might break through any moment by a single hearty and kindly feeling'.[161] Kingsley was a paternalist of the old school who, having found himself deeply disturbed by the existence of massive social misery, was never quite able to envisage the sort of structural changes which more vigorous radicals regarded as essential prerequisites for social justice.

It should also be noted, however, that in two rather important particulars, Kingsley's ideas about human suffering were limited. He was, first, an enthusiastic militarist – just as Maurice was. He came from a family of soldiers, and had a life-long fascination for military strategy. In 1854 he told Hughes that he could 'think of nothing but the war' – in the Crimea.[162] His pamphlet, *Brave Words to Brave Soldiers* was sent out in thousands to the soldiers. The war was 'honourable', for it was the suppression of evil 'by sharp shot and cold steel'.[163] In 1870 he supported Prussia, whose ideals he admired, against the French.[164]

---

[154] Kingsley, *Who are the Friends of Order?*, 14.   [155] *Letters and Memories*, I, 477.
[156] Kingsley, *Who are the Friends of Order?*, 8, 15; Hughes, 'Prefatory Memoir', 46.
[157] *Letters and Memories*, I, 477.
[158] Hughes, 'Prefatory Memoir', 29; Chitty, *The Beast and the Monk*, 134; Baldwin, *Charles Kingsley*, 108.   [159] *Politics for the People*, No. 2 (13 May 1848), 17.
[160] Hughes, 'Prefatory Memoir' (Letter of January 1851), 30.
[161] *Letters and Memories*, I, 177.   [162] Ibid., I, 440.
[163] Charles Kingsley, *Sermons for the Times* (London, 1855), Sermon XIII, 'Providence', 210.
[164] Colloms, *The Lion of Eversley*, 324.

He was, secondly, a racist: not merely as part of the assumed texture of attitudes to race that was a feature of English society in the mid-century, but with a self-conscious belief that 'savages' who impeded the spread of enlightenment could properly be eliminated. In 1850 his description of the extermination of the Canaanites, in an article for *The Christian Socialist*, shocked Ludlow.[165] The rift between the two men was widened by Kingsley's support for Rajah Brooke's massacre of the Dyaks in Borneo. The episode was raised in Parliament during 1851. Kingsley had called Brooke 'my hero', and remarked of the genocide: 'One tribe exterminated, if need be, to save a whole continent'. He denied that the ill-fated natives were actually, by definition, 'human life' and said 'it is beast life'.[166] They were 'stupid', he later declared, who supposed that the 'race of Borneo are men at all – and not apes'.[167] The relations of Ludlow and Kingsley were further cooled by the latter's support for the Confederacy in the American Civil War. Kingsley was actually opposed to slavery, but regarded it as the best available way of conducting a society of those who – like the blacks, as he imagined them to be – were incapable of civilized life. The war, he thought, would in the end be seen as 'a blessing to the poor niggers'.[168] When Kingsley supported the Committee to defend Governor Eyre of Jamaica in 1866 – who had been accused of brutality towards the blacks – the relationship of Kingsley and Ludlow came virtually to an end.[169] Kingsley seems to have thought that black people 'are not as God intended them to be, but are falling, generation after generation, by the working of original sin'. Some blacks, like the Australian aboriginals, were 'too stupid' even to understand the Gospel.[170] In a letter to Professor Lorimer of Edinburgh, written in 1866, Kingsley spelled out his dismal opinions on race. He denied human equality, and upheld the view that 'congenital differences and hereditary tendencies' clearly divided mankind into those who were responsible and those who were 'unfit for self-government'.[171] Not all those who were white belonged to the first category. Gypsies were 'savages',[172] and the Irish were 'white chimpanzees'.[173]

These opinions, so frightful to modern judgment, ought not to be allowed to obscure Kingsley's real contribution to social advance in the nineteenth century. Through his novels he was one of the great popularizers of progressive reform in the conditions of human life, and he served religion by associating the Church with the alleviation of suffering in areas sometimes too familiar to be recognized. He gave 'ordinary folk', in the words of G. M. Trevelyan, 'the idea that they could be religious without being ascetic or gloomy or censorious'.[174]

[165] Pope-Hennessy, *Canon Charles Kingsley*, 103; Chitty, *The Beast and the Monk*, 142.
[166] *Letters and Memories*, I, 222.   [167] Kingsley, *Who are the Friends of Order?*, 11.
[168] Martin, *The Dust of Combat*, 258.   [169] Colloms, *The Lion of Eversley*, 294.
[170] Charles Kingsley, *Sermons on National Subjects*, Second series (London, 1854), Sermon XVIII, 'The Fall', 33, 234.   [171] *Letters and Memories*, II, 241–3.
[172] Kingsley, *Sermons on National Subjects*, Second series, Sermon III, 'The Value of Law', 33.
[173] *Letters and Memories*, II, 107.   [174] Quoted in Kendall, *Charles Kingsley and his Ideas*, 10.

In one thing, in particular, his legacy had enduring qualities: in his work for sanitary reform. It became his major preoccupation, sweeping aside Christian Socialism by the mid-1850s. He lobbied public men over health issues, and he consulted Edwin Chadwick,[175] the greatest sanitary reformer of the century. The interest began in 1849, when, after reading Mayhew's account of the cholera epidemic at Jacob's Island, in the *Morning Chronicle*, he went to Bermondsey with Mansfield to see conditions for himself. He was so shocked by the urban squalor that he began agitation for reform at once – and also undertook practical measures. He, Mansfield, and Ludlow, bought water-carts and toured the district distributing 'pure' drinking-water to the poor. The enterprise was terminated when the poor stole, first the brass taps from the barrels, and then the barrels themselves.[176] Not deterred, he gave considerable publicity to the environmental pollution and dreadful housing that promoted the spread of infectious diseases, emphasizing that cholera was not a punishment inflicted because of human wickedness, but a scourge whose control and elimination elicited gifts of God to men. Hence the tract of 1854, *Who Causes Pestilence?*. He had already come to see that the 'great and blessed plans for what is called sanitary reform' were a sign 'that Christ is revealing to us the gifts of healing far more bountifully and mercifully than even He did to the first apostles'.[177]

To some extent, Kingsley's sanitary interests revived his radicalism: because vested interests were often opposed to the required reforms, he frequently found himself attacking property owners.[178] In 1874 he was quite emphatic that it was 'society' which was collectively responsible for public health, for the individual was 'no more responsible for his own weakness than for his own existence'.[179] At the very end of his life, therefore, he had come to recognize the necessity of some measure of state intervention in the area of reform he held to be the most urgently necessary for the improvement of the social conditions of the people. It was a fitting last evidence of his struggle for social progress.

[175] *Letters and Memories*, II, 15 (Chadwick was at Eversley in 1857).
[176] Ibid., I, 216ff.
[177] Kingsley, *Sermons on National Subjects* (1852), Sermon III, 'The Kingdom of God', 35.
[178] Colloms, *The Lion of Eversley*, 174.
[179] Charles Kingsley, *Health and Education* (London, 1874), 7.

4

J. M. LUDLOW

Of all the Christian Socialist leaders of the middle years of the century, John Malcolm Ludlow was the most explicit in political analysis. Ostensibly, too, he was the most theoretical – he seems to get nearer than the others did to the exploration of philosophical bases to his socialism. But to some extent that is an illusory appearance: Ludlow's mind was in fact extremely practical, and what looks at first glance like a systematic assemblage of political ideas turns out, at a second, to be a characteristically French style of arranging information in a structured and ordered pattern. The information itself was characteristically English in its pragmatism. Ludlow had been born in India, and after two years, following the death of his father (who worked for the East India Company), the family moved to England – and then, in 1826, to Paris. He was educated at the Collège Bourbon and acquired the manners and intellectual styles of the French classes of privilege amongst whose sons he studied. He intended to remain in France, where many, including Guizot, predicted a brilliant career. Instead, in 1838, he settled in London, wishing to follow what his mother assured him would have been his father's will: that he became an Englishman.[1] He was only sixteen, and the intended personal transformation never quite happened. Emotionally still attached to France, he came to idealize aspects of its life and culture; he became suffused with the exile's enthusiasm for a remembered land. It was in the year following this upheaval – and clearly a product of it – that he underwent the almost simultaneous conversions to active Christianity and to Socialism. He studied for the bar at Lincoln's Inn, and eventually began thirty-one years' work as a conveyancer. Not until 1843, when he fell in love with his cousin, did he feel that 'England, and not France, was now my heart's home'.[2]

Yet it was not entirely so; Ludlow was fluent in the languages and followed the national and political events of both countries. He never quite belonged to

---

[1] John Ludlow, *The Autobiography of a Christian Socialist*, ed. A. D. Murray (London, 1981), 33.
[2] Ibid., 88.

either. This curious detachment was not of his wish. He very earnestly sought to identify himself with England – he had all that enthusiasm for English institutions that those cultivate who are drawn from the outside. It made him very different from the other Christian Socialists. He had, unlike the other leaders, no university background and no attachment to the English landed classes. His outlook was innocent of the paternalism of the old Tory order. His mind was French: he believed in methodical planning, and was 'often irritated by the amateurish, casual and haphazard approach to problems that he found among his English contemporaries'.[3] Until his middle years he even thought in French.[4] The texture of his formal learning was thus unlike that of the other Christian Socialists, too. He was not particularly attracted to English writers, and was critical of Carlyle; his most extensive reading, other than French authors, was in German. His religious background was French. Through sheer distaste for the Church of England, with what seemed to him its cold formalism, its trappings of social privilege, its wasted ecclesiastical machinery, and its pew-rents, he attended the French Protestant Church in London instead. The religious writers and personal influences were French also: Athenase Coquerel, minister of L'Eglise Reformée Nationale, who first introduced him to German thought, and to the synthesis of French Protestantism with contemporary developments in society and culture; Alexandre Vinet, who acquainted him with a reasoned version of Evangelicalism; and above all the Lutheran pastor Louis Meyer, whom he did not meet until 1846, and from whose *Société des Amis des Pauvres* – and not from any English source at all – Ludlow was fired with the ideal of Christian work among the poor of the industrial cities. It was typical of Ludlow that this ideal preceded any attempt at philosophical conviction. He was a practical man 'more concerned with events than ideas'.[5] His earliest English source of inspiration was not the theoretician of the state, Coleridge, but Arnold, whose *Life* by Stanley he had read on its publication in 1844, and had found 'a new turning point',[6] through identification with the subject's commonsense instincts for reform. One interpreter has correctly noticed that Ludlow 'decided to continue where Arnold had left off'; his study of the *Life* became 'the starting point for his subsequent idea of Christian Socialism'.[7]

Ludlow's adhesion to Christian Socialism had an immense personal importance, too. He was by nature a shy man, attractively unpretentious and undemanding, introspective and anxious to break out of it through the service of others. In the company of Maurice and his followers, Ludlow found a group

[3] N. C. Masterman, *John Malcolm Ludlow. The Builder of Christian Socialism* (Cambridge, 1963), 18.   [4] Ludlow, *Autobiography*, 33.

[5] A. D. Murray, in his introduction to Ludlow's *Autobiography*, xviii.

[6] Torben Christensen, *Origin and History of Christian Socialism, 1848–54* (Aarhus, 1962), 51.

[7] Ibid., 53.

of personal English friends for the first time: his life was for a time changed by the movement. After its dissolution in 1854, he returned to his withdrawn condition. At times he suffered depths of loneliness, and on at least two occasions in his life contemplated suicide. Though of quite outstanding religious conviction and perception of faith, he was afflicted – as he listed with characteristic precision – with seven spiritual crises. He settled for the conclusion that 'honest doubt' was 'simply the sincere struggling of a mind for truth';[8] that it was 'impossible without faith'.[9] He remained a layman, although he had thought of priesthood in 1843, linking the vocation with the work of social alleviation in an East End parish.[10] His writings were filled with religious reference, as was his personal life. His vision of social reform was itself a projection of this pursuit of sanctity. 'If, as I believe it to be', he wrote in 1850, 'all earthly society is the work of God and not of man – if it be appointed of God to be, as it were, the reflexion and image of the eternal brotherhood of the Church – if the word 'society' be the very mirror in which that image is glassed . . . if this be so, I say, then all we have to do, every one of us, is, having once learned of such things, to endeavour to understand them; having understood them, to endeavour to remedy them; and God will help us in so doing, if to Him we look for help'.[11]

As a boy and a young man in France, Ludlow had never lapsed from the formal practice of Christian worship, but it was in 1839 that he underwent a distinct conversion experience. The occasion was the earthquake in Martinique, and his sense of gratitude in the divine providence that had, as he understood it, spared the lives of his two sisters who were there at the time visiting relatives. It was, he later affirmed, 'the great spiritual crisis of my life'.[12] Despite the Evangelical style of this experience, and despite his acquaintance with aspects of French Evangelicalism, Ludlow never adhered to true Evangelical principles – or to the qualities of mind which generally characterized those who adopted them. He acknowledged that he had come to authentic spirituality 'by the Evangelical door', but eschewed the Evangelical outlook because of its 'narrowness'.[13] He was, however, extremely orthodox in his religious ideas – unlike, for example, the deism of Neale, or the various blends of pantheism that from time to time preoccupied his friend Mansfield – and he was, like the Evangelicals, soaked in Scriptural fundamentalism. It was Ludlow who first had the idea of holding Bible study evenings, as the centre of fellowship for the Christian Socialist circle.[14] Yet, unlike the Evangelicals, he was a convinced upholder of clerical authority – much more so than Maurice, and certainly

[8] J. M. Ludlow, 'A Dialogue on Doubt', in *Tracts for Priests and People* (Cambridge, 1861), VI, 3.
[9] Ibid., VI, 7.   [10] Ludlow, *Autobiography*, 308.
[11] 'J. T.' [Ludlow], 'Labour and the Poor', in *Fraser's Magazine*, XLI, (January 1850), 9.
[12] Ludlow, *Autobiography*, 57. See also Masterman, *John Malcolm Ludlow*, 26.
[13] Ludlow, *Autobiography*, 59.   [14] Masterman, *John Malcolm Ludlow*, 76.

much more than Kingsley's erastianism would allow. He believed that the head of the Society for Promoting Working Men's Associations should always be, by constitutional provision, a priest; and the grievous and fundamental dispute over the revision of the Society's constitution, in 1852, centred around his insistence that the co-operative movement should be linked with Christianity, in contrast to Maurice's belief that as Christ was in every man, anyway, there was no need for a formal link.[15] The Church to which the movement should be related of course required reform, especially since the Socialist order was 'the highest earthly embodiment of the Christian Church'.[16] From Arnold he got the idea of a broadly based national Church, incorporating Protestant Dissent. When 'more freely-constituted' and 'more livingly-organized', the Church of England could become a federation of denominations: each 'group' 'might be made to fall into its place as an order or fraternity devoted to some special function or functions, but all recognized as forming part of the body of the Church, and subject in the last resort to its general discipline, although ruled, as respects their special functions, by a special discipline of their own'.[17] The resulting Church must be truly national, if not actually formally established by law – this was essential 'for the proper development of a nation's character', and in order to give every person 'the value of the tie which binds him to his fellow-countrymen'.[18] The Catholic Church (as Arnold had also believed) would have to be left out. It was 'positively irreligious'.[19] Ludlow was opposed to voluntaryism in religion, and therefore to one of the mainsprings of Protestant Dissent in nineteenth-century England. 'Do you really feel satisfied with the power of the purse wielded by chapel seat-holders as a final test and bulwark of social doctrine?' he asked.[20] Voluntaryism was simply the hated principle of free economic competition applied to religion. What was needed was the release of the real message of Christianity from its class imprisonment – through Christian Socialism – and the reformation of the national Church to give it an institutional vehicle. 'Christ's gospel, let us be assured', he wrote in 1867, 'has not lost its power over the masses since the days when it was said of its First Teacher, that "the common people heard Him gladly"'.[21] His vision was that the Church 'put forth all her strength to grapple with the hundred-headed evil'; she had been 'supine for too long'. 'As I look upon her benefices and episcopal sees', he continued, writing in 1850, 'upon her deacons, her priests, and her bishops, I seem to see the skeleton of a great army'. The machinery lay ready for

[15] Christensen, *Origin and History*, 202, 314; Ludlow, *Autobiography*, 227.

[16] *Christian Socialist*, I, 244.

[17] *Tracts for Priests and People* (Cambridge, 1861–2), II, No. IX, *Dissent and the Creeds. A Lay Dialogue*, by J. H. Ludlow, 13–14.

[18] Ibid., 20.   [19] Ibid., 21.   [20] Ibid., 7.

[21] J. M. Ludlow and Lloyd Jones, *Progress of the Working Class, 1832–1867* (London, 1867), 281. (The authorship of the sections in this book is separately indicated: Lloyd Jones wrote the first chapter, and Ludlow the rest.)

use. 'Officers to command there are plenty', he noticed; 'but the privates are nowhere'.[22] The parishes could be transformed into cells of social activity: 'let the poor be no more helped *in* their poverty, but helped *out* of it'.[23] It was a noble vision, derived directly from the spiritual sensibilities of one whose religious convictions lay firmly at the basis of his public policies.

Ludlow was arguably the most important of the Christian Socialist leaders of the whole century. His life was actually so long that it spanned the entire sequence of Christian involvement: he lived to take part in the Christian Social Union of 1889, and he even appeared at the Pan-Anglican Congress in 1908. He died at the age of ninety-one in 1911, his remarkable mind still lucid, and his convictions intact. Though not particularly successful in his literary attempts, he was a respected contributor to periodicals; his collection of papers and reports on social work and social issues became a major resource for Church and co-operative reformers. He made decisive contributions to the legal protection of the associations and to the safeguarding of working-class savings. But in two things in particular Ludlow's quiet persistence, through so many years of difficulty, proved of enduring importance. It was he who introduced French ideas about co-operative enterprise, and it was also Ludlow who forged links between the co-operatives and the trade union movement. His legacy was emphatically practical. It was not really French socialist *thinkers* whose ideas Ludlow introduced to Maurice and his gathering circle: it was French co-operative *method*, and the ideals that went with it. Though indebted to the general atmosphere of radicalized France in the 1840s, Ludlow drew his inspiration from no single source – 'his views had been worked out independently'.[24]

As a schoolboy in Paris he had followed English politics through newspaper accounts and had early on decided that he was a sympathizer of the Radicals. At Lincoln's Inn, later, he was to discover that he was the only Radical in chambers, and 'had a good many political tussles with my fellow pupils'.[25] The July Revolution of 1830 turned his thoughts to French politics, and for a time they more or less completely preoccupied him.[26] This was the stage at which he first studied the thought of the French Socialists, though it seems clear that he was not especially attracted; their utopianism was too theoretical – he was dissatisfied with their failure to get involved with the practical issues of reform.[27] By 1848, indeed, it could be concluded that 'he had not the least inclination for Socialistic thinking'. This was the view of Christensen, who went on: 'at most, he may be said to have realised that Socialism constituted a

[22] 'Labour and the Poor', in *Fraser's Magazine*, XLI (January 1850), 17.
[23] Ibid., 18.
[24] Charles E. Raven, *Christian Socialism, 1848–1854* (London, 1920), 65.
[25] Ludlow, *Autobiography*, 40.   [26] Christensen, *Origin and History*, 36.
[27] Ibid., 44, 82.

challenge to the Church, but Christian Socialism as the solution to the problems of the relations between Christianity and Socialism had not then entered his mind'.[28] It is a conclusion which is perhaps a little overdrawn. While it is very probable that the policy of 'Christianizing' Socialism was a product of Ludlow's experience of the political events of 1848 itself, there is some evidence that his earlier acquaintance with the ideas of the French Socialists had been more formative than Christensen allowed. He had already associated himself with the ideas of Fourier, and regarded his debt to them as an enduring part of his political outlook. 'I was more of a Fourierist than anything else', he wrote of his state of mind in 1848. Fourier's Socialism, furthermore, was 'all-embracing', since 'he contemplated a new industrial and social world'. This, Ludlow remarked, showed that 'the working associations of the day in Paris could not be the satisfaction of my social aspirations'. He became, of course, the great advocate, together with Lechevalier, of adopting the practices of the French workshops to English use; but he was anxious, in the *Autobiography*, to establish the Fourierist pedigree of his political ideas. 'I mention this', he added, 'because the formation of the co-operative associations of producers in the various trades has been treated as if it had been the be-all and end-all of our Socialism'.[29] The move to London in 1838 had given Ludlow some knowledge of Owenism, also. But he came to regard it rather dismissively as 'a sect' rather than as a 'popular party'. It 'entertained opinions and sought to carry out principles not shared in, nor indeed understood by the great majority of the working people'.[30] This illustrated another feature of Ludlow's emphasis on the practical: popular politics really did have to be popular; their form should keep pace with, and never exceed, the general education of the working population. However much he may have had to hedge his desire for a universal suffrage within the limitations of evolving mass education, he was, unlike Maurice and Kingsley, a true democrat.

The same realism described his attitude to the Chartists. While he was open to acknowledge the essential moderation of the main body of them, and even to praise their restraint and obedience to the law during the 1848 demonstration,[31] he actually regarded most parts of their platform as premature, and the Chartists themselves as wrongly emphasizing political rather than social change. 'I had long since ceased to look for any substantial results from merely political reform', he wrote, in reflecting upon the failure of Chartism: 'Social reform alone was worth living for'.[32] For the Chartists themselves, he declared no sympathy – 'but neither did I sympathise with their opponents'.[33] In 1848 he went with Kingsley to try to moderate the Kennington Common demon-

---

[28] Ibid., 108.   [29] Ludlow, *Autobiography*, 153.
[30] Ludlow and Lloyd Jones, *Progress of the Working Class*, 296.
[31] *Politics for the People*, No. 1 (6 May 1848), 'The Suffrage – No. I', 11.
[32] Ludlow, *Autobiography*, 120.   [33] Ibid., 121.

stration. He feared the threat to order, not because of essentially middle-class adhesion to property, but because he could see no prospect of a genuine advance of the working class through disorder, given the conditions of political society and the limited development of working-class consciousness.

The move to London in 1838 had also resulted in a study of Political Economy, probably at the suggestion of Bellenden Ker, the Whig head of his chambers in Lincoln's Inn.[34] He found the ideas of the Political Economists to be lacking in humanity and deficient in ordinary social justice. The competitive principle was simply destructive of human worth; it abandoned people to blind forces; it was a 'let alone' system, divorced from authentic human aspirations for brotherhood.[35] This critique passed straight into Ludlow's general support of co-operative socialism as the immediate means of furnishing a practical alternative. The other consequence of the move to London was a study, now at first hand, of English party politics. Ludlow became, in fact, what Maurice and Kingsley certainly were not, a skilled and close observer of the political scene. He even, at one time, thought of a political career for himself.[36] But his involvement in public issues was, until the advent of the Christian Socialist movement, slight. He joined the British India Society and the Anti-Corn Law League, but was not particularly active in either. The latter was 'essentially a middle-class movement, of which a large and representative portion of the working class was distrustful'.[37] It did, however, give him some idea of the power of political organization and, even more, of the effectiveness of concentrating attention on a single issue. Despite his early identification with the Radicals, once in England Ludlow kept clear of party loyalty. This mostly represented his growing conviction that it was social rather than political action which pointed the way forward. There is also a sense in which he found political organization secularizing – 'It is because we are looking for earthly leaders that we cannot see the heavenly one'.[38] He only voted twice in his long life; once at Finsbury, in order to keep out a candidate who was 'a money-lender', and once at Wimbledon, in order to see how the new system of secret balloting worked. Party politics seemed at times to belong to a lower plane. 'Not being a party man', he recorded, 'it has almost invariably appeared to me that the candidates on both sides were just as good the one as the other'.[39] Yet Ludlow's observations of the political realm in England were very detailed. In 1848 he published a series of brilliantly perceptive articles in *Politics for the People* on the various party characteristics. They were also remarkable for their freedom from censorious comment. Toryism, which was 'rather a feeling than an opinion',[40]

[34] Masterman, *John Malcolm Ludlow*, 36.
[35] *Christian Socialist*, I, 2. See also *Tracts on Christian Socialism*, VI, 'Prevailing Idolatries' (October 1850).　　　　[36] Ludlow, *Autobiography*, 308.　　　　[37] Ibid., 72.
[38] *Politics for the People*, No. 17 (July supplement, 1848), 'We Want Leaders', 278.
[39] Ludlow, *Autobiography*, 73.
[40] *Politics for the People*, No. 4 (27 May 1848), 'Party Portraits – No. I. The Tory', 56.

produced, in his judgment, genuine concern for the poor through its traditional paternalism. The Tory, he wrote 'hates oppression, for he instinctively knows it to be the very worst foe of reverence and authority'. The Tory, in fact, 'rather likes a good Radical or Chartist, so long as they do not become seditious'.[41] He seeks 'harmonious co-operation' with the poor, and this elicits 'the feeling of true equality, for he sees a man in every begger'.[42] For the Conservative, also, he had respect, and would indeed claim the name for himself 'if I did not call myself a Radical'.[43] Conservatism was encountered 'in all ranks and classes' and was 'the groundwork of the English character'. It sought seasoned reform, and was 'firmly bottomed, healthy, reflective'. Conservatives were 'prone to experimentalize' in government; to seek the 'removal of political disabilities'.[44] There was, here, though he does not spell it out, a description of the pragmatism of Peelite Conservatism. Whigs, however, were recognized by 'party feeling'.[45] Their party was 'essentially intellectual, philosophical'. They were also 'the aristocratic element' in the nation; but though once a great party they would, he predicted – long before this became evident in fact – increasingly produce fewer great men. They were 'a progressive party, but with limits', that they 'can never pass'. Though good at the initiation of reform, they were obsessed by the need for precedents and 'cannot make it radical'.[46] As for the Radicalism itself, it was 'the latest outgrowth, the last realized development of Christianity in the field of worldly politics'. He cited the words of Christ: 'If thy right hand offend thee, cut it off'; that, he observed, 'is the Radicalism of Christianity'. He added, 'No man can be a Christian who is not, in this sense, a Radical'. At this point, however, Ludlow's analysis of English parties has moved into the ideal, for the Radicals of his day were clearly far removed from his description of Radicalism. 'No man can be a true Radical who is not a Christian', he emphasized,[47] as if to underline the paradox, for the Radicalism of his day was heavily tinctured with free thought and overt hostility to ecclesiastical institutions. Authentic Radicalism, Ludlow continued, was the Christian power to eradicate evil. 'It is the blind Conservative who looks upon the thorns and thistles as holy, instead of feeling that they are God's curse'.[48] Ludlow did not include the Irish party in his series, but it should be noticed that his great admiration for O'Connell in large measure derived from an appreciation of his political Radicalism. In O'Connell, he believed, 'the true sentiments of the people were found'.[49] Ludlow accepted most of the Repeal case. The union of England and Ireland was 'an invalid contract', carried by 'fraud and coercion'; it was 'a great national crime for England that Ireland

[41] Ibid., 57.   [42] Ibid., 58.
[43] Ibid., No. 7 (10 June 1848), 'Party Portraits – No. II. The Conservative', 115.
[44] Ibid., 116.
[45] Ibid., No. 12 (8 July 1848), 'Party Portraits – No. III. The Whig', 199.
[46] Ibid., 200.
[47] Ibid., No. 13 (15 July 1848), 'Party Portraits – No. IV. The Radical', 221.
[48] Ibid., 222.   [49] Christensen, *Origin and History*, 43.

should be what she is'. There followed an unflattering description of the Irish as 'knavish', 'fearfully false', 'bloodthirsty' and 'almost utterly godless'. Ireland, he concluded, 'is what we have made her'.[50]

To some extent, Ludlow's opinions about Ireland were a parallel to his interest in the cause of reform in the administration of India. For family reasons, he retained a life-long and active interest in Indian affairs, and wrote two books about them. His *British India*, published in 1858, was an extended, two-volume analysis of the condition and culture of India, based upon lectures originally delivered at the Working Men's College. To India, he reflected in its *Preface*, he was connected 'by almost innumerable ties'.[51] The matter was not marginal. Ludlow linked the reform of India with the reform of England, and for two essential reasons. The political and administrative systems, in the first place, were the same, in the sense that a single English governing class operated in both spheres. Colonial reform implied 'corresponding changes in the home system'.[52] In India, he argued, the East India Company had done nothing to initiate reform – that had always come from agencies outside government. The lesson, again, was a general one.[53] Yet he approved English rule in India, provided it was genuinely altruistic: they were 'setting before the Indian races a pattern of administrative excellence which they could never have realized for themselves'.[54] Ludlow's second reason for regarding Indian affairs as so important derived from his endorsement of the ideal of a global British presence. Hence his encouragement of emigration. Much is revealed here about Ludlow's sense of the unique virtues of British institutions. The English social transformation he sought, that is to say, was not intended to change the main structure of social life; it was intended only to widen the range of the beneficiaries. Emigration was both an interim solution to poverty in England – until the 'universal civil war' provoked by the competitive system could be phased out[55] – and also positively and enduringly desirable as a means of extending British civilization. He argued for 'one general system of legislation over the whole empire', with colonial representation in the imperial parliament. 'What a glorious empire would this be', he ruminated in 1848, 'when an Englishman could travel from London to Labrador, to Hong Kong, to New Zealand, and find everywhere parishes and boroughs, juries and English judges, churches and schools; when every fruit of the earth, every product of human skill, could circulate untaxed from one British shore to the other'.[56] Two years

[50] *Politics for the People*, No. 7 (10 June 1848), 'Repeal of the Union', 126–7.

[51] J. M. Ludlow, *British India, Its Races, and Its History. Considered with Reference to the Mutinies of 1857* (Cambridge, 1858), I, vii.

[52] *Politics for the People*, No. 14 (22 July 1848), 'The Colonial System', 239.

[53] Ludlow, *British India*, II, 279.

[54] J. M. Ludlow, *Thoughts on the Policy of the Crown Towards India* (London, 1859), Letter xxvi, 356.   [55] *Fraser's Magazine*, XLI (January 1850), 13.

[56] *Politics for the People*, No. 14 (22 July 1848), 'The Colonial System', 239–40.

later, Ludlow gave this picture a more explicitly religious backing. Emigration was now seen in fulfilment of the Scriptural injunction 'to be fruitful and multiply, and replenish the earth'. It was now England's 'duty as a nation' to send out to the rest of the world 'swarms from the parent Saxon hive', to establish 'the elements of her own organic life'.[57] Ludlow also entertained what he called his 'pet terror' that 'a half-million or more of Chinamen' would 'march westwards' and swamp European society.[58] The horror grew with the years, as did the spectre of a 'yellow peril' for many others: it added to his desire to see a strong British presence overseas.

Just as colonial questions were related to Ludlow's domestic political analysis, so his view of what constituted good government was also sometimes defined with first reference to colonial territories. It was therefore in consideration of India that he spelled out most clearly what were the required conditions. They were '1st. Protection of person and property; 2nd Honest and efficient justice; 3rd. An inoppressive fiscal system; 4th. Encouragement to agriculture, industry, and trade; 5th., finally, as a necessary consequence from these, a thriving and contented people'.[59] England should exemplify the same conditions; society was to be seen in organic terms – 'what is good for the whole people, and that only, must hold good of every man'. The entire people 'cannot be rich whilst it contains whole masses of poor'.[60] But what of the actual mechanisms of government? Ludlow really did believe in democracy, and wanted society to move towards the achievement of universal suffrage. Like Maurice, he recognized that the extension of the franchise would have to wait upon the spread of universal education; unlike Maurice, he welcomed the notion of democracy. 'I long for universal suffrage', he wrote in 1848. The qualification was an obvious one: 'so long as men are not capable of self-government, so long are they unworthy of sharing in the government of others; so long as there are wicked and foolish men, so long will it be wrong to allow those wicked and foolish men to control men better and wiser than themselves'.[61] In the end, however, he saw it as realistic that nearly everyone would possess the 'precious and honourable right' of the vote.[62] The scale of admission to the franchise should be set according to true principles of citizenship, and not merely according to numbers. What mattered here, Ludlow contended, was 'moral worth'. He believed that the behaviour of the public during the Chartist emergency of 1848 had shown that conditions were already favourable: 'Not, therefore, as a concession to brawling agitators, but as a reward to the unenfranchised supporters of law and order; not for the

---

[57] *Fraser's Magazine*, XLI, 13.   [58] Ludlow, *Autobiography*, 123.
[59] Ludlow, *British India*, II, 283.
[60] *Politics for the People*, No. 2 (13 May 1848), 'The "People"', 17.
[61] Ibid., No. 1 (6 May 1848), 'The Suffrage – No. I', 10.
[62] Ibid., No. 2 (13 May 1848), 'The Suffrage – No. II', 31.

turbulent Chartist minority, but for the bulk of the people, who have shown themselves not to be turbulent, do I claim an extension of the suffrage'.[63] Like Maurice he rejected the idea of numbers, as such, determining the franchise; like Maurice, again, he believed that education — both formal and in the sense of responsible social behaviour — would in practice result in universal suffrage. 'We are competent boldly to reject the Chartist claim for universal suffrage, as attempted to be enforced by the terror of numbers', he wrote. Yet 'inclusion should be the rule, not exclusion'.[64] How far the extension would finally go, he declared, he did not know, but he saw steps on the way. Property should be abolished completely as the basis of the franchise — this was a 'godless contrivance'. For 'moral worth is not to be fixed at any particular degree in the mere scale of wealth'.[65] He thus rejected household suffrage, which was at the time being promoted by middle-class radicals, since it was centred, still, in a property qualification. He decided for 'a Taxation and Education suffrage': all were to be included who paid 'towards the support of the State'.[66] The old Registration system should be swept away, and — a curious illustration of Ludlow's moral earnestness — victims of drink were to lose the vote. 'The making of drunkenness a disqualification would alone go far towards redeeming the credit of our electoral system', he said.[67] The advantage of a taxation franchise, he continued, was that by lowering the threshold of tax liability the franchise was automatically extended.[68] He also favoured some other reforms to the electoral system: the abolition of property qualifications for Members of Parliament (one of the Chartists' six points), payment of Members (but by their constituencies, not by the State directly), and, not annual Parliaments (as in the Chartist programme), but the election of Members on a phased basis so that a proportion changed each year.[69] Once an advocate of the ballot — a favourite demand on Radical platforms — Ludlow came to reject it. Secret voting was a 'makeshift of expedience'; the ballot was 'the admission that men dare not openly be honest'.[70] In France, under Louis Philippe, he pointed out, the ballot was in use, and corruption and intimidation were still widespread.[71]

Some of Ludlow's caution about the conditions for the extension of the franchise fell away with the experience of the years. The dissolution of the Chartist threat must also have helped, for Ludlow, like so many others, regarded the Chartists as posing a difficulty, a hindrance to reform. The present generation, he wrote in his *Autobiography*, 'has no idea of the terrorism which

[63] Ibid., 32.   [64] Ibid., No. 3 (20 May 1848), 'The Suffrage – No. III', 43.
[65] Ibid., No. 5 (May supplement, 1848), 'The Suffrage – No. IV', 85.
[66] Ibid., No. 6 (3 June 1848), 'The Suffrage – No. V', 103.   [67] Ibid., 104.
[68] Ibid., No. 7 (10 June 1848), 'The Suffrage – No. VI', 120.
[69] Ibid., No. 12 (8 July 1848), 203–4.
[70] Ibid., No. 10 (17 June 1848), 'The Ballot – No. I', 142.
[71] Ibid., 143.

was at the time exercised by the Chartists'.[72] By the time of the reform debates of the 1860s, he was, again like many others, persuaded by the conduct of the working classes, and especially by the restraint shown during the Lancashire cotton famine, that the franchise could safely be extended. Social advance, he saw, had not been matched by a corresponding political emancipation. 'We cannot suppose that men whose physical, intellectual, social condition has been raised', he wrote in 1867, 'are yet no more fit to be trusted with political power than they were thirty-five years ago'.[73] The changes really had been decisive. The working classes were not, he conceded, perfect, but 'their faults and their vices, if not always the same as those of the governing classes, have at least their equivalents among those classes'.[74] The enfranchisement of 'the operative classes' would constitute 'the completion of the national fabric, and not the usurpation of dominion by a class'.[75]

For Ludlow, democracy had always been a necessary accompaniment of socialism. There was, once more, a contrast here with Maurice and Kingsley. It was also an aspect of Ludlow's belief in the organic harmony which should characterize the life of the whole society. 'The Government of the People', he wrote in 1850, 'must mean not the letting loose of all the accumulated selfishness of the many, but the giant self-control of a nation, ruling itself as one man'.[76] When Maurice used his influence to suppress Goderich's tract in favour of democracy, in 1852, Ludlow drew out the difference between himself and Maurice, and in the process obliged Maurice to declare against democracy explicitly. Another contrast between the two men was seen in Maurice's loathing of public opinion and Ludlow's recognition of its value in the reform process. Opinion, Ludlow believed, was 'the queen of the world'. It was 'not by votes, but by ideas' that 'government is carried on'.[77] Government itself was not a matter of responsive action, 'a mere check upon the movements of a nation'; it was, or should be, the force which promoted the directions indicated by 'the national impulse' − by which he meant simply public opinion.[78] Agitation was necessary; it was 'the focus of that political life which the rulers have to shape'.[79] There was, of course, in the Maurician sense, a need to avoid 'the despotism of majorities'. Ludlow wrote 'that between the tyranny of the few and the tyranny of the many, I prefer the former'. Yet even the existing House of Commons, which did 'not directly represent the country, but a number of small oligarchies', in practice consisted of men responsive to opinion − to the 'vast unrepresented mass, perpetually pressing on and driving forward his own constituency'.[80] Opinion also checked the evil of class legislation

---

[72] Ludlow, *Autobiography*, 65.
[73] Ludlow and Lloyd Jones, *Progress of the Working Class*, 83.
[74] Ibid., 299.   [75] Ibid., 'Conclusion', 304.   [76] *Christian Socialist*, I, 49.
[77] *Politics for the People*, No. 2 (13 May 1848), 30.
[78] Ibid., No. 7 (10 June 1848), 124.   [79] Ibid., 125.
[80] Ibid., No. 13 (15 July 1848), 213.

'whether it comes from the monied classes, as with us, or from the working classes, as in France now', he observed in 1848. 'Class legislation is selfish legislation,' he declared; 'party politics are selfish politics'.[81] Too much centralization of government, Ludlow also contended, inhibited the 'true development of national life'. The 'efficiency of government grows in inverse proportion to its cumbrousness'.[82] There were clearly limits, here, to state action which would effect Ludlow's definition of Socialism. In fact he saw very severe limits to the proper sphere of political action.

Social transformation did not of itself make men free. What was needed was a change of heart, an inward cleansing of the sort which Christianity preached: then were men able to set themselves truly in the service of their brothers. But while social conditions degraded them, men could not attain the prior internal change. Hence the dialectical relationship of religion and politics. The suffrage would 'make no rogue honest';[83] the error of the French socialists, he argued, was to suppose that 'by a change in the social machinery' it was possible 'to work out all the purposes of humanity'.[84] This amounted to 'a deadly idolatry'. Machinery itself was 'but a means, not a principle'. That was no reason, he emphasized 'for not seeking better tools to work with'; but it was a reason for 'not breaking such as we have before we can get better ones'.[85] Governments, similarly, 'cannot create movement and life where there is none'.[86] The remedy to social ills, he concluded in his seminal article on 'Labour and the Poor' in *Fraser's Magazine* in 1850, 'lies not in any system or theory, not in any party cry or economical machinery, but in a thorough change of spirit'. He cited Scripture: 'Make me a clean heart, O God, and renew a right spirit within me'. That must be the call of 'this whole nation'.[87] Sceptical, therefore, of any extension of the powers of the state, setting clear limits to the proper realm of the political, and yet recognizing that the crucial interior transformation of men was only possible when social conditions were sufficiently elevated to allow it, it was inevitable that Ludlow would find in the co-operative idea something approaching a sympathetic way forward. It was socialistic, it did not depend on political or state action, it transformed and educated the participants, and it enshrined the principles of human brotherhood and mutual respect.

Ludlow's own knowledge of the social conditions of the working classes was not really much greater than that of the other Christian Socialist leaders in 1848. By selective involvement with schemes of social improvement, through a lifetime's study which made him an expert on the legal position of working-class organizations, and through a continuing connexion with aspects of the labour movement, he came over the years to have a much closer knowledge than the

81 Ibid., No. 2 (13 May 1848), 17.　　82 Ibid., No. 7 (10 June 1848), 125.
83 Ibid., No. 2 (13 May 1848), 30.　　84 Ibid., No. 3 (20 May 1848), 33.
85 Ibid., 34.　　　　　　　　　　　　86 Ibid., No. 7 (10 June 1848), 124.
87 *Fraser's Magazine*, XLI, 13.

others, however. It was his encounter with Louis Meyer in Paris, in 1846, and his *Société des Amis des Pauvres*, which impelled Ludlow – already heightened in a desire for social activism, through his enthusiasm for Arnold – into visiting the slums. The *Société* consisted of young professional men who visited the poor in their homes. Meyer suggested to Ludlow that he begin the same type of work in London.[88] This he did. On his return, he approached J. S. M. Anderson, the Preacher at Lincoln's Inn, who directed him to seek the advice of Maurice. But Maurice was not particularly interested,[89] and Ludlow therefore began to visit the slum courts and alleys on his own. He came, almost at once, to sense the dignity and patience of the poor – even the dignity of those forced into vice and crime by the conditions of their poverty: 'Let those who dare cast the first stone at these poor creatures, I will not'.[90] His was a realistic appraisal, shorn of any romanticism, born of his own suffering. He found no personal taste in the dreadful task he had set himself. 'The goodness of the good poor is unspeakably beautiful and Christ like', he later recorded; 'they are constantly giving out of their necessity, if not in money, in time'.[91] It was this mutual help which particularly surprised and attracted him: 'God's blessings be upon you, ye noble martyrs of labour, sent into this age of horse-race betters and railway gamblers to shew how those words of St. Paul can be fulfilled to the very letter – "Owe no man anything, but to love one another"'.[92] For all that, the work of visiting the poor left him deeply dissatisfied. 'It seemed to me', he reflected, 'that no serious effort was made in any single instance to help a poor person out of his or her misery, but only to help him or her in it'.[93] He came to regard himself as actually 'pauperizing instead of elevating the people', and gave up the work before the end of 1848. Nevertheless, as he remarked, 'I was learning social facts which would be valuable to me thereafter'.[94]

There was another French inspiration for work among the poor which also made a lasting impression on Ludlow. The Deaconesses or French Protestant Sisterhoods undertook works of social alleviation which Ludlow always recommended for emulation in England, and in 1865 he published a book on the need to revive this sort of women's ministry in the Church of England. There he noticed, in the style of Kingsley – and perhaps at his prompting – that the female diaconate had died out 'through the growth in the Church of the false ascetic principle'.[95] On previous occasions, Ludlow had suggested the setting up of public *crèches* for the care of children of working mothers, on lines

[88] Christensen, *Origin and History*, 56; Raven, *Christian Socialism*, 58; Masterman, *John Malcom Ludlow*, 48; Ludlow, *Autobiography*, 98–9.
[89] Christensen, *Origin and History*, 56–7.
[90] 'Labour and the Poor', in *Fraser's Magazine*, XLI (January 1850), 7.
[91] Ludlow, *Autobiography*, 106.   [92] *Fraser's Magazine*, XLI, 8.
[93] Ludlow, *Autobiography*, 103.   [94] Ibid., 104.
[95] J. M. Ludlow, *Women's Work in the Church. Historical notes on Deaconesses and Sisterhoods* (London, 1865), 72. See also Ludlow's article on sisterhoods in the *Edinburgh Review* (May 1848).

similar to those of the French Sisters of Charity.[96] These ideas made Ludlow a pioneer advocate of the development and extension of women's work in the ministry of the Church.

He had made his first visit to the industrial districts in 1841, and was not at all horrified by what he saw. In Birmingham, he found the working people 'fine looking and healthy', the young girls 'often quite roguishly dressed, with pretty pink frocks, often coral necklaces, ear-rings almost always'.[97] In Manchester the workers 'though sometimes pale, were healthy and cheerful'.[98] His next foray was in 1851, when he and Thomas Hughes set off to the north of England to see the co-operatives for themselves. He found 'the pick of our provincial working class' to be 'thoroughly frank and friendly'.[99] Between these two dates, however, he had discovered the nature of the injustices to which the working classes were subjected. Like the other leaders of the Christian Socialist movement, he was informed and moved by the articles in the *Morning Chronicle* in 1849, and in 1850 published his own article on 'Labour and the Poor' in *Fraser's Magazine* (subsequently republished as numbers 3 and 4 of *Tracts by Christian Socialists*). There he noted that the *Morning Chronicle* revelations were not of 'absolutely new facts', for the facts about social conditions had long been buried 'in the dust-heaps of parliamentary blue-books and reports of societies'. What was new was the publicity, and the effect in drawing public opinion 'from the particular to the general, from the effect to the cause'.[100] The plight of the agricultural labourers was the worst – men living like 'beasts' and 'stunted in all their faculties' by poor housing and low wages. The manufacturing districts were 'the most pleasing side of the picture' – 'manufacturing industry is decidedly conducive to the welfare of the people employed in it'.[101] London seemed to represent the competitive system at its worst: 'the employers for the most part have not the slightest connexion with the employed, beyond the giving out work and paying for it'.[102] This was not, he exclaimed, how society was meant to be; if the competitive principle resulted in this, it ought to be abandoned; 'if this be necessary, I say, in English society, then English society is the devil's own work'.[103] Charitable enterprise, however nobly pursued, was not the solution, he argued, for it failed 'in raising the condition of a class of sufferers'. The matter was one of justice. 'What is the meaning of "underpaid labour"?' he asked. It was 'robbery'. It was 'an insult' to the labourers 'and a lie to God'; for by their labour the workers have earned their right to maintenance: 'the money we pretend to give them is *their own*'.[104] There was no immediate solution, however, and for a time 'competition must be attacked with its own

[96] *Fraser's Magazine*, XLI, 2.   [97] Ludlow, *Autobiography*, 55.
[98] Ibid., 56.   [99] Ibid., 204–5.
[100] 'J.T.', 'Labour and the Poor', in *Fraser's Magazine*, XLI (January 1850), 1.
[101] Ibid., 2.   [102] Ibid., 3.
[103] Ibid., 9.   [104] Ibid., 12.

weapons'. Hence the idea of the co-operative workshops, a machinery 'to force wages up, instead of that complex one now existing to force them down'.[105] They must create in England equivalents of the *Associations Ouvrières* of France. 'The principle of association appears to me the only effectual remedy against this fearful beating down of wages', Ludlow contended; 'against this fearful realizing of capitalists' imaginary profits out of the starvation and degradation of the workman'.[106] It was a principle to be applied 'not in one shape, but in a thousand'.[107] The Church, too, must get involved in attacking the evils. He ended by asking his readers if these proposals were 'visionary and ideal'. Even if they were, he concluded, it was better to see 'how nearly we can realize them' than to do nothing.[108]

Ludlow's other great statement on the condition of society came in 1867. The *Progress of the Working Class* was written in co-operation with Lloyd Jones, a fustian-cutter, Owenite, and part-time lecturer on Radical politics. Though, in Ludlow's works, Lloyd Jones was 'singularly reticent in spiritual matters'[109] – he was in fact a free thinker until almost the end of his life – he became Ludlow's 'dear friend'[110] and a major source of his information about working-class opinion. Lloyd Jones had taken part in Chartism and was involved with a series of working-class political organizations, and with both trade unionism and the co-operative movement. The *Progress of the Working Class* was largely written by Ludlow, however, and comprised a lengthy analysis of the developments of the years following the Reform Act of 1832. It was written in order to amplify an essay in which he had outlined 'questions for a reformed parliament';[111] in the atmosphere, that is to say, of the reform discussions of the mid-1860s. There is a detailed analysis of legislation to help the working class, of their influence in public events, of popular education and the 'moral progress' of the people. There was heavy reliance on parliamentary blue book material, and on Ludlow's knowledge of the law. In the introduction, Ludlow observed of himself; 'without being able to boast of a very numerous acquaintance with working men, he has been fortunate enough to be placed in relation, from time to time, with a certain number of the most intelligent amongst them'.[112] Having laid out the main social and moral developments in the middle years of the century, Ludlow lamented that political reform had not kept pace, 'for we cannot reasonably suppose that political progress is inseparable from all other'.[113] The maturity of the class had been revealed in the co-operative movement, and in 'the improvement in the character of the working population generally by means of education', of which there were 'abundant' signs.[114] The Working Men's Colleges, in Sheffield, London, Halifax and

---

[105] Ibid., 13.   [106] Ibid., 16.   [107] Ibid., 17.   [108] Ibid., 18.
[109] Ludlow, *Autobiography*, 149.   [110] Ibid., 147.
[111] Ludlow and Lloyd Jones, *Progress of the Working Class*, Preface, v.
[112] Ibid., 3.   [113] Ibid., 83.   [114] Ibid., 151.

Salford, had shown the same, even though they were patronized by 'only the intellectual élite of the working classes'.[115] On a larger scale, there was every reason to suppose that popular reading matter pointed to the great moral improvement: publications like *The Lady Highwayman* and *Varney the Vampire* were no longer available.[116] Temperance was spreading, although, he feared, drunkenness was still 'the cardinal vice of the working man'.[117] In reply to commonly expressed accusations that the quality of workmanship was declining in England, he admitted a slide but judged that it was no greater than the decline in everything else – journalism, literature, even religion. He blamed 'the excessive pressure of competition';[118] the working class 'cannot be justly charged with having done more than share in the general lowering of tone in what may be called the morality of production'.[119] An important sign, for Ludlow, of the growth of working-class maturity was a decline in hostility to religion. The *Progress of the Working Class* showed Ludlow's own maturity too. Its tone is quiet, its assessments balanced; its realism and its breadth of knowledge still impress and inform the reader. It was through reading the German edition of the book that Lujo Brentano set out to study the co-operative movement in England, and produced, in 1872, his two-volume work.

Through his friendship with Maurice, Ludlow became a central figure in the Christian Socialist movement of 1848–54, and was, indeed, due to his continuing enthusiasm for its ideals, the most consistent and lasting of the leaders. He has, in fact, been rightly seen as 'the founder of the movement';[120] and as Frederick James Furnivall (whom Ludlow himself introduced to the group) observed, he was 'the true mainspring' of English Christian Socialism, for 'Maurice and the rest know nothing about Socialism', whereas Ludlow 'educated in Paris, knew all'.[121] What Ludlow contributed was a critical knowledge of the French Socialist thinkers, and, more importantly, actual first-hand knowledge of French Socialist practice. In 1848 he arrived in Paris on the first train to get through after the February Revolution in order to see that his sisters were safe; he also made a close assessment of political events. What he found was discussion of social as well as political issues. He was in Paris again in September 1849, to visit the *Associations Ouvrières*, and to collect papers and comments about their organization and rules. Although he recognized the limitations of the Socialists' thought – 'they are trying to manufacture a Paradise out of their own theories and imaginations'[122] – he was able to transmit important aspects of their social analyses to England. The English movement, he recorded in his *Autobiography* was, largely in consequence,

[115] Ibid., 178.   [116] Ibid., 182.
[117] Ibid., 266.   [118] Ibid., 268.   [119] Ibid., 273.
[120] Masterman, *John Malcolm Ludlow*, 1.
[121] Quoted in Raven, *Christian Socialism*, 55.
[122] Quoted in Christensen, *Origin and History*, 60.

'intimately connected with the contemporary French one'.[123] Ludlow was particularly impressed by the French mixture of politics and Christianity, and this encouraged his conviction that it was possible to 'Christianize' Socialism and, in the course of doing so, to revitalize the Church. Of the thinkers themselves, Ludlow owed his greatest debt, he declared, to Proudhon – whose first published work, 'never afterwards disavowed by him',[124] was on the necessity for Sunday observance. Even Buchez, whom 'not one of us had ever acknowledged as his teacher',[125] was a practising Roman Catholic. Louis Blanc, another influence, though plainly not a religious one, had shown him that the concept of 'liberty' included 'the idea of power'.[126] Ludlow never developed this last contribution into advocacy of a Socialist state structure, however, and although on one occasion he wrote about the building up 'brick by brick, generation by generation', through class consciousness, of 'a great and prosperous Socialist State'[127] he did not generally envisage Socialism as attainable in England through state power. It was to come through the education, moralizing, and transformation of working men through co-operative enterprise and religious practice.

It is arguable that Ludlow received as much of his knowledge of the *Associations* through Jules Lechevalier as he did from first-hand experience; it is also possible that English Christian Socialism owed as much of its French dimension to Lechevalier as it did to Ludlow. Lechevalier arrived as an exile in England, following Cavaignac's curtailment of Socialist organizations, in 1849. He had been a follower first of St Simon, and then of Fourier, and had joined with Proudhon in the *Banque du Peuple*. He was also Paris correspondent of the *New York Tribune*, for which he continued to work after his arrival in London. He had taken a leading part in the *Associations*, and made the crucial link, also made by Ludlow, between Socialism and Christianity through the practical work of co-operative production. Ludlow had known him in Paris, and introduced him to the Maurician circle when he settled in London. He joined the Church of England, gravitating (as a former Roman Catholic) to the High Church in 1851. The effect of Lechevalier's presence on Ludlow was decisive: it finally confirmed his social diagnosis, and, perhaps more importantly, finally made him abandon pietistic and philanthropic priorities for social activism.[128] Later, according to Ludlow's disillusioned account, Lechevalier 'sank to depths of hypocrisy and intrigue',[129] and eventually he returned to France, where he became a member of the secret police under Napoleon III.

The most decisive influence in Ludlow's conversion to active Christian

[123] Ludlow, *Autobiography*, 172.
[124] Ibid., 112.   [125] Ibid., 165.
[126] *Politics for the People*, No. 17 (July supplement, 1848), 'The Great Partnership', 274.
[127] *Christian Socialist*, I, 201.   [128] Christensen, *Origin and History*, 119.
[129] Ludlow, *Autobiography*, 152.

Socialism, however, was Maurice – who supplied no social or political dimensions, but a compelling religious motivation. When, in 1848, Ludlow addressed to Maurice that letter about the movements in France, and the urgent need to 'Christianize' Socialism, he was unacquainted with Maurice's theological attitudes. But Maurice, hugely impressed, replied saying that 'probably God had some work'[130] for him to do in England; from then onwards, as Ludlow began to go to his house in the evenings and to become acquainted with the rest of the gathering circle, their friendship increased. Ludlow was impressed by Maurice's conception of humanity; of the notion that Christ was in all men, and that the Church might become the means of an actual social regeneration. Though he found Maurice infuriatingly impractical, and disliked his refusal to countenance co-ordinated action – especially when this resulted in the suppression of Ludlow's own idea, in 1849, of a Health League – he acquired an 'exaggerated deference' for Maurice.[131] He was 'by far the greatest man I have ever known', to be ranked equally with Athanasius, Augustine, Anselm, Luther and Calvin.[132] Ludlow used his legal skills to compose a defence of Maurice when he was under attack for his opinions by the council of King's College,[133] and despite their differences of opinion, especially over the nature of the Kingdom and the emphasis to be given to educational rather than co-operative work within the movement, Ludlow always remained loyal to Maurice. 'Arnold, Meyer, Maurice', he recalled towards the end of his life: 'to these three men I owe under God my better self'.[134] The differences about the Kingdom were really very decisive. Whereas Maurice believed it was already in existence, and required only recognition by men, Ludlow saw it as a goal to be achieved in the future, through social transformation, sometimes by political means. For Ludlow, real changes were required in the social fabric, precisely because each man has legitimate claims 'as a social being, as the member of a brotherhood'.[135] The differences of emphasis and analysis between the two leaders also came out in the journalism of their movement. Ludlow was joint editor of *Politics for the People* with Maurice in 1848, and actually wrote about a third of the articles. But the paper was never specifically Socialist enough for Ludlow's taste, and he waited in vain for Maurice to give it a specific and political content.[136] The *Christian Socialist*, on the other hand (with two series, begun in November 1850 and July 1851) was the vehicle of Ludlow's own thoughts: he was sole editor, and saw the paper as 'peculiarly mine'.[137] He ventured to think, with some justification, that the paper 'did most to keep the movement together while it lasted'.[138] The *Christian Socialist* was practical

130 Ibid., 114.   131 Masterman, *John Malcolm Ludlow*, 78.
132 Ludlow, *Autobiography*, 114.
133 *King's College No. 1, the Facts, by a barrister of Lincoln's Inn* (London, 1854).
134 Ludlow, *Autobiography*, 98.   135 *Christian Socialist*, I, 234.
136 Ludlow, *Autobiography*, 130.   137 Ibid., 229.   138 Ibid., 188.

rather than theoretical in its advocacy of Socialism, but it encouraged real social change, the actual structures of society to be replaced – it was all quite unlike Maurice's moral exhortations.

In the last number of *Politics for the People* Ludlow sketched his idea of Socialism in a way which, more clearly than usual, showed why his understanding of it was best expressed within associationism. Socialism, he contended, arose in order to remind men of the imperative of 'human partnership'; it was 'but the recoil of individualism, of that splitting up of society under a thousand influences of sceptical and vicious selfishness'. Socialism, therefore, 'means nothing of itself but the science of making men partners'. It was 'a very old' truth, and afforded, as a science, 'the means of carrying out that partnership into new fields of material or intellectual exertion, of better husbanding of the common stock, of more simply and successfully carrying on the common business, of assigning more judiciously to every partner such duties as he is best able to fulfill. It is God who wills this for the life of the whole nation'.[139] In 1850 he declared that the principle of association appeared to be 'the only effectual remedy' against 'the starvation and degradation of the workman'.[140] At the same time he urged men to remember 'that all property, all talent, all strength, all learning, all labour, is but a trust for the benefit of all'.[141] To achieve some concrete expression of this, 'much must be done by the operatives themelves'; not 'by strikes and combinations, though even these have their worth', but by association, by co-operative workshops.[142] They should learn from the example of Paris, where the associations had revealed 'a sense of conscious freedom' which was 'peculiar to the co-operator'.[143] Personal regeneration was, indeed, the chief object of the co-operatives for Ludlow; it was the most effective and most moral way of elevating mankind from the thrall of capitalist self-interest. It was the working men themselves 'without advice or aid from any outsider' – he rather inaccurately recalled in 1867 – who had 'matured the plans' for the associations in England.[144] The result was the evolution of 'a new type of working man'.[145] The notion was elaborated in his *Thoughts*, produced in September 1852, as a guide to follow in the proposed reconstitution of the central machinery of the co-operatives. His idealism was not in fact followed. Maurice was more concerned with reconciling the working men to their true natures; Neale was preoccupied with their rights. Ludlow rejected any emphasis on rights, and, in the style of Mazzini, sought to redirect men to their social duties. He distrusted those who spoke about 'the Rights of Labour', he wrote, as much as he

---

[139] *Politics for the People*, No. 17 (July supplement, 1848), 'The Great Partnership', 273.
[140] *Fraser's Magazine*, XLI, 16.   [141] Ibid., 13.   [142] Ibid., 15, 16.
[143] Ludlow and Lloyd Jones, *Progress of the Working Class*, 144. There is an account of the Paris Associations in the fourth of the *Tracts in Christian Socialism* (1850).
[144] Ludlow and Lloyd Jones, *Progress of the Working Class*, 131.   [145] Ibid., 143.

distrusted those who spoke of 'the Rights of Property'. He added: 'I know of no inborn and inherent right in any man to any privilege or enjoyment whatsoever'. For we are 'what God makes us', and we 'receive what He gives us'.[146] The whole of society turned upon the point: 'We have Duties to fulfill, and from those Duties spring the Rights of others, not as a property in them, but as an obligation in ourselves'. It was, again, God who willed it. 'Love one another, therefore, that is the measure of human Duty'.[147]

The evidences of personal regeneration were not always apparent in the co-operatives that the Christian Socialists actually set up, following the Working Tailors' Association in 1850. Ludlow, who took the major part in the work, appreciated that the subsequent failures were due to financial causes, and to the diversion, as he saw it, of resources into the Working Men's College. But he also recognized 'that the raw material' of the associations was not 'promising'. The London working men, he came to believe, 'do not possess the energy, the enthusiasm, the spirit of self-sacrifice which in 1848–9 at all events distinguished those of Paris'. The result was that the associations, 'instead of containing the pick of the trades', were made up 'of what the French call the *déclassés*'.[148] Hence, also, the history of financial irregularities by managers of the various enterprises, and their failure to display signs of moral regeneration. Even Charles Sully, secretary of the Tailors' Association, had to be removed from the country in order to avoid a prosecution for bigamy.[149]

Ludlow did not object to the principle of the Working Men's College, and assisted its foundation in 1854; for a time he also gave a few courses of lectures. What he objected to was the priority over the associations which Maurice clearly gave to the College. As the Christian Socialist movement began to break up there were also differences between Ludlow and Neale over the Central Co-operative Agency, and, behind that, over the development of stores as well as workshops.[150] Fundamental, too, was Ludlow's insistence on identifying the work with Christianity. Where others fell away, or quietly allowed their enthusiasm for social reform to slide into near oblivion, Ludlow never departed from either his convictions or his activity. In the history of legislation to protect working-class organization he had an important place. In 1850 he gave evidence to Slaney's Select Committee of the House of Commons on middle and working-class savings; and he appeared, also, before the Royal Commission on Limited Liability set up in 1853. In 1870 he became secretary to Northcote's Commission on Friendly Societies, drew up the resulting legislation in 1875, and was himself, for seventeen years after that date, Chief Registrar of Friendly

[146] *Politics for the People*, No. 6 (3 June 1848), 'Rights and Duties', 105.
[147] Ibid., 106.
[148] Ludlow, *Autobiography*, 207–8.
[149] Masterman, *John Malcolm Ludlow*, 100.
[150] P. N. Backstrom, *Christian Socialism and Co-operation in Victorian England* (London, 1974), 36.

Societies. They were years which he remembered as 'the happiest of my life'.[151] He had also, like Hughes, taken a leading part in the organization of the Co-operative Congress of 1869, and had, in 1859, become a member of the Council of the Social Science Association, and of its committee on trade unions. Ludlow, indeed, had become a valuable link between the co-operative and the trade union movements, suggesting actual schemes for union involvement with model associations.[152] He assisted, in particular, the early development of the Amalgamated Society of Engineers. This enthusiasm had grown with experience. Ludlow had, initially, been sceptical of trade unions, regarding them as 'at best one-sided and one-eyed'; as existing only 'to protect or further a single class-interest'.[153] He preferred, and always preferred, co-operative enterprises. Yet the unions were the most effective school, he came to believe, for teaching the working men 'those powers of organization which, when rightly controlled and directed, make the will of the mass the will of one, and its might as that of millions'.[154] But it was associationism which developed 'organic fellowship', and which enabled men to realise 'in their fullness, and in their depth, those marvellous words of St. Paul, that we should be "members one of another"'.[155]

[151] Ludlow, *Autobiography*, 288.
[152] *Christian Socialist*, II (15 November 1851), 'Address and proposals of the Central Co-operative Agency to the trade societies in London and the United Kingdom'.
[153] Ludlow and Lloyd Jones, *Progress of the Working Class*, 227.
[154] Ibid., 228.   [155] *Christian Socialist*, I, 28.

5

THOMAS HUGHES

There was general laughter among the gathered Christian Socialists when Maurice announced that Thomas Hughes had joined them. That was in the autumn of 1848, some months after the beginning of the movement. 'We are not going to start a cricket club', someone said.[1] For Hughes was known as an extrovert and a sportsman, distinguished at Oxford not for his learning or his participation in ecclesiastical controversy, but for rowing and being a cricket blue. Of 'the high regions of scholarship, criticism, or science', he confessed, 'I have neither head nor time for such matters'.[2] There has been a general agreement among observers of the Christian Socialist movement that he was 'intellectually the least gifted'.[3] He was, Raven noted, 'unperplexed with doubts'.[4] Yet the case for his inclusion among the most influential of the leaders is a strong one. Hughes never lost his early faith in Christian Socialism, and devoted a lifetime to political activity to further the cause. He laboured extensively to preserve religious ideals within the developing co-operative movement, and, as a Liberal Member of Parliament, he became a central spokesman for working-class aspirations. After Kingsley, he was, through his writings, the great popularizer of the ideals of social reform which the Christian Socialist group had projected. He embodied, in fact, all that Kingsley sought to be – but never was: practical, athletic, and with an easy and unselfconscious rapport with the working classes. 'For many years I have been thrown very much into the society of young men of all ranks', Hughes wrote in 1861; 'I like being with them, and I think they like being with me'.[5] It was the truth. Hughes was at the centre of the movement because he exuded good-will and attracted the trust of the other leaders – men who were given to aggravated bouts of critical internal strife. Kingsley, in writing to encourage his political hopes, in

---

[1] Edward C. Mack and W. H. G. Armytage, *Thomas Hughes* (London, 1952), 52; Charles E. Raven, *Christian Socialism, 1848–1854* (London, 1920), 130.
[2] Thomas Hughes, *Religio Laici*, in *Tracts for Priests and People*, No. 1 (Cambridge, 1861–2), 7.
[3] D. O. Wagner, *The Church of England and Social Reform since 1854* (New York, 1930), 139.
[4] Raven, *Christian Socialism*, 131.   [5] Hughes, *Religio Laici*, 9.

the 1860s, remarked on 'the real spiritual good which you have done to men's hearts'.[6] There were, in Hughes' life, no hidden complications or unwholesome ambitions. His was a noble and selfless dedication to the cause of social harmony and reform, undertaken from impulses of patriotism, social romanticism, and practical Christianity. His religious faith, like his politics, was simple and deeply felt. 'I tell you that all the miseries of England and of other lands consist simply in this and in nothing else', he declared; 'that we men, made in the image of God, made to know Him, to be one with Him and His Son, will not confess that Son, our Lord and Brother, to be the Son of God and Son of Man, the living Head of our race and of each one of us'. If they would make that confession, Hughes continued, in a frame of reference that actually owed more to Arnold than to Maurice, they would see 'that the Kingdom of God is just as much about us now as it will ever be'.[7] His clarity of thought and expression, as much as his patent goodness, inspired the other leaders to give him their confidence. Ludlow, in particular, became a close friend. The two families actually shared a house together for a few years – 'The Firs', in Wimbledon, completed in 1854 by the North London Working Builders' Association, one of the co-operative enterprises got up by the Christian Socialists.

Hughes' personality was very unified: his life and his ideas were closely related and did not change significantly. At the heart of his social vision was the world of the country squires from whom he came; at the centre of his politics was an ideal of 'democracy' which had more to do with rustic *camaraderie* than it had with the palliation of the gritty sufferings of the industrial poor. Yet his involvement in the evolution of the co-operative movement, and his work to maintain a link between it and developing trade unionism, were real contributions to the advancement of the working classes. The pivot was the ideal of service, and the desperate urgency, as he saw it, of defeating the materialism of his day by educating the ruling classes out of their social selfishness. The enemy was 'the open and unabashed property worship', the 'Mammon worship of our time', the 'idolatry of mere hard cash'.[8] 'There is nothing which tries individual character so shrewdly as wealth coming suddenly and in plethoric abundance; and what is true of individuals is true of nations', Hughes observed in a talk at Rugby School in 1881: 'In the intoxication of this great materialist movement we English have somewhat lost our heads – have come to an alarming extent to acknowledge the heaping up of wealth to be the true end of all effort; and the hero, the man most worthy of admiration, the happy man, he who has succeeded best in his business'.[9] The task was to restore simplicity of living to the ruling classes, and to prevent the

---

[6] *Charles Kingsley: His Letters and Memories of his Life*, edited by his wife (London, 1878), II, 133.

[7] Hughes, *Religio Laici*, 37.

[8] Thomas Hughes, *Rugby, Tennessee, being some Account of the Settlement Founded on the Cumberland Plateau by the Board of Aid to Land Ownership Limited* (London, 1881), 8.

[9] Ibid., 122–3.

contamination of the working classes with materialism as they acquired what was, he believed, justly theirs – an enormous improvement in their material circumstances. However much he may have clung to the virtues of the rural social order from which he came, Hughes still sought a real alteration in the balance of society. 'Every change is a transformation to something higher', he reflected in 1859, in the sad days following the death of his son Maurice, for whom *Tom Brown's School Days* had originally been written.[10]

Tom Brown actually illustrated most of Hughes' social beliefs – both the *School Days*, published in 1857, and the later *Tom Brown at Oxford*, which appeared as three volumes in 1861. Ludlow, writing of the Christian Socialist movement from the perspective of his later years, noted that '*Tom Brown's School Days* belongs to it as truly as *Yeast* or *Alton Locke*'.[11] Ludlow also noted that he had 'not conceived him capable of producing anything so original and so good',[12] thus illustrating once again the consensus about Hughes' rather limited intellectual capacity. Both books, together with the popular biographical studies which Hughes produced in the 1880s, were crammed with his beliefs; they were moral tracts, in effect – in social harmony, in the ideals of service, in the virtues of simple and healthy living, in the superiority of practical action over intellectual criticism, in applied broad Christianity, and, above all, in helping the less fortunate to achieve dignity and independence. In the preface to *Tom Brown at Oxford* Hughes declared that the hero was not 'a portrait of myself'.[13] But that was not really so. The work, like the preceding *School Days*, has strong autobiographical qualities,[14] and in Tom Brown's awakening social conscience at Oxford there was an authentic, if exaggerated, description of Hughes' own experience. For there grew in the hero 'a true and broad sympathy for men as men, and especially for poor men as poor men, and a righteous and burning hatred against all laws, customs, or notions, which, according to his light, either were or seemed to be setting aside, or putting anything else in place of, or above the man'.[15]

It is not necessary, as it so often is with other men, to have to pick into the details of Hughes' family and educational background to assemble some elements of his later attitudes: for in Hughes the whole background became the groundwork of his mature thought. He was born at Uffington, in the Vale of the White Horse, in 1822, and went to school first at Twyford (where he met Charles Mansfield, another pupil) and then at Rugby. Both the home at

[10] Mack and Armytage, *Thomas Hughes*, 104.
[11] John Ludlow, *The Autobiography of a Christian Socialist*, ed. A. D. Murray (London, 1981), 192, 263.   [12] Ibid., 282.
[13] Thomas Hughes, *Tom Brown at Oxford* (Cambridge, 1861), I, xii.
[14] David Newsome, *Godliness and Good Learning. Four Studies in a Victorian Ideal* (London, 1961), 212. Norman Vance, *The Sinews of the Spirit. The Ideal of Christian Manliness in Victorian Literature and Religious Thought* (Cambridge, 1985), 134, 163.
[15] Hughes, *Tom Brown at Oxford*, III, 153.

Uffington and Rugby were to provide the permanent models of right social order for Hughes. The first seemed to typify the robust 'democracy' of rural England, and was described in *Tom Brown's School Days* and in *The Scouring of the White Horse* – an account, written in 1859 and published with illustrations by Richard Doyle, of the history and legends of his native countryside. There he frankly wrote of his possession 'by intense local attachment, love for every stone and turf of the country where I was born and bred'.[16] At Rugby, between 1833 and 1842, he cultivated friendships which were to last a lifetime, enjoyed games, and was academically idle. He moved on to Oriel, which was his father's college. 'With the exception of Christ Church', he recalled, 'there was at this juncture probably no College in Oxford less addicted to reading for the schools, or indeed to intellectual work of any kind'.[17] He fitted in perfectly. His academic capabilities were rather like those of most who at the time proceeded to Holy Orders in the Church of England, and Hughes thought of the idea,[18] but entered Lincoln's Inn instead, where he shared chambers with Neale, and later with Ludlow. In 1847, after a long engagement, he married. That his life did not enfold upon a quiet and unremarkable professional course was due to two conditions of his education. The second of these was his adhesion to social reformist ideas while at Oxford; the first was the legacy of Rugby School.

Just as Ludlow, in his self-imposed exile from the France of his happy youthful years, created a half-mythical ideal of the land he was distanced from, so Hughes spent a lifetime idealizing the Rugby of his school days. The central figure was, of course, Thomas Arnold. It is not clear that the great headmaster took much note of Hughes, but the impact of Arnold on Hughes' development was enormous, providing him with a progressive openness to reform, with a latitudinarian Christianity, and with a sense of the unique virtue of England's historical development as the land of individual liberty. Arnold's weekly history lessons to the sixth form dwelt frequently on the theme of free Saxon institutions and democratic customs before the imposition of Norman feudalism. It was a theme common enough among radical and liberal writers of the early nineteenth century. Arnold employed the historical myth to show the origins of social class estrangement: the background to the social unrest of the day.[19] Hughes later recollected that Arnold's influence was never brought directly to bear on English politics – 'What he did for us was, to make us think on the politics of Israel, and Rome, and Greece, leaving us free to apply the lessons he taught us in these, as best we could, to our own country'.[20] One of the legacies, doubtless, was Hughes' project, in co-operation with Ludlow, to further Christian Socialism by 'a series of historical novels bringing out the

[16] Thomas Hughes, *The Scouring of the White Horse; or The Long Vacation Ramble of a London Clerk* (Cambridge, 1859), vi.
[17] Mack and Armytage, *Thomas Hughes*, 27. [18] Ibid., 48. [19] Ibid., 24.
[20] Thomas Hughes, *Memoir of a Brother* (second edn., London, 1873), 89.

socialist or communist element in the past history of England'.[21] None were written. Much as he enjoyed Rugby, it should be noticed, the effect of Arnold on his developing progressivism was delayed. There was little evidence of it during his first two years at Oxford, and it was only with the publication of Stanley's *Life of Arnold*, in 1844, that Hughes seems to have adopted him as the first and greatest of his social teachers. The *Life*, Hughes wrote, 'had come like a revelation to many of us'.[22] Phrases of Arnold's thereafter became his watchwords: he was 'haunted' by the sentence 'If there is one truth short of the highest for which I would gladly die, it is democracy without Jacobinism'.[23] When Hughes spoke or wrote about the 'Kingdom of Christ' he inevitably quoted Arnold, not Maurice. 'Making the kingdoms of the world become the kingdoms of Christ; not partially, or almost, but altogether', Arnold had said, was a real possibility – 'the means are yet in our hands'. Hughes cited the words as the purpose of public life.[24] That was in a book on church reform dedicated to W. E. Forster, a man who earned his approval not only because of his Liberal principles but because he had married one of Arnold's daughters in 1850. Hughes saw the influence of Arnold on all the Rugbeians he knew, and recruited some of them into the Christian Socialist movement. Thus George Grove, G. G. Bradley, and Septimus Hansard were signed up. Hansard had been head boy of Rugby at the time of Arnold's death, and, as Ludlow perceptively noticed, 'formed with Hughes the main link between the Arnold school and the pure Maurician one'.[25]

Arnold was a progressive Liberal, perhaps even a Radical (at least in his attitude to church reform), but he was not remotely a Socialist. How, then, did it come to pass that his disciple and practical interpreter became so tenacious a Christian Socialist? Hughes himself, in ruminating at length over the failure of his brother George to remain in the movement, admitted that the word Socialist itself had only a limited application. They called themselves 'Socialists', he recalled, because 'our trade principles [co-operation] were on all-fours with Christianity, while theirs [the upholders of the competitive principle] were utterly opposed to it'.[26] Yet he agreed with his brother that use of the word 'socialist' identified them with the opponents of property – 'which they were not'. Hence their unfortunate tendency to repel rather than attract many who 'were inclined theoretically to agree with us'.[27] Hughes adhered to the Christian Socialist movement in 1848 for very much the same sort of reasons as the other leaders: because of his enthusiasm to do something for humanity which would progressively release the working classes from the thrall of

21 Ludlow, *Autobiography*, 316.
22 Hughes, *Memoir of a Brother*, 89.   23 Ibid., 89.
24 Thomas Hughes Q.C., *The Old Church; What shall we do with it?* (London, 1878), 22.
25 Ludlow, *Autobiography*, 138–9.   26 Hughes, *Memoir of a Brother*, 112.
27 Ibid., 114.

existing economic relationships. That something was co-operative enterprise. In *Tom Brown at Oxford* the hero had set out to learn more about 'the condition-of-England problem', and had done so by the study of Political Economy.[28] He had found it unsatisfactory. So did the real Thomas Hughes. Tom Brown had gone on to become, for a time, 'little better than a physical force Chartist'.[29] Hughes omitted this development himself (though he did admit that for a time the Charter had 'a strange attraction for me'[30]), but he did seek to follow one of his other fictional characters in the book, Grey, in undertaking social work among poor young men in London.[31] It was at Oxford, in the summer of 1844, that Hughes gave up the traditional Toryism of his family for political Liberalism. If the publication of Stanley's *Life of Arnold* was the catalyst, the actual occasion appears to have been a discussion with some travellers encountered at Lancaster while he was *en route* to Scotland.[32] Thereafter he designated himself 'an advanced liberal',[33] and continued to do so for the rest of his life. Christian Socialism he seems to have regarded as an additional dimension to this; as something *practical* to help the poor. There was also some influence of Carlyle. Tom Brown had experienced 'exultation' on reading *Past and Present*; 'he had scarcely ever in his life been so moved by a book before'.[34] Hughes was a little more selective than his fictional creation. Yet he was attracted by Carlyle's lack of respect for existing social arrangements, and by his insistence that the world was God's world, and that all men had a duty as men to find their work in it. Together with Arnold, and the example of the rural squires with their traditional obligations, Carlyle furnished Hughes with his ideal of service.

Hughes had in his study what he called his 'prophetic bookcase'. Its contents disclosed the chief influences in his social attitudes. These were to be found among the works of Maurice, Kingsley, Carlyle, Emerson and Lowell. In 1881 he listed the 'prophetic voices' of the nineteenth century as those of Carlyle, Arnold, Maurice and Newman.[35] Neale was remembered as the person who had acquainted him with the French socialists and with Marx and Lasalle.[36] Although he owed a lasting debt to Maurice, it was probably less than most of the other leaders; Maurice seems merely to have confirmed the optimistic view of humanity, and the idea of the immanence of the kingdom, which Hughes had already got from Arnold. Maurice also gave these concepts – an idea that would have horrified him – a kind of systematic basis for Hughes. *Tom Brown at Oxford* was actually dedicated to Maurice. Hughes had first heard him as he

---

[28] Hughes, *Tom Brown at Oxford*, III, 37.   [29] Ibid., III, 114.
[30] Hughes, *Memoir of a Brother*, 89.   [31] Hughes, *Tom Brown at Oxford*, III, 263–4.
[32] Mack and Armytage, *Thomas Hughes*, 43; Hughes, *Memoir of a Brother*, 89.
[33] Hughes, *Memoir of a Brother*, 117.   [34] Hughes, *Tom Brown at Oxford*, III, 41–2.
[35] Hughes, *Rugby, Tennessee*, 11.
[36] P. N. Backstrom, *Christian Socialism and Co-operation in Victorian England* (London, 1974), 31.

preached in the chapel at Lincoln's Inn, in the late summer of 1846. He was impressed, as he said, because 'his views nearly coincide with Arnold's'.[37] He came to have 'an unbounded confidence in Maurice and was always ready to follow his advice'.[38] Maurice, that is to say, became the substitute for the dead Arnold. In reality Hughes and Maurice can have had little in common: Hughes was practical and non-theoretical in his approach to social issues, whereas it was of the very essence of Maurice that he shied away from actual involvement with political realities. But Hughes summarized him, finally, as 'a bold and earnest social reformer'.[39]

With Kingsley, matters were more on the surface. What Hughes chiefly shared with Kingsley was a love of trout fishing, and that was what their letters were mostly about.[40] The two men had first met at Maurice's house in 1848. Kingsley discovered in Hughes just the common-sense athleticism that he projected as his ideal. In Hughes' writings he professed to find a confirmation of his own distaste for asceticism and feminity. 'The day of "pietism" is gone, and "Tom Brown" is a heavy stone in its grave', Kingsley wrote to Hughes in 1857. '"Him no get up again after that", as the niggers say', he added.[41] The two men did in fact have a reasonably close identity of views on both church and social matters; both were broad churchmen, hostile to Tractarianism and exclusivity in religion, and both urged practical measures for social alleviation. Hughes' admiration for James Russell Lowell, the American poet, began in the later 1850s, though the two men did not actually meet until 1870, when Hughes called to see him at his house in Boston while he was on an American tour. Lowell believed in the destiny of the Saxon race, upheld the Saxon peoples as the great exponents of freedom and individual liberty, was suspicious of mob democracy but upheld popular institutions, and combined his liberalism with a strong conviction of the truth of Christianity. He was 'the last of Hughes' gods: the peer of Arnold and Maurice'.[42]

Hughes' understanding of Christian Socialism was centred in his ideas about democracy. He regarded himself as a thorough democrat. Democracy, he wrote in 1878, 'was a cause well worth the devotion of a life'; it was an 'early faith' from which he had never departed.[43] Originally he had seen it as a kind of folk spirit; the natural harmonious good-fellowship of the rural countryside from which he came, where the sons of labourers and the sons of squires played sports together and judged one another by their manly qualities and not by the accidents of birth or status. There is a description of such relationships in the first

[37] Quoted in Mack and Armytage, *Thomas Hughes*, 52.
[38] Torben Christensen, *Origin and History of Christian Socialism, 1848–54* (Aarhus, 1962), 362.
[39] Thomas Hughes, *Memoir of Daniel Macmillan* (London, 1882), 226.
[40] Thomas Hughes, 'Prefatory Memoir' to the 1881 edition of Kingsley's *Alton Locke* (London, 1881), 42.   [41] *Charles Kingsley: Letters and Memories*, II, 27.
[42] Mack and Armytage, *Thomas Hughes*, 133.   [43] Hughes, *The Old Church*, 9.

part of *Tom Brown's School Days*, and there, too, was the mature embodiment of the true democratic spirit, as envisaged by Hughes, in Squire Brown's impeccable performance of his traditional social duties towards the people. He thought 'It didn't matter a straw whether his son associated with the lord's sons or ploughmen's sons, provided they were brave and honest'.[44] His wife 'dealt out stockings, and calico shirts, and smock frocks, and comforting drinks to the old folks'.[45] In later life Hughes confessed that, in remembrance of such conduct, he had 'never been able to hate or despise the old-fashioned Tory creed'.[46] His belief that traditional relationships were being ruined by the rise of the commercial spirit, and by 'the further separation of classes consequent on twenty years of buying cheap and selling dear',[47] was characteristically Tory. As a Liberal politician, Hughes continued to believe in the permanence of social class stratification, and sought reforms that guaranteed its safe existence by removing the grievances of those who were less favourably placed within the stack. Much remained to be done, he wrote in 1881, 'before we can feel anything like security as to the foundations of our social pyramid'.[48] There was no suggestion here that the pyramid was itself an injustice. Hughes, like so many Liberals in the second half of the nineteenth century, was shocked by the idea of the rule of numbers; his understanding of democracy did not include the sovereignty of the masses. But he did give his concept of 'democracy' some real political content. The electorate was to be widened in recognition of the inherent worth of the working men – who were then expected to support the virtues and enlightenment preached by men of education and position. The 'true democrat', Hughes wrote, 'will destroy nothing which others value merely because he doesn't value it himself'.[49] He will also value the inheritance of the past, and not root up institutions and practices indiscriminately. 'At such a time as that in which we live', he advised, 'we should not rashly cut off any of our old links with the past without trying very steadily, and testing very severely, whether they won't stand the strain of the present – whether they are not better for this time than anything we should be likely to make under new circumstances'.[50] At Birmingham, in 1872 (where he called himself 'a Radical'), he defined his political practice as 'the greatest good (not happiness) of the greatest number'.[51] The qualification was an important one: there was to be no slavish palliation of the mere wants of the masses. That he regarded as the evil legacy of Jeffersonian democracy to the American political tradition. It had proceeded by 'dressing Jacobinism in cheap philosophical robes, and professing to fall down and worship "the great voice of the people"'.[52] In the end, Hughes

---

[44] *Tom Brown's School Days, (by An Old Boy)* (London, 1889 edn.), 43.

[45] Ibid., 13.

[46] Hughes, *Memoir of a Brother*, 117.

[47] *Tom Brown's School Days*, 33.

[48] Hughes, *Rugby, Tennessee*, 16.

[49] Hughes, *The Old Church*, 10.

[50] Ibid., 45.

[51] Quoted in ibid., 23. His speech was on the 'Advantages of a Public Church'.

[52] Ibid., 130.

expressed his understanding of democracy most coherently in his description of the purpose of the self-help community he inspired in Tennessee in 1880. 'Our aim and hope are to plant on these highlands', he said, 'a community of gentlemen and ladies; not that artificial class which goes by those grand names, both in Europe and here, the joint products of feudalism and wealth, but a society in which the humblest members, who live (as we hope most if not all of them will to some extent) by the labour of their own hands, will be of such strain and culture that they will be able to meet princes in the gate'.[53] But Hughes did support an extensive widening of the franchise in England as well. Indeed, he had shown his early adhesion to democracy when, against Maurice's successful protests, he had promoted Lord Goderich's tract, *The Duty of the Age*, with its frank advocacy of democratic principles, in 1852. Nearly thirty years later he told public men that they should realize 'that labour is going to be King'.[54] Though opposed to the ballot (and for the same reasons as Ludlow – that it was unmanly), Hughes supported most movements for parliamentary reform. Throughout the agitation for the second Reform Bill, in the mid-1860s, he worked for the Reform League. His maiden speech in the House of Commons, in 1866, advocated a democratic suffrage. He supported the North in the American Civil War, thus associating himself with the democratic forces in England who used public feelings on the American question as a vehicle for the propagation of their ideas. 'If the North is beaten', he wrote in 1861, 'it will be a misfortune such as has not come upon the world since Christendom arose'.[55] It was a broad canvas. Hughes, similarly, represented the purpose of political life, and his part in it, in large terms. Speaking of 'the object of politics' in 1873, he said 'the chief means of making a wise and understanding people is by training them up in wisdom and understanding'. He added: 'The State wants men who are brave, truthful, generous; the State wants women who are pure, simple, gentle'.[56] Hughes' advocacy of political democracy did not extend very far into the possibility of female emancipation.

The quality which made Hughes known to the Christian Socialists when he joined them was also significant in his own attitude to public affairs. For he regarded sport as tending to democracy. 'The charm of cricket and hunting', he wrote, 'is that they are still more or less sociable and universal'.[57] The need was to secure their place in the new mass society of the industrial heartlands. 'Don't let reformers of any sort think that they are going really to lay hold of the working boys and young men of England by any educational gospel whatever, which hasn't some *bonâ fide* equivalent for the games of the old country "veast" in it', he declared.[58] Hughes carried his devotion to the cause of athleticism into

[53] Hughes, *Rugby, Tennessee*, 106.
[54] Ibid., 19.   [55] Mack and Armytage, *Thomas Hughes*, 134.
[56] Hughes, *The Old Church*, 41. His speech was 'Established and Voluntary Churches in Contrast'.   [57] *Tom Brown's School Days*, 23.   [58] Ibid., 33.

the Christian Socialist movement. At the Working Men's College he organized boxing classes – to the astonishment of Maurice[59] – and also got up a corps of Volunteers during the French invasion scare of 1859. It 'attracted men interested in uniforms rather than in intellectual culture'.[60] Hughes also organized cricket matches between the co-operative associations. He even insisted on taking Matthew Arnold for early morning swims, and on one occasion remained in the water for an hour, 'with the swans looking at them'.[61] Athleticism was not a legacy of Arnold;[62] it may, in Hughes' case, have gone back to that first school in Twyford which was, as Hughes himself recalled, 'before its time' in encouraging gymnastics.[63] The Christian part of his Christian Socialism was 'muscular'. He was forthright in asserting it. Muscular Christianity, he wrote, 'has hold of the old chivalrous and Christian belief, that a man's body is given to him to be trained and brought into subjection, and then used for the protection of the weak, the advancement of all righteous causes, and the subduing of the earth which God has given to the children of men'.[64] Here, then, was a clear link: those who would perform practical work for the betterment of the poor were those who disciplined themselves first. In 1879 Hughes published a book called *The Manliness of Christ*. Its purpose was to show young working-class men that religious belief, far from showing weakness, as was popularly supposed, was a sign of strong moral character. True manliness, furthermore, 'is as likely to be found in a weak as in a strong body':[65] there was to be no élite of the fit, since muscular Christianity was authentically democratic. Hughes was fully aware of the dangers inherent in a cult of physical strength, and therefore went to some lengths to emphasize that 'athleticism is a good thing if kept in its place, but it has come to be much over-praised'.[66] With strength went simplicity of living. In the best schools 'extravagance is sternly controlled and simple habits are encouraged'.[67] He taught that there was no effective way of preventing the rich from falling into a vulgar dependence on their wealth, or of preventing the poor from envying that very weakness. 'But you may live simple and manly lives yourselves, speaking your own thought, paying your own way, and doing your own work', he insisted. Then 'you will remain gentlemen so long as you follow these rules, if you have to sweep a crossing for your livelihood'.[68] Hughes came to lament the professionalization of sport, and the growing luxury of life in public schools – where 'boys are made to feel

---

[59] Mack and Armytage, *Thomas Hughes*, 179.
[60] Wagner, *The Church of England and Social Reform*, 115.
[61] Mack and Armytage, *Thomas Hughes*, 62.
[62] Newsome, *Godliness and Good Learning*, 80. See also Vance, *The Sinews of the Spirit*, 71.
[63] Hughes, *Memoir of a Brother*, 17.   [64] Hughes, *Tom Brown at Oxford*, I, 199.
[65] Thomas Hughes, *The Manliness of Christ* (London, 1879), 25.
[66] Ibid., 25. For a general discussion, see J. A. Mangan, *Athleticism in the Victorian and Edwardian Public School* (Cambridge, 1981), 6–9, 107.   [67] Hughes, *Rugby, Tennessee*, 4.
[68] Hughes, *Memoir of a Brother*, 96–7.

uncomfortable who do not conform to the fashion, or who practise such useful and often necessary economies as wearing old clothes or travelling third-class'.[69] Like Maurice and Kingsley, he had a firm conviction that values should be maintained by physical force; he differed from them in supposing that valour was expressed in individual tenacity rather than in military action. In an illustrative homily to 'The Fight' at Rugby, in *Tom Brown's School Days*, Hughes observed, 'From the cradle to the grave, fighting, rightly understood, is the business, the real highest, honestest business of every son of man'. For everyone 'worth his salt' had enemies, 'who must be beaten'. Quakers and other pacifists, he argued, were merely unrealistic. 'Human nature is too strong for them'. He concluded: 'The world might be a better world without fighting, for anything I know, but it wouldn't be our world'.[70] In *The Manliness of Christ* he added, 'we are born in a state of war; with falsehood and disease, and wrong, and misery in a thousand forms, lying all around us and the voice within calling on us to take our stand as men in the eternal battle against these'.[71] It was thus part of the dynamics of Christian Socialism, for Hughes, that those who would take up the task of social reform must first cultivate an interior life of religious dedication, made active and socially useful by strength and simplicity of living.

Just as there were differences of emphasis between Hughes' idea of physical force, and Maurice's and Kingsley's, so his strong sense of nationalism and patriotism was rather different from theirs. Hughes' was more concerned with the preservation of the old England of the squires and the shires; theirs had wider overtones of national interests in opposition to those of other nations. Hughes saw the nation as 'a family, bound together to work out God's purposes in this little island and in the uttermost parts of the earth . . . and to sink in their proper place the miserable trifles, and odds and ends, over which we are so apt to wrangle'.[72] The destiny of the nation and of Christianity were one.[73] The dons, in *Tom Brown at Oxford*, were blamed for converting the University into a 'learning machine', when it should be 'the heart of dear old England'.[74] Hughes' patriotism looked to the preservation of a world that was rapidly passing away; it was a romanticizing of the rural relationships that had survived from the pre-industrial age. Much of Hughes' Christian Socialism was an attempt to humanize the new world with the values and personal styles of the old. It was, to put it simply, even obviously (but accurately), to convert the whole of England into a kind of Rugby School, with the social reformers, like Arnold, teaching manly virtues to the emergent masses. Hughes was as alarmed by the lack of true patriotism within the working classes as he was by their disregard of religion. At one of the Christian Socialists' meetings with working men at the Cranbourne Tavern he sprang to the chair and threatened to fight the Chartists

[69] Hughes, *The Manliness of Christ*, 165–6.   [70] Hughes, *Tom Brown's School Days*, 231.
[71] Hughes, *The Manliness of Christ*, 34.   [72] Hughes, *The Scouring of the White Horse*, x.
[73] Hughes, *The Old Church*, 25.   [74] Hughes, *Tom Brown at Oxford*, I, 124.

who had hissed when the National Anthem was played on the piano.[75] His patriotism was, unlike Kingsley's, devoid of race prejudice. He observed black society in America closely, particularly at the time of the Tennessee Settlement in 1880 – though his interest had begun with opposition to slavery at the time of the Civil War – and believed 'that the black race have a great future in America'.[76] He could see no qualities which were not universal and human ones. 'The negro will loaf and shirk as often as not when he gets the chance', he noticed, 'but he has not the white craving for knocking off altogether as soon as he has a couple of dollars in his pocket'.[77] Kingsley regarded blacks as scarcely human.

The English settlement on the Cumberland Plateau in Tennessee was Hughes' great attempt to preserve the old values he so cherished. His interest in model villages had been stimulated in 1878 and 1879 when he and Neale had produced the *Manual for Co-operators* at the request of the Co-operative Congress held at Gloucester. There is much in it about model factories and villages, and although it is true that Hughes only actually wrote the preface (and Neale the rest), he had conceived the original idea and was completely identified with the finished work. He had also been inspired by the allotment movement – there was a description of the allotments at 'Englebourne Village' in Berkshire in *Tom Brown at Oxford*.[78] They encouraged self-help and independence. During the 1870s he had frequently addressed working men's gatherings on the advantages of emigration, but the foundation in Tennessee was not intended for the working class. It was, Hughes himself said, for 'young men of good education and small capital, the class of which, of all others, is most overcrowded today in England'.[79] Here, then, was no experiment in primitive socialism; there is no influence of Fourier. Rugby in Tennessee was intended to re-create the sturdy independence, simplicity of living, and practical democracy that Hughes identified as the strength of old England. Nowhere was his understanding of Christian Socialism so clearly revealed. The settlement, he wrote, was intended to transcend 'the present caste prejudice against manual labour'. It would provide conditions so that 'the English public school spirit – the spirit of hardiness, of reticence, of scrupulousness in all money matters, of cordial fellowship – shall be recognised and prevail'.[80] The name itself, as Hughes acknowledged,[81] indicated the objects. Land was purchased by a board, of which Hughes was president, and was sold off in small lots to the settlers. There were a hundred and twenty after a year. A 'commissory', or public store, arranged for the co-operative marketing of the fruits of their labour. The board put up the public buildings – a library, an hotel called 'The Tabard', and a church at which non-denominational services were held. A cricket ground was

[75] Mack and Armytage, *Thomas Hughes*, 59.
[76] Hughes, *Rugby, Tennessee*, 83.
[77] Ibid., 79.
[78] Hughes, *Tom Brown at Oxford*, II, 21.
[79] Thomas Hughes, *Rugby, Tennessee*, v.
[80] Ibid., 25.   [81] Ibid., 26.

laid out, and Hughes was indeed delighted to see, on his visit for the formal opening in October 1880, a boy 'in flannels, with racquet in hand, on the way to the lawn-tennis ground'.[82] So far from encouraging a socialist equality of goods, the settlers were intended to receive a sound return on their investment: the purpose of Rugby was to stimulate petty capitalism. Yet personal regeneration was also expected; Hughes said that the settlement was 'to begin the world anew'.[83] In his inaugural address, he disowned any sympathy 'with the state communism of Europe, represented by Lasalle and Karl Marx'. He had 'no vision whatever to realise of a paternal state, the owner of all property, finding easy employment and liberal maintenance for all citizens, reserving all profits for the community, and paying no dividends to individuals'. He had no intention of emulating, at the new Rugby, the communistic communities tried elsewhere: 'We are content with the laws relating to private property and family life as we find them, feeling quite able to modify them for ourselves in certain directions as our corporate conscience ripens'.[84] But the venture was under-capitalized and collapsed after a few years. Nothing in his entire life so distressed him.

In his religious convictions Hughes was both simple and deeply serious. He did not regard Christianity as a moralistic ally of social reform, as Neale did, but as the very centre of all national and social life. Christianity, too, was for him a peculiarly democratic creed. Though he disapproved of the heterodoxy of the authors of *Essays and Reviews*, in 1860, for example, he applauded the publicity which had allowed a debate about faith to 'come down to the every-day working world'. Ordinary people, he supposed, 'who are earning their bread in the sweat of their brows' had come to feel involved.[85] The church, he said on many occasions, was 'a truly popular democratic institution'.[86] He even believed this of the Church of England, and sought broad reforms which would make the nineteenth-century reality correspond to what it was intended to be. The Church, he told the audience at Hull in 1876, was 'a creation of the people themselves'; they 'have the ultimate control over it' because it is governed by Parliament.[87] Hughes' erastianism, like his vision for a reformed church, derived from Arnold. 'There is no wider basis possible for a National Church than the nation'.[88] Tom Brown, at Oxford, did not want a Church if it was 'an exclusive body, which took no care of any but its own people'.[89] Hughes was opposed to the voluntary principle in religion for reasons which echoed those of Thomas Chalmers in the 1830s – that those most in need of religion were the least able and the least likely to make financial provision for it.[90] A national church was, at least in theory, the church of the poor. The reforms required to give greater substance to this almost exactly corresponded to those laid out in

[82] Ibid., 51.   [83] Ibid., 25.   [84] Ibid., 96.   [85] Hughes, *Religio Laici*, 7–8.
[86] Hughes, *The Old Church*, 10.   [87] Ibid., 148.   [88] Ibid., 149.
[89] Hughes, *Tom Brown at Oxford*, III, 39.   [90] Hughes, *The Old Church*, 93, 151.

Arnold's *Principles of Church Reform*, published in 1833. The Church was to be 'remodelled', according to Hughes, so that it should incorporate all Protestants, and should therefore 'be made wide enough to include all English Christians who own no human allegiance outside their own nation'. Most 'Liberal churchmen', he believed, could support such a plan, even though he acknowledged the possibility of differences of view over particular details.[91] The evil was sectarianism, exclusivity in religion.[92] He commended the ecclesiastical ideals of that other Rugbeian and erastian, Dean Stanley.[93] The union of Church and State, Hughes argued, consecrated the work of civil government; it obliged public men to see that 'the nation in its corporate capacity has a spiritual as well as a material life'.[94] It was 'a protest against the notion that the nation can repudiate its highest functions and duties'.[95] As the Liberal Party, to which he owed allegiance in Parliament, moved progressively into the hands of the Liberation Society, in the 1870s and 1880s, Hughes found that his support of the establishment of religion placed him in an increasingly isolated position within the wing of the party to which he belonged. In 1870 he had joined the churchmen's National Educational Union rather than the Education League, the body supported by most Liberals and Radicals. In 1878 he produced a considered defence, in the form of published speeches and addresses on the church issues. Of the policy of Disestablishment itself – then being actively advocated by most of his Radical colleagues – he wrote that 'there is too much common sense left in our people to commit such an act of stupidity'.[96] It was a correct prediction. In Hughes' case the whole idea of Disestablishment went against the grain of English tradition; the Church was an organic part of the old English world of values that reform and social adaptation would enable the new classes of the nineteenth century to enjoy. At a discussion got up at the Working Men's College, the participants 'were practically unanimous, that from the democratic point of view it would be more patriotic, not to sever, but to maintain the connection' of Church and State.[97] Increasingly he found himself espousing Whig and Conservative opinions on issues which excited enormous amounts of passionate feeling among the working men of the constituencies and the associations.

Of all the Christian Socialists of the 1848 movement, Hughes was the most active in public life. Like Ludlow he took a leading part in the co-operatives, and continued his involvement through later stages of development. But he also carried his beliefs into formal politics. It was Holyoake who persuaded the Radicals of Lambeth to adopt Hughes as their parliamentary candidate, in 1865, and with the support of the Reform League, he was elected, as a Liberal, and took his seat in 1866. He made it clear from the start that he expected a considerable measure of independence from his Radical backers, however, and

91 Ibid., 16.   92 Ibid., 29.   93 Ibid., 20.
94 Ibid., 28.   95 Ibid., 90.   96 Ibid., 3.   97 Ibid., 112.

when this took the form of speaking on behalf of stricter liquor licensing the enthusiasm for him in Lambeth began to evaporate. In 1868 he got himself elected for Frome in Wiltshire – a seat nearer to the heartlands of his beloved boyhood years. In a speech of 1873, he defined his position. 'I stand before you as a Liberal politician', he told his audience, at Norwich; 'a Liberal politician is a man, who looks to the future and not to the past; he looks for progress; he desires to see the whole nation raised . . . he holds that every institution must be tried by its worth and its value to the nation; – he holds above all things that there should be equality before the law for every institution, for every society, and for every individual citizen'.[98] Hughes never spoke of himself, in parliamentary terms, as a Socialist: he did not think it necessary. Socialism, for him as for most of the others in the movement, was an ethical insight, an additional dimension to public service – it was not a separate and sovereign political creed. Walter Morrison and Lord Goderich also sat as Liberals in Parliament, and did not regard their simultaneous profession of Christian Socialism as a *political* identity.[99] Hughes' defence of his independence was very self-conscious. 'I care comparatively little whether you turn out Liberals or Tories', he wrote; 'those who are most useful and powerful in supporting a cause are those who know best what can be said against it', and 'your opponents are just as likely to be upright and honest men as yourselves'.[100] Such sentiments were not particularly well suited to the realities of party division in the House of Commons, and by early in the 1870s Hughes was disclosing a measure of disillusionment with parliamentary life. He simply did not fit. By turns, he managed to cut himself off from each particular interest and pressure-group. For several years he was the acknowledged spokesman for the working men in Parliament, but by early in the 1870s he was displaced in this role by A. J. Mundella. On the questions of liquor licensing, sabbatarian legislation, education, and the establishment of the Church, he was increasingly out of touch with influential groups within Radicalism and Liberalism; his actions over parliamentary enquiries into labour laws and trade unionism alienated more of his supporters. He was an articulate opponent of the rise of the Birmingham caucus, the most dynamic and formative expression of Radicalism of the time. It was a machine which was, he said quite simply, 'dangerous'.[101] He eventually fell out with the Gladstonian section of Liberalism as well, through his opposition to Home Rule. But by then he was out of Parliament. Growing opposition in Frome led to his being dropped as candidate in the 1874 election, and after failing to get adopted at Marylebone, he retired from party politics – though he always regretted his departure and

[98] Ibid., 46–7.
[99] Backstrom, *Christian Socialism and Co-operation*, 66.
[100] Hughes, *Memoir of a Brother*, 118–19.
[101] Hughes, *The Old Church*, 7.

hoped, vainly as it transpired, for a return. Trusted, respected, and admired, Hughes' political idiosyncracies and combinations of beliefs did not attract confidence. Electors sought men less independent.

His work for the co-operative movement was not much smoother, but it continued until his death in 1896. It was in associationism that Hughes saw the real work of Christian Socialism. 'Co-operative associations *are* socialism', he declared boldly in 1850.[102] 'We cannot repudiate the name "Socialist"', he told the Co-operative Congress at Bolton in 1872; 'but we have never looked to the state' for the re-organization of society – 'we have only asked the state to stand aside and give us breathing room and elbow room to do it for ourselves'.[103] His view of this work derived from a straightforward acceptance of the regenerative power of self-help among the workers. He later came to acknowledge that it was too linear a view. 'It was right and necessary to denounce the evils of unlimited competition, and the falsehood of the economic doctrine of "every man for himself"', he wrote in 1873; 'but quite unnecessary, and therefore unwise, to speak of the whole system of trade as "the disgusting vice of shop-keeping", as was the habit of several of our foremost and ablest members'.[104] He recalled the enthusiasm of the heady days of 1848 with some amusement: he had then been convinced that all they had to do was to announce 'the solution of the great labour question' – co-operative enterprise – 'in order to convert all England and usher in the millennium at once'.[105] In fact 'we were young, saucy, and so thoroughly convinced we were right'.[106] It is not clear that this was a description that Maurice would have cared to apply. But as to the 'solution' itself, Hughes never changed his mind. He came to see, it is true, as others did, that many working men were not yet ready for the responsibilities of association; even the best of the 'aristocracy of trades' were less fitted than he had originally imagined.[107] But in a life's work for the co-operative movement he came to see its ideals and purposes gradually unfold in a way which gave him considerable satisfaction. He weathered the frequent controversies well – supporting the Central Co-operative Agency against Ludlow after 1851, fighting hard to preserve the religious orientation of the work against Holyoake and the secularists at the Co-operative Congress of 1881. He became a member of the original Council of Promoters in 1850, edited the *Journal of Association* in 1851, and in the second of the *Tracts on Christian Socialism*, which described the start of the Working Tailors' Association, he disclosed an impressive grasp of the purposes and problems of co-operation. His tour of the associations in the north of England, with Ludlow, in 1851, introduced him to what became a

---

[102] *Christian Socialist* (2 November 1850).
[103] Quoted in Mack and Armytage, *Thomas Hughes*, 202.
[104] Hughes, *Memoir of a Brother*, 115.   [105] Ibid., 111.
[106] Mack and Armytage, *Thomas Hughes*, 63.
[107] *Journal of Association* (24 January 1852).

close and permanent acquaintance with industrial society. In 1860 he became one of the two secretaries (with P. M. Rathbone) of the Committee on Trade Societies and Strikes of the Social Science Association, and distilled a decade of experience of the evolving co-operative and trade union movements in his report, taking the opportunity to advocate what had by then become his major policy – the legal recognition of trade union practices.[108] Hughes had supported the Iron Trades strike of 1852, and the experience gave him a lasting commitment to the development of trade unionism. His support for the builders' strike in 1860 introduced him to a new generation of moderate union leaders, to William Allan and Robert Applegarth, whose general attitudes he greatly approved. He even supported the unions during the notorious Sheffield 'outrages' in 1866, and his subsequent appointment by the Conservative government to the Royal Commission to enquire into trade union activities gave him the opportunity to act as spokesman for Applegarth and the 'Junta'. Together with Frederic Harrison, he produced a minority report favourable to the unions. Yet, independent as ever, Hughes endorsed the Criminal Law Amendment Act of 1871, which many trade unionists saw as an assault upon industrial action. He was further out of step when he accepted appointment to the Conservatives' Royal Commission on trade union legislation in 1874, and in 1875 he signed its report.

In the campaign to secure legal recognition of co-operative enterprises Hughes worked closely with Slaney, and gave evidence to his 1850 Select Committee. Throughout the 1860s and 1870s he was at the centre of the movement, and it was Hughes who in 1869 was Chairman of the convening committee of the first Co-operative Congress. For him, co-operation was always 'the most remarkable social movement of our time'.[109] By the 1880s, he could look back with some satisfaction to the achievements of the movement. The 'spirit of co-operation', he felt able to declare, was 'in the air'. *Laissez-faire* had been discredited, he believed, and 'the change is an entirely wholesome one for the nation, bringing back health and social prosperity to trade'.[110] It was, perhaps, a pardonable exaggeration. Hughes' clear integrity, his religious faith, and his trustworthiness, had attracted the respect of very many during his extended work for the alleviation of social suffering. He was always open to new ways of furthering the causes to which he held, and in 1891 he joined the Executive Committee of Christian Social Union, then two years old. He was thus a link between the first Christian Socialist movement and the second, as Ludlow also was. In 1878 he was the inspiration behind the founding of the

[108] Wagner, *The Church of England and Social Reform*, 130.
[109] Thomas Hughes, *James Fraser, Second Bishop of Manchester* (London, 1887), 152.
[110] Hughes, *Rugby, Tennessee*, 13.

Guild of Co-operators, and became its first Chairman. The Guild was intended as a propagandist body to promote the ideals of associationism. When Hughes recruited Stewart Headlam as a member the link between the past and the future of Christian Socialism was considerably strengthened.

6

STEWART HEADLAM

There was a recklessness and perversity in Headlam which hung about him all his life, Caustic expression, straining after effect, and the bald statement of paradoxes as though they were the commonplace of all but the insensitive or the malign, while sometimes acceptable in youth are rarely so in the more mature, and Headlam accumulated large numbers of influential opponents. His own biographer – in a work read and approved by Headlam[1] – referred to 'an imp of mischief' that seemed to rest upon him.[2] Yet the same work speaks also of his courage,[3] and this was echoed by others who have assessed his life and ideas.[4] To many of his contemporaries he seemed eccentric: a clergyman who praised the insights of atheists and secularists, a member of the 'respectable' professions who mixed in theatrical and artistic circles, who embraced Fabian Socialism, who supported outcasts like the Ritualist priests prosecuted under the Public Worship Regulation Act, and who befriended Oscar Wilde at the time of his trial. Headlam actually revelled in the seeming incompatibilities. 'It is because we are Communicants that we go to the Theatre', he said on one occasion; 'because we are Priests that we believe in Progress'.[5] To the modern ear such sentiments will not seem strange. To late-Victorian sensibilities they could sound profoundly shocking, and Headlam's vaunting tone did not help. He may, indeed, be rightly accused of poor judgment over the expression of his ideas; for ideas, to be influential, have in some measure to be acceptable to the generation who receive them, and Headlam lacked both the historical sense and the balance of temperament needed to adjust his opinions to the expectations

---

[1] F. G. Bettany, *Stewart Headlam: A Biography* (London, 1926), preface, vi.
[2] Ibid., 61.   [3] Ibid., 87.
[4] Peter d'A. Jones, *The Christian Socialist Revival 1877–1914. Religion, Class, and Social Conscience in Late-Victorian England* (Princeton, 1968), 99; Reg Groves, *Conrad Noel and the Thaxted Movement* (London, 1967), 28.
[5] Stewart D. Headlam, *The Sure Foundation. An Address Given before the Guild of S. Matthew, At the Annual Meeting, 1883* (London, 1883), 13.

and common assumptions of the Church and the society he served. The ideas themselves, however, were quite another matter. Headlam really was one of those few men who are able to stand outside their immediate circumstance and to see truths which the generality cannot recognize. His opinions were not so much 'revolutionary', as some have supposed,[6] as prophetic: his understanding of Socialism and the political processes was neither remarkable nor original, but his sense of the damage done to the interior lives of men by their wrong social priorities, their inability or unwillingness to elevate collective needs above individual, and their blinkered cultural perspectives, which made men mistake the transient for the permanent in human orderings of society, gave Headlam a quite astonishing series of insights into values which are today much esteemed. Headlam is not to be treated seriously because he chanced to fall upon attitudes which subsequent generations find sympathetic, of course, but because his moral critique of his own society had unusually penetrating qualities. So the first condition in evaluating Headlam's contribution to Christian Socialism is to set the eccentricity and perversity and poor judgment of personal reactions into one dimension of his life, and to recognize his social criticism as belonging to another. His courageous foolhardiness, indeed, gave his ideas a currency they might not otherwise have achieved, so the two dimensions are linked. They were joined, also, by Headlam's quarrels with authority. How much of the case he made out so well for Church Reform derived from intellectual conviction, and how much from antipathy to the bishops who had kept him out of the beneficed ministry by refusing to license him? It was Bishop Jackson of London who first prohibited Headlam from preaching. That was in 1878, and followed Headlam's lecture in support of theatrical art.[7] After he appeared on the same platform with Michael Davitt, the Fenian politician, in a Hyde Park rally (where he advocated the abolition of the House of Lords), Jackson removed his licence altogether. When Frederick Temple became Bishop of London he, too, refused to license Headlam to preach – noting that Headlam 'has a tendency to encourage young men and women to be frequent spectators of ballet dancing'.[8] Since Headlam esteemed his own priesthood as the most important thing in his life, the blow was terrible and left enduring scars: all brought about, as he ruefully observed many years later, 'for saying a few kind words about dancers on the stage'.[9] But it was not only the few words that had done the damage. The episcopal authorities were equally offended by Headlam's tactless insensitivity to received opinions and to the paradoxes implicit in his support of the Secularists. His political opinions, as such, were less likely to cause offence.

[6] Kenneth Leech, 'Stewart Headlam', in *For Christ and the People. Studies of four Socialist Priests and Prophets of the Church of England between 1870 and 1930*, ed. Maurice Reckitt (London, 1968), 84.

[7] Bettany, *Stewart Headlam*, 44. [8] Ibid., 69.

[9] Stewart D. Headlam, *The Meaning of the Mass. Five Lectures with other Sermons and Addresses* (London, 1905), 'The Holy Eucharist' (1901), 39.

Headlam was himself aware that his conduct was unconventional, and he knew the consequences. 'The people whom we have to shock', he said, 'can practically by the stroke of one of their pens force some of us to live on charity'.[10]

Headlam survived without this extremity, however, because he had private means. He came from a prosperous family. He was born at Wavertree in 1847, the son of a Liverpool underwriter; the family moved, when he was still a young boy, to Tunbridge Wells. He was educated first at a small school in Wadhurst and then, from 1860, at Eton. The experience proved to be of great significance – Headlam regarded Eton as a 'liberating influence'[11] and retained a life-long and even growing affection for the school (not unlike Hughes' preoccupation with Rugby). As an adult he came to see Eton as a home of social equality, where they 'did not bother who so-and-so's father was'.[12] This, to say the least, was an unusual and élitist judgment. His fag at Eton was the son of Archbishop Tait of Canterbury. Headlam even claimed that his convictions about the rightness of secular education had seeds in his Eton days, for there was, in the school's official Anglicanism, he supposed, no 'definite Church teaching'.[13] Eton certainly did not stimulate any very noticeably intellectual qualities in Headlam, nor did Cambridge, where he just managed a low third-class degree in classics in 1868. His was not the sort of mind, in fact, which flourished in academic learning: contemporaries of his mature years, friends and opponents alike, noted a permanent disposition to intellectual rigidity. His ideas, Sidney Webb observed, 'were seldom subject to modification under argument'. He added, 'What he said once in every topic he said always'.[14] This view was offered in relation to Headlam's contributions at Fabian Society meetings, but it applied equally to gatherings of the Guild of St Matthew – Headlam's most important Christian Socialist organization – and to his sermons. The repetitions in his writings, giving them an extraordinary consistency over the years, disclose a rather limited intellectual range. But Headlam's mind had other qualities which amounted to a kind of genius. His sympathy for the effects of culture and environment on human development, if in origin almost instinctive, was given, in his various writings and speeches, a treatment which those outside the benefits of any formal learning or social advantage at all could understand.

His simplicity of response to human suffering was independent of intellectual processes and yet was not naively detached from social realities. He managed to stand outside the class assumptions which hedged the liberalism of even the

[10] Headlam, *The Sure Foundation*, 9.
[11] Bettany, *Stewart Headlam*, 11.   [12] Ibid., 13.
[13] Stewart D. Headlam, *The Place of the Bible in Secular Education. An Open Letter to the Teachers under the London School Board* (London, 1903), 25.
[14] Quoted in Bettany, *Stewart Headlam*, 138.

most advanced of the reformist bishops of his times, and Headlam's most active years in Church campaigning, it should be remembered (the 1870s and 1880s) were also years which saw the emergence of a considerable band of socially-conscious prelates within the state church – men like Fraser, Mackarness, Westcott, King, and Creighton. Headlam's clarity of view is easily criticized by those who suppose that clarities of view should always result from the distillation of a thick mixture of complicated learning. In fact in Headlam it derived from a wealth of feeling, an unerring ability to sense and to identify the treasures lying undiscovered in the socially marginated and the inarticulate. He believed in humanity. The impatience and tactlessness he so often showed in his dealings with the leaders of the Church, and with conventional opinion, were strangely absent in his responses to social misery: Headlam's ideas, though not intellectually original, and though expressed with panache, were actually restrained. He was not a 'hot-head'. His interior refinement of senses was revealed not in academic disquisition but in aesthetic appreciation and religious devotion. Both were made to look eccentric by hostile contemporaries, and Headlam has therefore been remembered as much for his patronage of modish interior decoration, his love of ballet, and his Ritualism, as for his social vision and his actual residence, for many years – and until he was removed through the action of the Bishop of London, against his will – among the poor of Bethnal Green.

Headlam was ordained a priest in 1872. He was at the time a curate in Drury Lane, at St John's Church. There he met, for the first time, the theatrical people whose art and integrity he came to champion at so much cost to his own reputation and prospects. In 1873 he moved to Bethnal Green, as curate to Septimus Hansard, the Rugbeian Christian Socialist and friend of Hughes. Hansard's combination of Broad Church theology and social consciousness passed to Headlam; from Hansard, also, he learned the importance of parish-visiting among the poor, and of working to foster good relations with trade unionists. It was Hansard who encouraged him to join the 'Commonwealth Club', the local vehicle of Radical politics. At Bethnal Green, Headlam's social beliefs were formed and set. They did not greatly change thereafter, although in the 1880s he added what became his great preoccupation – indeed obsession – with land reform. There he was happy, for perhaps the only time in his life, and it was to Bethnal Green that he asked to be taken as he lay dying, at the age of seventy-seven, in 1924. From the time of his dismissal from the curacy at Bethnal Green in 1878 Headlam never held a post in the Church of England. Without an episcopal licence, and with an increasing reputation for unconventional opinions and precipitate behaviour he could not get a benefice. His priestly ministry was therefore performed at the altars of friendly colleagues who invited him into their Churches, and in the campaigns he launched for social reform and for the reform of the Church itself. The second half of his life, from 1888, was largely devoted to educational work, on the London School Board and on educational committees of the London County Council.

There can be no uncertainty about the origin of Headlam's Christian Socialism. It was due to the influence of F. D. Maurice, whose lectures he attended while at Cambridge. He never really knew Maurice personally, but the impact of his ideas was immediate and enduring, and it was due to Maurice's example that he decided to seek holy orders.[15] 'Long before the Fabian Society was founded', Headlam declared in his Fabian Tract on *Christian Socialism*, 'I learnt the principles and was familiar with the title of "Christian Socialism" from Maurice and Kingsley'.[16] However, Headlam did not really get his *socialism* from Maurice, but his ideas about humanity. It was Maurice who taught him to eschew the doctrine of human depravity, and to reject Evangelical emphases on individual salvation. Eternal punishment, Headlam told the East London Secular Society in 1876, was 'a horrid doctrine'.[17] In another place he said it was 'a monstrous libel upon God'.[18] Maurice's theology, in fact, had helped his emancipation from the rigid and informed Evangelicalism of his father – who, indeed, fought back (unsuccessfully) by sending him from Cambridge to assist an Evangelical minister for a year, in the hope that his newly acquired Maurician notions would be extinguished. Headlam, however, had found a new world of religious values. Men and their needs now became the centre of his Christianity. 'The Church exists to bear witness to men that they are brothers', he wrote in 1875: 'that God is now and for ever, here and everywhere, the Father of all men'.[19] To Maurice's Christian humanism, Headlam added a more distinct sense of social reformism and of Socialism, gained from working with Septimus Hansard in Bethnal Green. This gave a practical content to the socialist ideas he had encountered in Thomas Wodehouse, author of *The Grammar of Socialism*, during his time at Drury Lane. The origins of his Socialism may even go back to William Johnson, who taught him in Cambridge, and who was a friend of Maurice and Kingsley.[20] Headlam sometimes quoted Ruskin, in support of his ideals of human brotherhood; and from Selwyn Image, Slade Professor of Fine Art at Oxford, and a close friend in the 1880s, he acquired something of the folk romanticism of the arts-and-crafts movement. It was from Image that Headlam sought advice about interior decoration.

[15] Ibid., 22.

[16] Stewart D. Headlam, *Christian Socialism* (Fabian Tract No. 42, London, 1892), 2. For a second version, see *Socialism and Religion*, by Stewart Headlam, Percy Dearmer, John Clifford and John Woolman (Fabian Socialist Series No. 1, London, 1908).

[17] Stewart D. Headlam, *Priestcraft and Progress* (London, 1878), 'Some Popular Mistakes About the Church's Teaching', 85.

[18] Stewart D. Headlam, *The Service of Humanity*, 'The Church and Liberalism', 131.

[19] Stewart Headlam, *The Church Catechism and the Emancipation of Labour* (London, 1875), 3.

[20] Jones, *The Christian Socialist Revival*, 101.

In his Church affiliations, as in his social opinions, there were some paradoxes. Largely from the liturgical drama practiced at St Michael's, Shoreditch, Headlam experienced a gravitational pull to Anglo-Catholicism. His own services were suffused with Ritualism, and he nearly always referred to the Anglican Service of Holy Communion as 'the Mass'. Yet it is not clear that he really was an Anglo-Catholic. He saw himself as standing in the tradition of the Oxford Movement,[21] but his modernist approach to Biblical criticism, and his disregard for most structured views of authority, placed him very far from it in reality. Headlam was in fact a Broad Churchman: he welcomed *Lux Mundi*, and was more indebted (though he did not acknowledge it) to men like Arnold and Stanley than he was to Newman or Pusey. He saw no conflict of science and religion; evolutionary teachings were to be supported – 'Creation, by means of gradual, orderly development'.[22] There was, he insisted, no verbal inspiration in Scripture; religious doubts were 'probably of divine inspiration', and the real danger he perceived in submission to authority, 'to some Pope, Protestant or Roman, or to some book'.[23] There was a sad personal element in Headlam's difficulties with Church authorities which cannot be overlooked. In January 1878, the very month in which he received notice to leave St Matthew's, Bethnal Green, he was married. After a very short time the marriage dissolved away, and Headlam never referred to it throughout the rest of his life.[24] But Frederick Temple, when Bishop of London, cited Headlam's marital irregularity as among the grounds for his refusal of a licence.[25]

During his early years in the ministry Headlam cultivated a number of friendships with other young priests which became the basis of the Guild of St Matthew. They formed themselves into the Junior Clergy Society, with meetings in the vestry of St Martin-in-the-Fields. Here Headlam found companionship and an exchange of radical ideas; with George Sarson, John Elliotson Symes, and Thomas Hancock. After the social privilege of his upbringing and education, Headlam entered the Church with almost no first-hand knowledge of the working classes. The discussions among the young men supplied a grid of social interpretation – and the incentives for activism – but Headlam's actual knowledge of social conditions came from the work in Drury Lane and in Bethnal Green. He visited the people in their homes, and, through a conviction that it was the right thing to do (rather than through financial necessity) chose to live among them. In Bethnal Green he took a flat, No. 135 in the Waterlow Buildings, and can therefore really be judged to have known about the social conditions he denounced. The Buildings were model dwellings

---

[21] Leech, in *For Christ and the People*, 68–9.
[22] Headlam, *Priestcraft and Progress*, 92.
[23] Stewart D. Headlam, *The Doubts of the Faithful Sceptic the Confirmation of True Theology. A Sermon Preached in the Church of S. Matthew, Bethnal Green, 1875* (London, 1875), 4.
[24] Bettany, *Stewart Headlam*, 46.   [25] Ibid., 71.

for the working classes: from there he involved himself in social and religious work – reading classes, drama and literature appreciation groups, and the encouragement of healthy games, and especially swimming, for the poor boys of the district. It has rightly been noted that he 'gained immense knowledge of urban social conditions'.[26]

So closely were Headlam's own beliefs expressed in the Guild of St Matthew, and so decisively did he dominate its proceedings and policies through the entire length of its existence, as its Warden, that any attempt to assemble an analysis of his Socialism must begin with an account of the nature of the Guild. The element of sacramentalism, so much a part of Headlam's religious constitution, was present in its very origins: the Guild was begun by some of the girls in the Bethnal Green parish in order to secure regular attendances at early-morning celebrations of the Eucharist. That was in 1877. With Headlam's dismissal from St Matthew's, the following year, the Guild, which had already attached strong social interests to itself, became organized on a national basis, with local branches, got together by sympathetic High Church priests, in a number of provincial centres. London and Oxford, where F. L. Donaldson set up a branch at Merton College in 1884, were always the most influential areas, however. From Bethnal Green, Headlam moved the headquarters to St Michael's Boys' School in Shoreditch; annual meetings were held at Sion College. The house which Headlam had purchased at the time of his marriage was used, for a time, as a meeting place as well. There were originally forty members of the Guild, and despite some fluctuations, this rose to a peak of between 350 and 400 early in the 1890s. About a quarter of the membership consisted of priests: it was a clerical, sacramentalist, Anglican and Socialist organization, existing for largely propagandist purposes.[27] George Bernard Shaw used its meetings 'as a training ground for public speaking and debate'.[28] It also moulded the radicalism of a number of Christian Socialists who were to take a significant part in Anglican social discourse in the decades which followed – Conrad Noel, Percy Dearmer, J. G. Adderley, P. E. T. Widdrington, F. L. Donaldson, and, the Guild's only member to receive preferment, C. W. Stubbs, who later became Bishop of Truro. Especially in the early years Headlam and other members attended the annual Church Congresses, making occasional contributions to debate, but usually in order to sell their literature and generally to establish a Socialist presence. In 1884 Headlam used his own financial resources to buy up a newspaper, the *Church Reformer*, and to convert it into what was virtually (though never officially) the mouthpiece of the Guild. It ended in 1895, with a small readership and a cost by then too great for Headlam to undertake. Throughout its existence, and despite an atmosphere of slight eccentricity that

[26] Jones, *The Christian Socialist Revival*, 102.
[27] Bettany, *Stewart Headlam*, 81; Jones, *The Christian Socialist Revival*, 99, 113.
[28] Bettany, *Stewart Headlam*, 87.

attached to some of its proceedings and personnel, the Guild managed to secure an influence quite out of proportion to its size. Its members were extremely active in addressing themselves to the press on public issues, and the professionalism of its social analysis was markedly better than that available in most other sections of the Church – as seen in the address it sent to the Lambeth Conference in 1888.

The purposes of the Guild of St Matthew were originally expressed in three points. First, it was to eliminate prejudices against the Church, 'especially on the part of Secularists', and (in a phrase taken from Kingsley) 'to justify God to the people'. Secondly, it was to promote sacramental worship. Thirdly, it was 'to promote the study of social and political questions in the light of the Incarnation'.[29] This last stated object pointed to Headlam's neo-Maurician understanding of the immanence of divinity in all human affairs, and was the key to understanding his whole outlook. With Headlam's enthusiastic adhesion to Henry George's Land Reform programme in 1883, the Guild was reorientated – to include agrarian priorities. This became apparent in the resolution passed at the Trafalgar Square demonstration, got up by the Guild in 1884, and which thereafter tended to serve as its manifesto. 'Whereas the present contrast between the great body of the workers who produce much and consume little, and of those classes which produce little and consume much is contrary to the Christian doctrines of brotherhood and justice', the Guild's resolution urged, they should work 'to restore to the people the value which they give to the land [George's Single Tax proposal], to bring about a better distribution of the wealth created by labour', to 'give the whole body of the people a voice in their own government', and to 'abolish false standards of worth and dignity'.[30] Whatever difficulties may have surrounded George's land schemes, and however intellectual and impractical this kind of analysis may have been in the event, the fact is that it marks Headlam as the first really serious Socialist, in the modern sense, in the Church. Unlike his predecessors of the Maurician tradition, Headlam really did intend basic changes in the social state in the interests of justice, and the Guild, whatever its shortcomings, was the first Christian body in England to achieve some real insight into the dynamics of Socialism.

At the start, due to Headlam's preoccupation with the Secularists, and with protecting their rights, the Guild spent much of its time debating the Oaths Bills then before Parliament, arising out of the Bradlaugh controversies early in the 1880s. The Guild was also, at this time, agitating for the repeal of the blasphemy laws. With its increasing absorption by social questions, however, there came internal dissensions; like many such bodies inspired by those who are both moralists and practitioners of social ideology, the Guild was filled with

[29] Ibid., 79.   [30] Quoted in ibid., 83–4.

doctrinal divisions. Headlam's own inability to consult with others, or to try to arrive at a sense common to most of the membership, added to the difficulties. He simply behaved as if the Guild was the automatic agent of his own ideas. Headlam's support for the policy of Church disestablishment was contested by some members; his advocacy of universal secular education was rejected by most of the other High Churchmen; his priority for land reform, after 1883, offended more orthodox Socialists like Conrad Noel. The Guild came nearest to wreck in 1891 when Headlam, characteristically, issued a manifesto on behalf of secular education without consulting the members and was attacked by Sarson and Symes.[31] Fortunately for Headlam, he had in Frederick Verinder a loyal and extremely efficient Secretary of the Guild, who held things together. Verinder had been a pupil-teacher at the Bethnal Green National School when Headlam met him; he became, eventually, as General Secretary of the Land Restoration League, the foremost exponent of George's ideas in England. Even Verinder's organizing abilities could not overcome the fact that by 1908 the Guild of St Matthew was nearing its end. There were, in that year, further quarrels over the possibilities of an alliance with either the Fabians or the Social Democratic Federation. Headlam, who upheld the religious priority of the work, just as Ludlow had against Maurice early in the 1850s, was successful in averting this. In the following year, however, with a membership reduced to a couple of hundred, and with many who anyway had simultaneously adhered to the Church Socialist League (begun primarily as a northern movement in 1906), the Guild was dissolved by Headlam himself. By then it appeared rather out-dated to some of the younger men,[32] and Headlam's emphasis on his educational work for the L.C.C. robbed him of the energy he needed to breathe new life into the Guild. He had seen the Guild as an endeavour to bring the 'great principle of the Oxford Movement home to those who might not otherwise have grasped it'[33] – the Eucharistic centre of Christianity, the religious basis of all their work. Instead, as he observed disconsolately in 1909, 'the only thing we do is to talk about a definition of Socialism'.[34]

How, then, is Headlam's own Socialism to be defined? His public career began with his challenge to the London Secularists, whose meetings he attended in order to argue with them about their – as he maintained – erroneous attitudes to Christianity and the Church. He later said he had been 'in constant communication' with them.[35] Quite rapidly he moved from attack to defence. The Secularists, he then contended, for all their wrong assumptions about religion, were workers for humanity. The shift was illustrated by his attitude to

[31] Ibid., 89; Jones, *The Christian Socialist Revival*, 131–2.   [32] Groves, *Conrad Noel*, 29.

[33] Headlam, *The Meaning of the Mass*, 'The Church' (1896), 59.

[34] Bettany, *Stewart Headlam*, 92.

[35] *The Official Report of the Church Congress held at Leicester, 1880* (London, 1881), 650 (Headlam's speech in the debate on 'Existing Forms of Unbelief').

Charles Bradlaugh, the atheist propagandist whose campaign to remove the oath which inhibited free-thinkers from taking seats in Parliament so disrupted the life of Gladstone's second ministry. Headlam at first clashed with Bradlaugh, in 1875; but in 1880, when Bradlaugh was briefly detained in gaol at Northampton, Headlam sent him a telegram of sympathy – an act of solidarity which was regarded as scandalous by Church opinion.[36] He had come to regard the secular ethicists as actually doing God's work. 'If, then, we want to get rid of Secularism', he declared in 1880, 'we must let people see that the Christian Church is the great Secular Society, that the Kingdom of Heaven, of which Jesus Christ spoke, was not merely a place to which people were to go hereafter, but a Divine Society established in this world'.[37] Headlam's Christian Socialism rested on this fundamental conviction that all men were in Christ, that there was no distinction between the sacred and the secular because all work for humanity was God's work, and all human experience conveyed divine truth. It was a development of Maurice's view of man, and clearly anticipated some twentieth-century theological insights. Headlam's Socialism was therefore intended to be secular: it sought to reinterpret Christianity and to reorientate the Church, to correspond to existing and non-religious radical ideas. In this it was in sharp contrast to Maurice and Kingsley, and even to Ludlow, who had wanted to assemble a version of Socialism which was compatible with conventional Christianity. Maurice's doctrine of man was, it is true, unlike the usual Church one, but the main body of Christian understanding was left unreconstructed in Maurician thought. The use of the Bible as an authority shows the difference. Maurice's Biblical scholarship was conservative; Headlam's was progressive, and accepted most of the criticisms of the historical value of Scripture made by the Secularists.

This was why Headlam had especially singled out the third rule of the Guild of St Matthew – the promotion of social reform 'in the light of the Incarnation' – as 'the *raison d'être* of all our Christian Socialism'.[38] Secularism, Socialism, and Sacramentalism represented a common area of human experience. They conveyed the essential truth, as Headlam saw it, that the material nature of things disclosed the will of God for mankind. Of the Church he concluded: 'The Incarnation compels us to regard it as a great Co-operative organized institution for human welfare and human righteousness in this world'.[39] For 'the head of *every* man is in Christ', and '*mankind* is constituted in Christ'.[40] It was the failure of the Church to recognize this which had created the moral

---

[36] Bettany, *Stewart Headlam*, 62.
[37] *The Official Report of the Church Congress held at Leicester, 1880*, 650.
[38] Bettany, *Stewart Headlam*, 81. See also Stewart Headlam, *The Laws of Eternal Life*, (London, 1887), for a full exposition of this theme.
[39] Headlam, *The Service of Humanity*, 'The Cultus of Our Lady', 59.
[40] Ibid., 'Church and State', 68.

conditions in which Secularism was able, unconsciously, to do religious work instead: 'the Secularists have, in fact, absorbed some of the best Christian truths which the Churches have been ignoring, and can now give them out as something new and unchristian'.[41] The Church, if only she could see it, 'owes them a debt for sweeping away her cobwebs and opening her shutters'.[42] Instead of faithfulness to a Christ who came to liberate men from injustice, Headlam believed, Christianity had 'over and over again been found opposed to progress'.[43] The object of the Guild of St Matthew, he told the members in 1883, was to 'restore' Jesus as he really was,[44] and Headlam's writings and addresses were full of references to a Christ of material action. Jesus was 'the social and political *Emancipator*, the greatest of all secular workers, the founder of the great Socialistic society for the promotion of righteousness, the preacher of a Revolution'.[45] Their task was to rediscover 'the Christian Communism of the Church of the Carpenter';[46] to proclaim 'the Carpenter with his moral force revolution'.[47] All the attributes of contemporary political radicalism – 'solidarity, brotherhood, co-operation, socialism' – were 'vividly present in Jesus Christ's teaching'.[48] His miracles prefigured social welfare; they were 'all distinctly secular, socialistic works: works for health against disease, works restoring beauty and harmony and pleasure where there had been ugliness and discord and misery'.[49] The Church existed 'for doing on a large scale throughout the world those secular, socialistic works which Christ did on a small scale in Palestine'.[50] In another place Headlam wrote that the 'miracles are a direct command to the Church to spend a large part of her time and energy in fighting against all circumstances and conditions of life which foster disease or hinder health, in delivering people from an evil environment' and in seeing that resources 'are used not for the aggrandisement of the few but the well-being of the many'.[51]

The sacraments of the Church pointed to material conditions as well. The Mass was the 'Feast of National Emancipation', and Headlam's evidence to the Royal Commission on Ecclesiastical Discipline, which reported in 1906, was a set-piece on the social significance of liturgy.[52] Baptism he regarded as 'the great sacrament of equality'.[53] Devotional practices in honour of the Virgin 'are helping to make the Church once more, and more fully than ever, the great Secular Society',[54] for 'the cultus of the Blessed Virgin Mary, telling us as it does

[41] Headlam, *The Sure Foundation*, 10.
[42] Headlam, *The Service of Humanity*, 'The Church and Liberalism', 129.
[43] Stewart Headlam, *Priestcraft and Progress* (London, 1878), 2.
[44] Headlam, *The Sure Foundation*, 4.   [45] Ibid., 6.
[46] Headlam, *The Service of Humanity*, 3.   [47] Ibid., 12.
[48] Headlam, *The Meaning of the Mass*, 'The Ethical Value of the Parables of Jesus' (1896), 73.
[49] Headlam, *Christian Socialism* (Fabian Tract No. 42), 2.   [50] Ibid., 7.
[51] Headlam, *The Service of Humanity*, 10–11.
[52] Leech, in *For Christ and the People*, 71; James Bentley, *Ritualism and Politics in Victorian Britain* (Oxford, 1978), 92.   [53] Headlam, *Christian Socialism*, 7.
[54] Headlam, *The Service of Humanity*, 'The Cultus of Our Lady', 58.

of the sacredness of Humanity as revealed in Jesus Christ, pledges us to do our best to be Christian Socialists'.[55] All these beliefs constituted, in Headlam's thinking, the materials for the construction of a just society. He never tired of pointing out that Jesus had said very little about the after-life, but a great deal about the present one. The conventionally religious stood indicted of failing to accommodate this – 'they have thought that the Church, the body of Christ, should confine herself to religious matters; that the material, political, and social well-being of a parish, a nation, or of humanity, should be left to others'.[56] In 1901 he told the members of the Guild of St Matthew that the Church existed 'not for its own sake, but for the sake of the whole human family: the elect people of God are sanctified, not in order that they may develop an exotic hot-house of piety, but in order that every human family, every fatherhood, may realise its sacredness'.[57] The Kingdom of Heaven was not ethereal; it was 'the righteous society to be established upon earth'.[58] The words of Jesus 'tell of a Kingdom of Heaven to be set up upon earth, of a righteous Communistic Society'.[59] The Bishop of Newcastle once expostulated to Headlam, in 1884, during an exchange in the Athenaeum: 'Why, you talk as if you believed that Christ's Kingdom were coming here on earth!' Headlam replied, 'What else should I believe? Of course I do'.[60]

Headlam's sense of the immanence of the divine, that all life disclosed religious truth for those with unclouded vision, and that the secular yields authentic spiritual value, first received public attention because of his attitude to the theatre. It is perhaps difficult, from modern perspectives, to appreciate just how greatly the worlds of drama and dance horrified conventional opinion in Victorian England: the stage was seen as a place conducive to corruption, the performing arts as encouraging nameless vices. In his first acquaintance with theatrical society, during his time at St John's, Drury Lane, Headlam came to identify the men and women of the entertainment world with the social outcasts to whom Christ had addressed himself. In October 1877, he delivered his lecture on 'Theatres and Music Halls' to a radical club in Bethnal Green, and allowed its subsequent publication in the press. In it, he praised theatrical entertainment as 'pure and beautiful' and encouraged young people to go to music-halls.[61] The effect was catastrophic. The Bishop of London denounced the lecture; Hansard was obliged, because of the uproar, to prohibit Headlam from preaching at St Matthew's; and three months later Headlam was removed from the parish. Undeterred, he went on, in 1879, to found the Church and Stage Guild, a propagandist body aimed at educating Church opinion out of its prejudices against the theatre. Ruskin and Shaw were supporters. The press

---

55 Ibid., 59.   56 Ibid., 4.
57 Headlam, *The Meaning of the Mass*, 'Christian Democracy', 122.
58 Headlam, *Christian Socialism*, 3.
59 Headlam, *The Service of Humanity*, 11.
60 Quoted in Bettany, *Stewart Headlam*, 82.   61 Ibid., 43.

received its activities with ridicule. The Guild was intended 'to help to heal one of the wounds of humanity'; it was 'to try to get the clergy to take a Christian view of the stage'.[62] The Christ who entered all human activity was present here: 'He is with us now in the Theatre as well as in the Church'.[63] The stage, furthermore, was a place of education; it provided 'art for the people'.[64] It also gave amusement and pleasure, and for that, also, theatre people 'deserve the blessing of the Church'.[65] The professions of acting and dancing were 'as sacred as the other callings'.[66] This was not a fringe matter. It entered deeply into Headlam's view of his ministry and affected his social diagnoses. In one sense obviously prophetic – Headlam's moralistic appreciation of the theatre and dance as art anticipate modern dispositions – in another it showed his inability to operate within the common assumptions of his contemporaries, and so made him less effective. His Anti-Puritan League was the same, and it was through an artist friend in this body that Headlam supported Oscar Wilde at the time of his trial in 1895. His support for Wilde, who seemed to him to be suffering through the prejudices of society, was noble and altruistic: it cost him, however, a lot in terms of his own reputation and even led to defections from the Guild of St Matthew. C. L. Marsh, for example, a close colleague in the Guild, said he was all for building up the new Jerusalem but not for 'wading through Gomorrah first'.[67] Headlam was of course aware that his campaign for the theatre was unpopular with the Church, but he elevated his understanding of Incarnational truth above personal disadvantage; 'If the Church is to be the Kingdom of Heaven upon earth', he said, 'if human life is the most sacred and interesting thing possible, then the drama which interprets human life should have indeed the Church's support'.[68]

An aesthetic element was certainly important in Headlam's Socialism, and it is true that he belongs, to that extent, to the strain of English radicalism that represented an 'aesthetic reaction' to industrialism.[69] But he belonged also, and formed a link with, the collectivist Socialism of the later nineteenth century. Part of his critique of Fabianism, it is true, derived from his suspicion of Socialist bureaucracy and of too great a use of state power to achieve moral social ends. Yet Headlam was not an anti-collectivist, and his Christian Socialism incorporated solidly political as well as moral objectives. His fears about the growth of the state were directed towards the preservation of individual liberty. For Headlam, however, this was not a reflection of bourgeois liberal values, of a desire to do good for others at no cost to the existing structure of society – as it

[62] Headlam, *The Service of Humanity*, 'The Stage' (1881), 31.
[63] Ibid., 27.   [64] Ibid., 22.
[65] Headlam, *The Meaning of the Mass*, 'The Holy Eucharist' (1901), 39.
[66] Ibid., 'The Attitude of the Church Towards Drama' (1904), 129.
[67] Jones, *The Christian Socialist Revival*, 149; Bettany, *Stewart Headlam*, 131.
[68] Headlam, *The Meaning of the Mass*, 134.
[69] Jones, *The Christian Socialist Revival*, 48.

was for so many others in the English reformist tradition – since Headlam did believe in radical social change, to be achieved by real political means. He supported collective bargaining and trade union rights, 'municipal socialism', a redistribution of wealth by state interference, and full state education. As in all other aspects of his personality and conduct, however, Headlam's view of the functions of the state was muddied by contradictions. While he argued that the Church was a 'true Commune', for example, he contended, at the same time, that it was wrong 'to compel people by *law* to live as brothers': the duty of the Church was 'to persuade'. The actual means were sometimes left unclear as well. The Church was to support 'any means by which a more just distribution of the wealth of the country may be effected'.[70] But what of the state? Was compulsion for social ends any more appropriate there? On the whole Headlam thought that it was. The duty of all good men, he declared in his Fabian Tract, was 'to seize the State and to use it for the well-being of the masses instead of the classes'. They must 'get delegates or deputies returned to parliament who will carry out the people's will'.[71] He even believed it was an obligation of the bishops in the House of Lords 'to initiate such legislation as will put a stop to the robbery of the poor that has been going on for so long'.[72] He was, above all, impatient of the empty declamations of good intention made by the religious people of his day: change had to be concrete, an actual shift of power was needed. For Christ 'meant us to do as He had done, and not to take the whole meaning out of the works by spiritualizing them; He meant us to work for health against disease, to fight against the evil circumstances which make the death rate of St. Luke's so much heavier than the death rate in Belgravia: He meant us to be an organized society, to work for the physical as well as the moral and spiritual well-being of the Humanity He lived and died to save'. In a return to his perpetual theme, Headlam added, 'He meant us to do secular works in His name'.[73] Righteousness could only derive 'from some tremendous social reorganization'.[74] Headlam regarded his opinions as a natural continuation of the ideas of Maurice,[75] but his advocacy of collectivist reforms, his belief in actual social transformation and in the redistribution of wealth, and his co-operation with party political groups to do these things, was very far removed from Maurice's vision.

Like that of Maurice and his circle, however, Headlam's social diagnosis assumed the evils of economic competition – 'that most evil spirit of individual

[70] Headlam, *The Service of Humanity*, 'Church and State', 72.
[71] Stewart Headlam, *Christian Socialism* (London, 1892), 9.
[72] *The Official Report of the Church Congress Held at Wolverhampton, 1887* (London, 1887), 175.
[73] Headlam, *The Service of Humanity*, 7.
[74] *The Official Report of the Church Congress Held at Reading, 1883* (London, 1883), 428 (Headlam's speech in the 'Sunday Observance' debate).
[75] Leech, in *For Christ and the People*, 79.

selfishness'.[76] It was 'the principle of every man for himself and the devil take
the hindmost'.[77] A simple matter of justice was involved, for, as presently
constituted, the economic system guaranteed that 'those who work the hardest
and produce the most have the least of the good things of this world for their
consumption'.[78] A radical redistribution of wealth was 'of the first importance'.[79] The working class was entitled to 'a better share of the profits arising
from the wealth which they produce'.[80] Christian Socialism should be directed
not merely to the alleviation of the symptoms of poverty, but to 'getting at the
very root and cause of it'.[81] It was here that his collectivism and political
methods diverged from the Maurician advocates of social reform. In his Fabian
Tract, of 1892, Headlam listed three priorities: reform of education, to provide
free, secular schools, with a better pupil–teacher ratio, and encouragement to
the arts and healthy exercise; reform of the economic system, to establish a
minimum wage and a maximum length of the working day; reform of the land,
enacting the principles of George's Single Tax.[82] In 1905 he added two others to
the list: the nationalization of public houses, to encourage 'rational drinking in
connection with rational amusements'; and better housing.[83] He also advocated
female emancipation: an education 'on an equality with men', equality before
the law, equality in employment, and the acceptance by society 'that they have
political rights and duties which they are bound and able to perform'. Like
Ludlow, he believed that the revival of convents, because of their social work
'for humanity', were 'examples of Christian Socialism on a small scale'.[84] Part
of Headlam's collectivism was dependent on his traditional Christian belief in
the state as a divine institution.[85] It was the state's character as a 'sacred
organization' which should enable churchmen to 'unite with Socialists of every
sort' in using political power for social transformation.[86] Headlam defined
Christian Socialism as a great 'experiment'; it was 'to try and live in a rational,
organized, orderly brotherhood'.[87]

In order to effect the Christian dimension of Christian Socialism, the leaders
of the mid-century had envisaged reforms of the Church, to render it more
suited to a rôle which society would accept. Headlam also produced a series of
ideas for Church reform, but they were considerably more advanced. He
defined the Church, in the first place, in social language. It was an essay in
authentic communism, a true brotherhood, in which 'radical reform received
not only human but divine sanction'; the Church was 'as much opposed to
aristocracy of intellect or of correct opinion' as it was 'to aristocracy of land or

[76] Headlam, *Priestcraft and Progress*, 'The Militant Nation and the Militant Church – Joshua and
the Fight for Health' (1876), 48.   [77] Headlam, *Christian Socialism*, 3.   [78] Ibid., 6.
[79] Headlam, *The Service of Humanity*, 'The Cultus of Our Lady', 60.   [80] Ibid., 61.
[81] Headlam, *Christian Socialism*, 6.   [82] Ibid., 9ff.
[83] Headlam, *The Meaning of the Mass*, 'The Lord's Supper', 21–2.
[84] Headlam, *The Service of Humanity*, 'The Cultus of Our Lady', 63.
[85] Ibid., 77.   [86] Headlam, *Christian Socialism*, 9.   [87] Ibid., 3.

family', since 'its members are admitted simply on the ground of their humanity'. The Church was 'essentially democratic'.[88] Headlam's dislike of Nonconformity, which was stimulated through his association with Thomas Hancock in the Junior Clergy Society in 1873 – Hancock linked the Non-conformists with capitalism[89] – was because Dissent encouraged exclusivity and so destroyed the idea of the Church as a brotherhood of all men, knit together for social advancement. It was knit together, also, by sacramentalism, with the Eucharist at the centre of its witness to the Lord whose works it existed to continue. This was 'the Church Militant against social evil'.[90] The Church had to be free to be properly sacramental – free from the state which was, in his own day, prosecuting Ritualists; and it needed freedom 'to develop ourselves as the great Socialist Secular Society'.[91] The result was Headlam's policy of disestablishment of the Church of England: 'a complete Christian Socialism cannot be brought about until the Church is free to use influence and discipline for the establishment of the Kingdom of Heaven upon earth'.[92] Other High Churchmen in Headlam's day proposed disestablishment, and sometimes, like Gore, associated it with social reformism. But Headlam's advocacy was slightly embittered. Behind the social arguments lay his rejection of the ecclesiastical system which had withdrawn his licence and left him without a conventional ministry. 'The whole body of baptised people and the unbeneficed clergy', he pointed out, 'are practically in almost complete subjection to those few whom the state establishes in their arbitrary authority'.[93] The solution appeared simple. In reality it imposed a contradiction in his thinking. As an upholder of the divine office of the state (reinforced, indeed, by his conception of its high social duties), Headlam was directly opposed to the atomistic view of the state propounded by his Nonconformist allies in the disestablishment campaign, the Liberation Society. The contradiction remained unresolved. Headlam concerned himself with the practical details of the matter – with the elimination of the system of church patronage. The Guild of St Matthew, the *Church Reformer*, and the campaigning by Headlam and his friends at the Church Congresses, all concentrated on that issue. 'No wonder that on the whole', he said, the clergy were opposed to political enlightenment: 'if you allow the Squire to nominate the Parson what else can you expect?'.[94]

Education had emerged as the priority for Maurice, and the same was the case with Headlam. For the first wave of Christian Socialists education was the prerequisite for admission to political society; the working classes were to be

[88] Headlam, *The Service of Humanity*, 'The Church and Liberalism', 124.
[89] Jones, *The Christian Socialist Revival*, 110.
[90] Headlam, *The Service of Humanity*, 'Is Life Worth Living?' (1878), 93.
[91] Headlam, *The Service of Humanity*, 'The Church and Liberalism', 134.
[92] Headlam, *Christian Socialism*, 9.
[93] Headlam, *The Service of Humanity*, 'The Church and Liberalism', 122.
[94] Ibid., 123.

made fit to exercise the franchise through an education programme which changed them, by heightening their moral horizons, but which left the social structures more or less the same. For Headlam, education was directly linked to social transformation. 'It seems to me, to be the duty of every minister of Christ', he wrote, 'to do all he possibly can to stir up a divine discontent in the hearts and minds of the people with the evils which surround them'.[95] Education was to associate the acquisition of knowledge with political understanding – a process known to radical churchmen of the second half of the twentieth century as 'conscientization'. Headlam used the phrase 'divine discontent' frequently. It was the means of breaking up the thrall of social class deference. Church teaching itself, he contended, should encourage 'a noble ambition, a divine discontent' which leads men to see that they were called 'out of one state into another'.[96] In a tract of 1875, *The Church Catechism and the Emancipation of Labour*, Headlam constructed the Church of England's teaching to mean that social respect was due to 'betters', to those of moral goodness, and 'not to the rich or high in rank as such'.[97] The theme recurred in his Fabian Tract, where the catechism is represented as 'the principles of Christian Socialism' and the *Magnificat* is seen as a statement of Socialism also, for the humble were exalted and the rich were sent empty away.[98] In all social dealings, for Headlam, it was necessary to make 'moral worth the only standard of excellence'.[99] The schools where these ideals were to be pursued were to be free, open equally to all classes, and secular. Headlam's insistence on secular education divided him sharply from most other Anglicans – who were fighting a long battle in the later decades of the nineteenth century to prevent national education from losing an element of religious instruction. Most were prepared to settle for non-denominational Christian programmes in the Board schools, and leave full confessional teaching to the Church schools. Headlam wanted fully secular education for everyone, with no religious teaching of any kind; a view which allied him with the secularists and with a number of Nonconformists. Most Nonconformists, however, even those who spoke favourably of 'secular' education, actually intended to preserve some sort of 'common Christian' teaching – simple Bible reading. Headlam was at times prepared to concede that references to the divine were sometimes appropriate in the classroom, but well-integrated with a generally ethicist approach. He was vigorous and characteristically outspoken about it. Secular education was required on grounds of justice: it was suited to a society of mixed religious affiliation; and it was in itself desirable because of the immanence of the divine within the secular. Headlam's High Church Anglicanism included a very clear understanding of certain

---

[95] Headlam, *Christian Socialism*, 5.
[96] Stewart Headlam, *The Church Catechism and the Emancipation of Labour* (London, 1875), 1.
[97] Ibid., 2.   [98] Headlam, *Christian Socialism*, 8.
[99] Headlam, *The Service of Humanity*, 'The Cultus of Our Lady', 61.

dogmas, and they were to be taught by the suitable body – the Church. Hence the importance he attached to Sunday schools. Explicit religious teaching 'must come from the Church and not from the State: it is the business of the Minister of Religion, not of the Schoolmaster'.[100] The Church had a duty, Headlam argued, 'to bless and support' the Board schools.[101] Such schools, despite the absence of precise religious teaching, were not godless; they were – another of Headlam's triumphalist paradoxes – 'most divine institutions'.[102] In 1882 he was elected to the London School Board to represent the London Borough of Hackney, and entered into the work of educational administration and reform which was to occupy the rest of his life. Even the Guild of St Matthew came to take a second place. His election address in 1882 was a manifesto for secular education, and referred to the great purpose of education as generating 'divine discontent'.[103] He got in because Verinder organized the vote in co-operation with local working-class political leaders. He was, together with Mrs Annie Besant and A. W. Jephson, one of three Fabians on the London School Board.[104] When, in 1903, the Board was wound up, and its work absorbed by the Education Committee of the London County Council, Headlam was for a short time without an outlet for his educational zeal. In 1907, however, he was elected to the L.C.C., and his work was resumed, for seventeen years. Control of policy passed out of the hands of the Progressive Party, for whom he sat in the L.C.C., and for most of those years he found himself in a minority. It was something he was used to.

The other great preoccupation of Headlam's mature years was the Land question, and this, also, tended to place him in a minority even within the Guild of St Matthew – though he never acknowledged the fact, and gave off his opinions on land taxation as if they were the consensus of the membership. The ideas of Henry George had in fact come to exercise a quite extraordinary hold upon radical social thinking in England, and Headlam's adhesion to the cause, in 1884, was not idiosyncratic. George, indeed, came to replace Maurice as Headlam's major inspiration. The two men met a number of times, during the six visits to Britain made by George in the 1880s. George's *Progress and Poverty*, the Bible of the land reformers, was published in New York in 1879 and in London the following year. The work reflected American conditions; George was unaware of Maurice and of the Christian Socialists of the 1850s in England.[105] It soon acquired devotees amongst radical groups. George did not, as was so often supposed, favour the nationalization of land: his plan was for the progressive increase of taxation of land values to the point at which the state was

---

[100] Stewart D. Headlam, *The Place of the Bible in Secular Education*, 5.
[101] Headlam, *The Meaning of the Mass*, 'The Church and National Education' (1901), 86.
[102] Ibid., 88.   [103] Bettany, *Stewart Headlam*, 146.
[104] A. M. McBriar, *Fabian Socialism and English Politics, 1884–1918* (Cambridge, 1962), 198.
[105] Jones, *The Christian Socialist Revival*, 49.

receiving the full value of the economic rent. The simplicity of the Single Tax Scheme appealed to Headlam as soon as he heard of it. The agents of his conversion were two of George's first English disciples – H. H. Champion and J. L. Joynes (son of Headlam's housemaster at Eton, and himself an Eton master until he left to take up land reform agitation on a full-time basis). In 1883 Headlam joined the Land Reform Union, on its foundation, and soon began to speak of the Single Tax Scheme as the most important of the reforms that Christian Socialism should pursue. Land reform was 'the main plank in the platform of the Christian Socialist, the chief political reform at which he aims', for it went 'to the very heart' of social injustice in England, and was 'not tinkering' merely.[106] It would produce a 'revolution', once they could 'get the land, which is the main means of production, into the hands of the people'. It was 'the root question'.[107] *Progress and Poverty* was soon being sold on bookstalls run by the Guild of St Matthew and by Headlam and his friends at Church Congresses. 'It is because the earth is the Lord's that we say it is therefore not the landlords,' Headlam used frequently to say.[108] There was a Christian duty, he believed, to act immediately upon the truth that God had given land to men on an equality – 'and it is blasphemy on their part if they allow that most important and valuable of all material gifts to be lightly filched away from them by the Duke of Westminster or the Duke of Northumberland [two particularly prominent landowners in London], or any of the landlords of this country'. That, he declared, was the 'moral line which the Christian Socialists – which the Guild of St. Matthew, for instance – take in regard to these questions'.[109] The Biblicism of Headlam's views on land owed much to Frederick Verinder, the Secretary of the Guild. Verinder found in the early land codes of Israel the authority for radical agrarian reform, and he educated the Guild to see that the Mosaic agrarian legislation, was 'absolutely fatal to what we know as landlordism'.[110] In fact he was arguing in detail what Kingsley had suggested, in circumstances of some controversy, in his sermon at St John's Church, Charlotte Street, in 1851.[111] Verinder accepted the main conclusions of critical Biblical scholarship, as developed by his time, and observed that it was 'to the underlying principles of the Hebrew social philosophy, rather than to the details of the Mosaic legislation' that his analysis was directed.[112] He depicted Henry George as the 'expositor' of the laws of Moses.[113] In 1911 he summarized these ideas in a short work which vilified the notion that any private property in land could have moral sanction,[114] and argued that justice, not convention, should

---

[106] Headlam, *Christian Socialism*, 3.
[107] Ibid., 11–12.   [108] Headlam, *The Sure Foundation*, 12.
[109] *The Official Report of the Church Congress held at Wolverhampton, 1887* (London, 1887), 175.
[110] Leech, in *For Christ and the People*, 78.   [111] See Chapter 3, p. 46.
[112] Frederick Verinder, *My Neighbour's Landmark. Short Studies in Bible Land Laws* (London, 1911), 14.   [113] Ibid., 15   [114] Ibid., 18.

be the foundation of laws relating to the distribution of resources, as Moses, in the arrangements made for Israel, had appeared to declare.[115] Verinder became General Secretary of the English Land Restoration League in 1884, and gave the rest of his life as an organizer and propagandist to George's land reforms, just as Headlam increasingly gave his to education. Despite their original close co-operation, when Verinder came to write a detailed explanation of his policies, in 1935, there was no mention of Headlam in the book.[116] This was not surprising. Headlam's importance lay in his critique of contemporary social practices; he was not an original economic thinker.

Although Headlam never found himself entirely at home inside a political party he did not share the suspicion and distaste for parties which had characterized the earlier Christian Socialists. His difficulty was not the idea of party as such; it was that his range of interests, and the priorities he set to each, were not easily accommodated within the party options on offer in his day. On public platforms he called himself simply 'a Christian Socialist'.[117] During the period when Headlam's political formation was most critical, in the 1880s and 1890s, there also lacked a coherent definition of Socialism. Various groups attached their own meanings, and even organized parties, like the Fabians, incorporated a range of opinions within themselves. Many Socialists felt quite able to operate within local Liberal Party organizations, and Headlam was among them. 'I am a Socialist', he once declared, 'but I thank God I am a Liberal as well'.[118] There was even practical work: in 1882 he was chairman of the Bloomsbury Ward of the Liberal Party. F. L. Donaldson, a sympathetic observer, and a member of the Guild of St Matthew, said at the memorial service for Headlam, in 1924, that he was 'a true Liberal, a Conservative and a Socialist'.[119] Headlam's highly personal combination of interests and causes quite often led to such combinations of political labels. His own addiction to paradox was thereby reflected in the views of others about him.

Yet his Socialism was not diluted, and at some stages of his life he found himself on the left of the Fabians. As time passed he did not become more conservative in any political sense: he merely became more aware that his internal contradictions imposed difficulties in the way of easy party identification. In 1884 he had given some support to Hyndman's Democratic Federation.[120] But he belonged to the world of literary radicalism, to the artistic élite in London, and despite his genuine sympathy for, and real knowledge of, working-class society, he never felt happy with the idea of a working-class political party. He refused to get involved with the Independent Labour Party, regarding its Socialism as virtually token – in which opinion he was not without

---

[115] Ibid., 98.   [116] Frederick Verinder, *Land and Freedom* (London, 1935).
[117] At Church Congresses, for example. See the *Official Report* of Wolverhampton (1887), 174.
[118] Bettany, *Stewart Headlam*, 142.
[119] Ibid., 242.   [120] McBriar, *Fabian Socialism*, 9.

some justification – and its leadership, and especially Keir Hardie, as unworthy. To some extent his dislike of such a party derived from his educational priorities: the working people were not yet ready for a real transformation of society. That placed him, in the end, in the same category as Maurice, though for different reasons. But most of his dislike was actually personal: the politicians who were emerging within the I.L.P. did not seem, to him, to have elevated enough ideals for the advance of the people to their just inheritance. They did not appear to set the cultivation of theatre and the arts alongside the redistribution of wealth and other social reforms as among the primary objectives. Their vision for the future of the working class was too material, even for Headlam's understanding of the moral value of the 'secular'. The priorities of the Fabian Society were not particularly non-material, either; but in the artistic and intellectual interests of so many of the leading members Headlam could find some companionship. In their company, as Shaw noticed, 'he did not talk about religion', and 'kept tactfully to politics, letting the priest be seen and felt rather than heard'.[121] According to Headlam's biographer, he 'joined the Society in default of anything better of its kind'.[122] Having declared the religious 'duty' of political action,[123] he felt the need, not surprisingly, to find a means of expression for himself. But he can never have been entirely at one with the Fabians – among whose members were many noted for precisely the kind of austere ethicism that Headlam had campaigned against in his Anti-Puritan League. Sidney Webb believed that Headlam joined the Fabians because the Society was 'the nearest thing in Socialism that suited his views'.[124] He disliked the trend towards collectivist authoritarianism within the political thinking of the Fabians, sniffing out threats to individual liberty. It was always Headlam's problem that he could discover no satisfactory political ideology – one with solidity and internal consistency, at any rate – that combined his radical social reformism with his endorsement of the eclectic and the eccentric in personal choice. He was happy to give his simultaneous approval to Liberalism because he saw it, just as so many Victorian intellectuals did, as the protector of individual genius and high culture against the destructive potential of Conservative insensitivity to the need for change on the one hand, and of the political power of mass ignorance on the other. Suspicions of Gladstone, whose Midlothian campaign, and eventual Irish Home Rule policy, looked like pandering to the mob, were fuelled by these beliefs. Headlam did not join the intellectuals and the Whigs in the Liberal Party who thought this, and, with characteristic individualism of response, remained a Gladstonian. There ought especially, he taught, to be 'close sympathy' between 'liberal Churchmen and liberal politicians', for that would, among other benefits, help to advance the

121 Bettany, *Stewart Headlam*, 139.   122 Ibid., 133.
123 Headlam, *Priestcraft and Progress*, 'Patriotism' (1876), 38, 43.
124 Bettany, *Stewart Headlam*, 136.

cause of disestablishment, or, as Headlam put it, 'help to restore the Church in this country to its true position of a great democratic society'.[125]

Headlam joined the Fabian Society in 1886, within two years of its foundation, and he served on its Executive Committee on three separate occasions between 1890 and 1911. In 1887 he helped, as a member of the special committee of fifteen, to draw up the 'Basis' of the Society. He was thus a very active member, closely associated with policy throughout much of his thirty-eight years of membership. In 1892 he contributed a Tract to the famous series. But it is doubtful if his influence upon the Fabians was in the end very significant. His policy of not intruding religious issues, or of speaking from a distinctly Christian perspective, meant that his one great insight – the sacramental Socialism of his Incarnational theology – was excluded from their counsels. Headlam was correct, however, in recognizing that the Fabians would not have been interested in such matters anyway, and he joined them to give practical content to his imperatives for social reform. He was disappointed that the Society did not take up George's Single Tax ideas, and that only a few of the members appeared to share his enthusiasm for putting Land Reform at the top of the social agenda. Headlam applied the same kind of separation of functions that he practised within Fabianism to his preaching activities. In the pulpit he attempted – in a manner later associated with William Temple – to distinguish between generalities and details of politics. He declined, he said to the Guild of St Matthew in 1901, 'to suggest any definite action on the social and political problems', regarding it as his duty to point out 'the principles'. But he added, in what was unavoidably a political injunction, that it was also his business 'to warn' about 'what prevents those principles from being carried out'.[126]

Headlam was at his best when actually working among the poor, as his affection for Bethnal Green and its cramped social misery had disclosed at the beginning of his ministry. Where others were outraged by moral behaviour which seemed to breach the most religious of canons, he saw only outcasts whose lives needed the understanding and appreciation of a Christianity purged of social respectability and made to reflect the teachings of its founder. As he declared himself: 'Priesthood binds me to Radicalism'.[127] It was not his Socialism which shocked his contemporaries so much as his moral originality, and his sense of the transience of apparently established social practices. Seemingly so secular, his work was probably, as he believed himself, fundamentally religious, whatever his contradictions and eccentricities. 'Happy are those', he said in 1881, in the unlikely setting of Westminster Abbey, 'who know that in washing the tired and dusty feet of any human wayfarer, in

---

[125] Headlam, *The Service of Humanity*, 'The Church and Liberalism', 126.
[126] Headlam, *The Meaning of the Mass*, 'Christian Democracy' (1901), 123.
[127] Headlam, *The Service of Humanity*, 'The Church and Liberalism', 121.

ministering to any human want, they are at one with Jesus Christ'.[128] Headlam's sacramental Socialism, though so personal in origin and development, did not disappear: a generation of Christian Socialists, most of them active in the first decades of the twentieth century, were indebted to his vision, and in the Guild of St Matthew received their first intimation of the Social Gospel.

[128] Ibid., 14.

7

JOHN RUSKIN

It has been usual to divide Ruskin's life around the year 1859/60, when he was forty years old. Before that time he was essentially an art critic concerned with changing received attitudes to art, and after it he was a social critic obsessed with the evils of industrial society and preaching a new and radical social order. The first phase was dominated by the influence of Turner, the second by Carlyle. The division is basically sound, provided it preserves some impression of the unity of Ruskin's thought. There was, clearly, development with the unfolding of the years, and with the addition of new themes, but Ruskin's chief characteristic as a thinker was his consistency. In the later parts of his life his writing, often emerging from beneath overlapping sequences of mental instability, was increasingly filled with seemingly disjoined and sometimes even intellectually incoherent illustrations and subjects: but despite first appearances the consistency actually held; there was 'conscious design'[1] beneath the 'wide diversity of interests'.[2] Interpreters have appreciated the astonishing penetration of Ruskin's analysis, whether of art or of society, and they have sympathized with the power and sentiment of his assault upon the social evils of his day. Despite the evident clarity of his writing, however, he actually remains difficult to categorize.

He has been known as a Christian Socialist. The title does not rest easily upon him. His Christianity was not susceptible to an institutional expression, and his understanding of religious belief underwent several changes during his life and was rarely precise. It had great beauty about it nonetheless, and an understanding of Ruskin's rootedness in a religious vision of the world is essential for a comprehension of all his thought. His political radicalism was not really 'Socialist', as his most recent biographer has rightly noticed;[3] yet he un-

[1] J. A. Hobson, *John Ruskin, Social Reformer* (London, 1898), vi.

[2] F. W. Roe, *The Social Philosophy of Carlyle and Ruskin* (Port Washington, 1921), 149.

[3] Tim Hilton, *John Ruskin. The Early Years, 1819–1859* (Yale, 1985), xiv. For the same conclusion, see B. E. Lippincott, *Victorian Critics of Democracy* (Minneapolis, 1938), 59.

questionably inspired some elements within later Socialist thinking – and especially influenced William Morris and the practitioners of the Arts-and-Crafts movement.[4] Ruskin was far too much of a social traditionalist to be an authentic Socialist in any of its various nineteenth-century meanings. Nor was he, however, simply another Tory paternalist, like some of the others around whose persons an atmosphere of Socialism has sometimes seemed to appear. He was not in fact at all interested in politics. There was a difficulty here: he sought extensive social changes – nothing less than the dismantling of the existing economic order – and he sought them by the use of state power as well as by private 'Utopian' schemes, yet he had no belief in the political apparatus necessarily required for the task. He had no personal links with political society, and very few with society of any sort. He was among the most solitary of men. His social criticisms were not only made from a position outside the affairs of men, they were made by one who had no real expertise in them either. Admired by Mazzini as 'the most analytical mind in Europe',[5] the data upon which his intelligence rested was very narrow. His assault upon the Political Economists is most appreciated by those who have not read the authors Ruskin was attacking, and have taken his highly exaggerated caricatures of their arguments and opinions too seriously. His criticisms are deceptively attractive because of the enthusiasm for humanity that so obviously inspired them. There were also some very good direct hits on some particular targets. But the importance of Ruskin's writing on Political Economy does not derive from his close knowledge of the science: in the preface to his famous Manchester lectures on the Political Economy of Art, in 1857, he declared that the absence of textual references was 'because I have never read any author on political economy, except Adam Smith, twenty years ago'.[6] This rather large omission was later to some extent corrected, but by then Ruskin's opinions had formed, and he was on the lookout for illustrative material for his existing analysis. Yet his critique of Political Economy remains of great importance, because of its implied vision of a counter-world of humanized social values. Ruskin used a crudely assimilated understanding of the real and existing system of economic organization to produce a vivid model of an alternative.

The same is probably true of his 'political' radicalism or 'Socialism'. It has been conventional to regard this as largely Utopian. The problem has always been to decide where Ruskin is suggesting actual social changes possible within existing social structures, and where he seems to be fantasizing about a perfect society in another time. Different interpreters of his work have drawn lines in different places. Ruskin was conscious of the problem himself, and said that he

[4] E. T. Cook, *The Life of John Ruskin* (second edn., London, 1912), I, 311.

[5] Ibid., II, 12.

[6] John Ruskin, *A Joy For Ever* [The title under which the two Lectures were later re-issued] (London, 1887), xi.

had become accustomed 'to hear my statements laughed at for years'.[7] He knew himself to be spoken of as 'a delirious visionary'.[8] It is actually doubtful if Ruskin was ever fantasizing about the perfect society. The prescriptions for a just order appear side by side with ordinary social reformism throughout his writings – there is no late development, as some have supposed, which found a dreamy and unreal detailed expression in *Fors Clavigera*. In that chaotic and prophetic set of writings, it is true, Ruskin spells out the 'Utopian' arrangements for the St George's Guild, and superficially they look very similar to the kind of ideal communities sometimes produced at the social margin by apocalyptic analysis. It would probably be mistaken to leave the matter there, however. It may be that Ruskin was not projecting a Utopia at all; that the descriptions of the ideal society were not intended for implementation in the real world, but were to be held up as a model against which to test and evaluate the injustices of the prevailing order. 'I know not if a day is ever to come when the nature of right freedom will be understood', Ruskin once wrote.[9] It is clear that towards the end of his life he came more and more urgently to see social evils in prophetic terms;[10] the age was disclosing permanent truths about mankind through the horrors of life in a wrong social order. More horrific still was Ruskin's realization that the moral calamity of men in industrial society, as he saw it, was never going to be recognized for what it was. 'The reason why the educated and cultured classes in this country found Ruskin incredible', Shaw noticed, 'was that they could not bring themselves to believe that he meant what he was saying'.[11] The realization gave Ruskin's writing that 'ideal' quality which so easily passes for Utopianism. In fact he saw himself as a practical thinker holding out model sketches of salvation to an age sinking into a condition unfit for humanity. 'I feel constantly as if I were living in one great churchyard', he wrote in 1867, 'with people all round me clinging feebly to the edges of the open graves, and calling for help, as they fall back into them, out of sight'.[12]

Ruskin was also moved, as were so many men in the 1840s, by a sense of impending political catastrophe. The age of the Chartists and of the European revolutions was a time when violent disruption seemed just about to break the surface. Ruskin shared with the Christian Socialists, and especially with Kingsley, a belief that social disaster could only be averted if social righteousness became the object of public policy. He envisaged a struggle of classes, and a

---

[7] John Ruskin, *The Crown of Wild Olive. Four Lectures on Industry and War* [1866] (eighth edn., London, 1894), 10.

[8] John Ruskin, *Praeterita* [1885–9] (Oxford, 1978), 363.

[9] John Ruskin, *The Stones of Venice* (London, 1853), II, 163.

[10] Peter Quennell, *John Ruskin. The Portrait of a Prophet* (London, 1949), 121.

[11] Bernard Shaw, *Ruskin's Politics* (London, 1921), 9.

[12] John Ruskin, *Time and Tide, by Weare and Tyne. Twenty-five letters to a Working Man of Sunderland on the Laws of Work* (second edn., London, 1868), Letter XIX, 'Broken Reeds', 115–16.

struggle between wealth and poverty. Here, the analysis is obviously more approximate to real events. What Ruskin's version of the impending disruption lacks, however, is historical perspective. Although he devoted a lifetime to visiting the historic cities of Europe, and produced what are probably the most beautiful descriptions of historic buildings in the English language, he actually had almost no historical sense. He seems unaware of the historical nature of change, and describes social transformation in moral, not historical, terms. This to some extent accounts for the lack of systematic treatment: there is no clear statement of social principles in his writing, no class analysis that related to his day, and no appreciation of existing social movements. He envisaged Florentine guilds, for example, and not trade unions, as securing the protection of labour. There were, of course, obvious reasons, from within his own set of references, why that had to be the case. But the result was a collection of themes, illustrated by models, not a uniform and coherent explanation of social dynamics. Ruskin emerges, however, as a social writer of quite extraordinary penetration and force – within the boundaries he had set for himself. His influence on Christian Socialism was surprisingly slight, perhaps because of his conscious withdrawal from association with its leading figures, in the Working Men's College in the 1850s. His influence, as is well known, was very considerable within the intelligentsia, though even so there has been a tendency to approve his searing depictions of industrial society and the splendour of his appreciations of art, rather than to take him seriously as a practitioner of actual reform. A case may still be made out for regarding him, if not as 'the greatest social teacher of his age',[13] at least as a very inventive social critic. It was the work for which Ruskin himself wished to be remembered. 'Political work', he recorded in his autobiography, 'has been the most earnest of my life'.[14] It was the more noble for being undertaken at considerable personal cost. 'I have no particular pleasure in doing good', he observed early in the 1870s; 'I entirely hate the whole business'.[15]

Ruskin was unlike the other Christian Socialists discussed in this study. He took almost no part in any of the various movements for social reform, and remained largely beyond the edge of public life which they inhabited. Above all, he did not look to the Church as a primary agent of social policy. In what sense, in fact, may he be categorized as Christian at all? Students of Ruskin's life have emphasized his religious scepticism, the apparent priority of his doubts. The discovery of religious doubt, indeed, has become almost an essential preliminary for the admission of any past thinker to the esteem of the modern secular intelligence. Like most Victorians, however, Ruskin himself made a very earnest job of his own religious difficulties: what must impress the observer who looks closely enough at his analysis of them, nevertheless, is how much he

[13] Hobson, *John Ruskin Social Reformer*, v.   [14] Ruskin, *Praeterita*, 378.
[15] Ruskin, *Fors Clavigera*, I, 3; II, 283.

continued to believe. His religious journey was not unfamiliar: the rejection of the Evangelicalism he had imbibed from his mother, the middle years of uncertainty as he sought vainly for a satisfactory substitute, and his eventual return to a kind of orthodoxy. Although at times he doubted the immortality of the individual soul, and although he found his confidence in the veracity of the Scriptures progressively eroded, he never lapsed from belief in God. He continued to pray throughout his life, and his daily study of the Bible, despite the difficulties of interpretation, never lapsed, even when he found that it provided 'less ground of belief'.[16] In his later years he recorded: 'whatever I know or feel, now, of the justice of God, the nobleness of man, and the beauty of nature, I knew and felt then, no less strongly' – he was referring to his crisis of faith in 1845 – 'but these firm faiths were confused by the continual discovery, day by day, of error or limitation in the doctrines I have been taught, and the follies and inconsistencies of their teachers'.[17] Ruskin developed a kind of benevolent Deism, which still employed the familiar images of Christianity to convey religious meaning. It was related not to the Church as an institution but to the higher qualities of man. 'No man more than I has ever loved the places where God's honour dwells, or yielded truer allegiance to the teaching of His evident servants', he wrote.[18] But the places of God's habitation were not the churches (except, perhaps, for those in Italy), and God's 'evident' servants were not the clergy: they were the men elevated by work and moral beauty. Just as in his social analysis Ruskin had no sense that men existed in real class relationships that affected their conduct as much as the interior qualities of personal fulfilment, so in his religious attitudes he had no feeling for institutional religion. Belief, for him, was isolated and personal. It depended on perceptions of beauty and human nobility, not on creeds or structures of holiness. When he approached organized religion at all, it was generally in a form notably bereft of external ornament. As a youth he had been taken by his parents to a Dissenting chapel in Walworth, and in his maturity the only religious minister with whom he seems to have enjoyed friendship and a satisfactory exchange of opinions was Charles Spurgeon, the Baptist popular preacher whose style and capabilities were not noted for elegance or intellectual grandeur.[19] Visitors to his house in Denmark Hill noticed the same extraordinary absence of signs of taste in the furnishings and decorations. It was, perhaps, a characteristic of Ruskin's persistent Protestantism that he could be so insensitive to some aspects of enriched living. At some points in his life he was attracted to the ritual of Catholic worship, and the splendours of Catholic iconography. In his Oxford lectures of 1884, Carpaccio's St Ursula was represented as the normal mode of

---

[16] Cook, *Life of Ruskin*, I, 227.   [17] Ruskin, *Praeterita*, 356.
[18] John Ruskin, *The Lord's Prayer and the Church. Letters to the Clergy* (second edn., London, 1880), 376.
[19] Hilton, *Ruskin*, 260; Cook, *Life of Ruskin*, II, 21.

Catholicism, and one of Bewick's engravings of a pig as the mode of Protestantism.[20] But he was never really likely to have departed from his Protestant foundations. Far too much of his intellectual endeavour was centred in a life-long attempt to reconcile the human nobility of Catholic art in southern Europe with the Biblical Protestantism of his earliest religious perceptions.

Ruskin's religion lacked esoteric qualities. His heterodoxy was within well-defined and even conventional limits. He hated sectarianism, and the greatest spiritual crisis of his life, in fact, occurred near Turin, in 1858, when he heard a Protestant Waldensian preacher condemn the world and all those who did not adhere to exclusive doctrines of salvation. Ruskin was repelled: here, momentarily, he saw the face of the Evangelical religion he had been brought up to believe. The incident did not, as some scholars of Ruskin have supposed, result in 'a tearing up of his entire religious faith by the roots'.[21] He spent the next thirty years trying to work out exactly what his religious position was.[22] But the crisis gave a particular point to Ruskin's growing realization that the evidences of God were not to be sought in formal institutions but in the works of men inspired directly by intimations of his presence. 'Between the Campo Santo and Santa Maria Novella', he had realized, a decade earlier, he 'had been brought into some knowledge of the relations that might truly exist between God and his creatures'.[23] Ruskin attended chapel in his years as Slade Professor at Oxford. He received books from, and maintained an acquaintance with, Cardinal Manning. He continued to study the Bible, and to practice daily spiritual exercises. He was, in fact, a very religious man, not a mere moralist of vaguely held religiosity. But he was not a churchman. Was he a Christian? It is difficult to be precise, and by Ruskin's own standards, which rejected religious exclusivity, it would be improper to conclude that he was not. Ruskin always used the moral furniture of Christianity, and his religious insights were always expressed with Christian symbolism. It was a version centred in humanity, like Maurice's; but it was very far from Maurice in its blindness to the organized Church. Ruskin had been untouched by the Oxford Movement – at its height during his student years at Christ Church. His mother had destined him for the Christian priesthood: Ruskin had himself substituted the service of humanity. The high moral purpose remained the same, however. Ruskin clung to the end to his conviction that he had a special vocation; that he was called by Providence to open men's eyes to the beauty and authentic religion that would be evident when society set its priorities right. For men were fundamentally moral. What they needed was religious purpose. It was to be found in the proper working relationships of the past. In medieval crafts and in Gothic ornament – it is

---

[20] Joan Evans, *John Ruskin* (London, 1954), 398.

[21] William Burgess, *The Religion of Ruskin* (New York, 1907), 55.

[22] Hilton, *Ruskin*, 254.   [23] Ruskin, *Praeterita*, 345.

Ruskin's most well-known contention – men were reconciled to themselves; 'Christianity having recognized, in small things as well as great, the individual value of every soul'.[24] Then alienation (though Ruskin does not use the word) was overcome, and men and society were at one. His life's purpose was to lift the prophetic vision into the industrial world of the nineteenth century. It remained essentially a religious vision. At times, it looked as if it might pass into a version of the Religion of Humanity, yet Ruskin's sense of human frailty, an inheritance from orthodox Christianity, held him back. 'Every faculty of man's soul, and every instinct of it by which he is meant to live', he wrote in 1867, 'is exposed to its own special form of corruption: and whether within Man, or in the external world, there is a power or condition of temptation which is perpetually endeavouring to reduce every glory of his soul, and every power of his life, to such corruption as is possible to them'.[25] The difficulty was to find a structure to contain the slide into wrong values and moral imperfection. The Church was too flawed by its own corruptions, though Christianity was the means of personal alleviation – Christianity as understood by Ruskin. The structure which he substituted for the Church was authoritarian education. Much of Ruskin's social writing was preoccupied with getting the exact educational details right. As those refinements became more and more precise, the outline of institutional religion became less and less so. By the 1880s he was referring to 'the breadth of his own creed or communion'.[26] The simplification was regarded by him as quintessentially Christian. Dogmas were human artefacts, shrunk by the forceful religious magnificence of other artefacts – the art of truly free men. The inheritance of tradition was not relevant to the determination of truth, which was known by interior satisfaction. Ruskin wrote of his 'total ignorance of Christian history'.[27] The exaggeration was not gross. Yet the conclusion was recognizably Christian: 'What a child cannot understand of Christianity, no one need try to.'[28]

Recognizing that the Church of their day was inadequate to the task of social reform, other Christian Socialists had produced proposals for Church reform. Ruskin's lack of respect for institutional Christianity meant that he left his criticism of the Church at the level of observation: he had no plans for a restructured Church. In his model of the ideal society, it is true, he provided that 'bishops' were to assume functions of social administration; but the Church of which they were presumably a part was not described in any great detail. He did uphold the union of Church and State. In his early work of 1851, *Notes on the Construction of Sheepfolds*, written before his writings began to scatter around the fragments which collectively made up his model state, Ruskin observed

---

[24] John Ruskin, *The Stones of Venice* (London, 1853), II, Chapter vi, 'The Nature of Gothic', 159.
[25] Ruskin, *Time and Tide*, Letter X, 'Wheat-Sifting', 55.   [26] Cook, *Life of Ruskin*, II, 451.
[27] Ruskin, *Praeterita*, 227.   [28] Ibid., 320.

that to separate Church and State was 'to limit the sense in which it seemed to me that the word "Church" should be understood'.[29] As properly conceived, the Church was probably intended by Ruskin to approximate to Maurice's 'universal and spiritual Kingdom'. Ruskin was as opposed to the limiting exclusivity of religious sectarianism as Maurice. The universal beauty of art told him that Christianity was 'absolutely general for the whole Christian world'; there could be no 'question of sect or schism whatsoever'.[30] In *Sesame and Lilies* (1865) there was a ferocious assault upon religious persons who 'think themselves exclusively in the right and others wrong' and who 'hold that men can be saved by thinking rightly instead of doing rightly'. They were 'bag-pipes for the fiends to pipe with – corrupt and corrupting'.[31] But it was not only the small religious sects who thought these things: Ruskin's disapproval of dogma – of expressing religious truth in verbal and authoritative formulae – indicates that he imagined the fault to be characteristic of the historical churches, too. For Ruskin 'all dogmatic teaching was a matter of chance and habit', for 'the life of religion depended on the force of faith, not the terms of it'.[32] Religious truth derived from men's discovery of their interior qualities when, through satisfactory work, they were at one with the natural order and not divorced from it, as in his own day, by false social values. His criticism of religious people was twofold. In the first place they were not active for social justice: if men are told that their religious beliefs should affect their conduct of business they reply 'what you say is very beautiful, but it is not practical'.[33] Religious people were continually given to 'talk of acting for God's glory, and giving God praise', but Ruskin declared that they should 'think less of praising, and more of pleasing Him'.[34] In the second place, the religious were simply not religious enough – they did not live in expectation of their own doctrines being true: he noted that the exploitative upper classes of Europe, engaged in 'one large Picnic Party' for eight hundred years at the expense of the labouring poor, had all been, or claimed to be, religious.[35] Indeed, 'half the baptised people in the world are very visible rogues'.[36] Doctrines were given no practical effect: 'I know few Christians so convinced of the splendour of the rooms in their Father's house, as to be happier when their friends are called to those mansions, than they would have been if the Queen had sent for them to live at Court'.[37] The criticism turned also to the ordinary hypocrisy of conventional believers – 'the great mass of men calling themselves Christians do actually live by robbing the poor of their bread'. Political Economy itself, that most destructive of all social and economic doctrines in Ruskin's view, was upheld by Christian men; but it was

[29] John Ruskin, *Notes on the Construction of Sheepfolds* (London, 1851), 6.
[30] Ruskin, *Praeterita*, 322.
[31] John Ruskin, *Sesame and Lilies* (London, 1865), 33.   [32] Ruskin, *Praeterita*, 313.
[33] Ruskin, *The Crown of Wild Olive*, 13.   [34] Ruskin, *Fors Clavigera*, I, 237.
[35] Ibid., I, 33.   [36] Ruskin, *Notes on the Construction of Sheepfolds*, 13.
[37] Ruskin, *The Crown of Wild Olive*, 17.

theft from the poor. 'True Christianity is known – as its Master was – in breaking of bread, and all false Christianity in stealing it'.[38] The Church had to be radically changed if it were to exist without 'pollutions and hypocrisies beyond all words'; it had to become 'wide in its offices of temporal ministry to the poor'.[39] The Christian Socialists would have agreed with that, but, unlike them, Ruskin had no actual proposals for a transformation of the Church. Instead, he looked banefully at an institution patently serving the purposes of social control promoted by the governing classes, preaching the 'soporific' untruths 'to keep the mob quietly at work'.[40] It was a religion maintained 'at point of constable's staff'; its 'paraphernalia being chiefly of high pews, heavy elocution, and calm grimness of behaviour'.[41] Ruskin's rejection of the institutional Church was not solely because of the breadth of his own religious understanding, therefore. It also resulted from his social criticism. 'Christian Justice has been strangely mute and seemingly blind', he said in 1866, 'and if not blind, decrepit, this many a day'.[42]

For someone whose life was passed so much out of society, and whose student years, even, were dominated by the company of his parents – his mother moved to Oxford with him, so that he could spend each evening with her, and his father arrived at weekends – it would have been surprising if Ruskin's social knowledge was based on personal experience. Apart from the chair at Oxford, he never did a job, never held any kind of office, had no acquaintance with public life, and lived a life of great personal solitude, interrupted only briefly, between 1848 and 1854, by his unhappy marriage. He claimed that he had 'seen and known too much of the struggle for life among our labouring population';[43] but in reality the life passed in the accumulating suburbs of South London did not allow a very extensive knowledge. Ruskin is important and impressive because of his instinctive sensitivity to social misery, and because of his yearning for action. His actual awareness of the fate of the suffering millions elicited great anguish and extended to the depths of his being, but it was not founded upon personal experience. Even when Ruskin was conscious of the slender basis of his social knowledge it would not have mattered to him: he believed that good social conditions produced good art and fulfilled men, and that bad conditions of society were reflected in servile or debased styles, in ornament and in people. By an examination of art and of men, therefore, it was possible to deduce the state of society without any other social data. It has been noticed that his period as a teacher of art at Maurice's Working Men's College, after 1854, was 'a gallant and not unsuccessful attempt to get into close touch

---

[38] Ruskin, *The Lord's Prayer*, 31.
[39] Ibid., 32.   [40] Ruskin, *Sesame and Lilies*, 66.
[41] John Ruskin, *Modern Painters*, V (London, 1860), 296–7.
[42] Ruskin, *The Crown of Wild Olive*, 55.
[43] Ibid., 24.

with working men'.[44] At the time, another writer has suggested, he had 'little knowledge of the working classes save memories of his aunt's baker's shop at Croydon'.[45] If this was true, the Working Men's College was not the best place to make good the omission, for the men who resorted to its lectures were highly untypical of the working classes in general, coming, as they did, from specialized levels of the skilled trades. Ruskin did get involved with one or two small enterprises which gave him some additional social information: he financed an unsuccessful tea-shop in Paddington, intended to provide pure tea at moderate prices to the poor of the area; and he co-operated for a time – until they disagreed – with Octavia Hill in a scheme of model dwellings carved out of his properties in Marylebone. He met Arthur Helps and Sir John Simon in the mid-1850s and joined a committee concerned with the promotion of public health reforms. Here his acceptance of the need for state intervention in some areas of public policy was in contrast to that of most of the Christian Socialists, who had, indeed, pulled back from involvement in health measures precisely because they involved collective action and state participation – Kingsley alone excepted. It was not only a close knowledge of working-class society that eluded Ruskin; it was not until the 1870s that he came into occasional contact with the manufacturing entrepreneurs and the provincial bourgeoisie whose values and conduct he had by then spent over a decade assailing. He was surprised both by their social awareness and by their patronage of literary and artistic ideas. Most of Ruskin's knowledge of social fact came from his extensive reading. This quasi-academic source gave it an artificial quality, and accounts for his failure to recognize class phenomena. Ruskin was a genius at showing the effects of the industrial system and competitive economics in stunting the potential of individual men: his vision of the suffering of the working class was a collective made up of individual blighted people. He had no real sense of the class as a class. It was odd that in his autobiography there was almost no mention of social issues.[46] But then the book was written, as Ruskin declared, to give pleasure.[47]

If Turner was the chief influence on Ruskin's earlier work, as art critic – his 'Earthly Master'[48] – then, as already noticed, the major influence of his growing interest in social issues, the author of his formative reading matter, was Carlyle. The two men met for the first time around 1850 and at once seemed to enter into a firm and enduring mutual esteem. Ruskin was unrestrained in his devotion to Carlyle, 'the friend and guide who has urged me to all chief labour'.[49] His official biographer described Ruskin's visits to his friend's house:

[44] Hobson, *John Ruskin, Social Reformer*, 40.   [45] Evans, *John Ruskin*, 214.
[46] Kenneth Clark, in his Introduction to *Praeterita* (Oxford, 1978), xvi.
[47] Ruskin, *Praeterita*, Author's Preface, 1.   [48] Cook, *Life of Ruskin*, I, 107.
[49] John Ruskin, *Munera Pulveris. Six Essays on the Elements of Political Economy* (new edn., London, 1886), xxxii.

Carlyle 'reclining on a sofa, while Ruskin knelt on the floor, leaning over Carlyle as they talked and kissing his hand on taking leave'. He added, 'the description is typical of their relations'.[50] Ruskin told the working men that 'Carlyle is the only living writer who has spoken the absolute and perpetual truth about yourselves and your business'.[51] From Carlyle he derived most of his attitudes to the ills of industrial society, a doctrine of the nobility of work, a sense of the importance of inner resource in the individual, a loathing of democratic practice. Many of Ruskin's themes were clearly taken straight from Carlyle, and at one time, in fact, he had to deny that he had actually plagiarized his thought.[52] Yet Ruskin often penetrated deeper than Carlyle, particularly in the extent of his rejection of Political Economy, and it is probably true to say that what most marked out the common ground of the two men was the employment of the social language Carlyle had established as a basis of description.[53] Ruskin's critique of existing society was much more analytical than Carlyle's. Ruskin himself identified – surprisingly – with Rousseau. He was 'unhesitatingly' the man he believed himself 'to be grouped with'.[54] There was, it is true, a clear affinity in the desire of the two thinkers to find some ideal relationship in which the alienation of men in society could be overcome, but there was in reality little in Ruskin's thought which bears much similarity to Rousseau. He owed more to Pugin: a debt largely unacknowledged, for he patently disliked the Catholic convert for claiming Gothic as an exclusively Catholic style.[55] Pugin's belief in the relationship between the morality and government of an age and its artistic achievement plainly bore a close relationship to Ruskin's comparable thesis in *The Seven Lamps of Architecture* and *The Stones of Venice*.

The man who so inspired the Christian Socialists because of his doctrine of humanity, F. D. Maurice, was hardly an influence at all upon Ruskin. 'I loved Frederick Maurice, as every one did who came near him', Ruskin wrote, 'but Maurice was by nature puzzle-headed and, though in a beautiful manner, wrong-headed'.[56] In 1872 he declined to contribute to the Maurice Memorial Fund on the ground that he did 'not think of him as one of the great, or even one of the leading, men of England of his day'. He was only 'the centre of a group of students whom his amiable sentimentalism at once exalted and stimulated, while it relieved them from any painful necessities of exact scholarship in divinity'. He was 'harmless and soothing in error', offering 'consoling equivocations'.[57] There is some variation here from the fulsome tributes paid to Maurice's influence by the Christian Socialists. Ruskin and Maurice had corresponded between 1851 and 1853 over *Notes on the Construction of*

---

[50] Cook, *Life of Ruskin*, I, 475–6.   [51] Ruskin, *Fors Clavigera*, I, 203.

[52] Evans, *John Ruskin*, 206.   [53] Hobson, *John Ruskin, Social Reformer*, 189.

[54] Cook, *Life of Ruskin*, II, 549.   [55] Hilton, *Ruskin*, 149.

[56] Ruskin, *Praeterita*, 451.   [57] Ruskin, *Fors Clavigera*, I, 448–9.

Sheepfolds, but the letters, exchanged by the hand of F. J. Furnivall, another of the Christian Socialists in Bellenden Ker's chambers, failed to establish any common ground beyond a shared intention to do something for the working men. When Ruskin taught in the Working Men's College he met Maurice occasionally, received a low impression of his style of organizing the College, and seems to have remained impervious to the spiritual serenity that attracted others to Maurice's company.

The original group of Christian Socialists were moved to claim a Socialist identity by the stimulating events of the great Chartist demonstration of 10 April 1848. On that very day Ruskin was in Scotland, unmindful of the portentous happenings in London: it was the day of his marriage to Effie Gray. Ruskin's only real contact with the Christian Socialists came through the Working Men's College. It was, again, Furnivall who drew him into this, and who had, at the start of the venture in 1854, circulated reprints of Ruskin's famous essay on 'The Nature of Gothic', from *The Stones of Venice*, as a sort of advertisement for the kind of purposes the College was intended to promote. Ruskin, in turn, attracted Rossetti, Ford Madox Brown, and Burne-Jones to the College as occasional teachers of drawing. But Ruskin became disillusioned with the work, and when he gave up after four years he told Maurice that men 'trained to mechanical toil' found artistic appreciation 'unintelligible'.[58] The truth was that he also had very little in common with the Christian Socialists. Though he supported the principle of Co-operative Workshops he could not regard it as a satisfactory solution to the massive social evils that afflicted his consciousness. 'For the alternative', he wrote, in a discussion of co-operatives in *Time and Tide*, in 1867, 'is not, in reality, only between two modes of conducting business – it is between two different states of society'.[59] He actually reinterpreted the word 'co-operative' to mean a radical rejection of the whole system of production and competition, in a manner which had 'hardly yet entered into the minds of political inquirers'.[60] The Christian Socialists' enterprises were surface attempts at mere self-help; they left the structure of a wrongly conceived social order intact. Ruskin's own 'Socialism' has to be defined negatively: it resides in his critiques of industrial society and of the principles of Political Economy, and is perceptive and often very sensitive. When he comes to discuss the actions which were to bring correctives there are all kinds of complications – his is an attempt to restore the working relationships of the distant past, to dismantle the industrial society without destroying the wealth of an industrial economy, to give power to the state and yet preserve the priority of individual will, to enable government by enlightenment and not by the masses. However radical the social insights, the solutions are difficult to categorize as Socialist, and despite the depth of his feeling for the suffering of the

[58] Quoted in Evans, *John Ruskin*, 243.
[59] Ruskin, *Time and Tide*, Letter I, 'Co-operation', 2.   [60] Ibid., 5.

alienated labourers there is little that they are really offered beyond a return to better versions of a former paternalism. Ruskin's most recent interpreter has concluded that he had no 'real connection with the Labour movement'.[61]

Ruskin called himself 'a violent Tory of the old school' – and that was towards the end of his life, as he looked back upon his developments and intentions.[62] Though he took the idea of a 'science' of politics seriously, and believed it should be included in the school curriculum, he believed that 'a glance at the state of the world' would show that 'there was no such science', or that it was 'still in its infancy'.[63] He thought that there were 'everlasting laws',[64] and that the security of property had to be the basis of all political order:[65] 'to the enforcement of this, by law and police-truncheon, the nation must always primarily set its mind – that the cupboard door may have a firm lock to it, and no man's dinner be carried off by the mob'.[66] He was opposed to republicanism and rejected democracy; both tended strongly to social indiscipline and to the worship of wrong values, for the generality were incapable of exercising political power without corruption.[67] Egalitarianism had already, in Ruskin's belief, gone too far to enable the rule of the strong and the wise: in 1873 he wrote, 'as the working men have been for the last fifty years taught that one man is as good as another, they never think of looking for a good man to govern them'.[68] This sort of view was, of course, commonly found among the Christian Socialists, as, indeed, among intellectual Liberals. Ruskin revelled in his rejection of Liberalism, too. 'Liberty' as an abstract concept encouraged the negation of duty, of natural authority, and of individual genius. 'I am a violent Illiberal', he declared.[69] The 'follies of Modern Liberalism' could be summarized as the 'denial or neglect of the quality and intrinsic value of things'. Liberalism was the 'theology of universal indulgence', and 'the root incapacity of discerning, or refusal to discern, worth and unworth in anything, and least of all in man'.[70] These observations came from *Fors Clavigera*, that late exposure of Ruskin's genius (in a series of letters to the working class, published between 1871 and 1884) which, for all their hurried chaos still contain some of the richest insights of Ruskin's picture of the world. They are also the place where his juxtaposition of the real and the ideal is the most difficult to sort out.

There is a paradoxical quality about Ruskin's political concern. He wrote quite often to the newspapers about public issues, but his interest rarely extended to government itself – despite the enormous number of suggestions

[61] Hilton, *Ruskin*, xiv. See also, for a comparable conclusion, Roe, *The Social Philosophy of Carlyle and Ruskin*, 245.   [62] Ruskin, *Praeterita*, 5; *Fors Clavigera*, I, 188.

[63] Ruskin, *The Stones of Venice*, III, Appendix 7, 'Modern Education', 215.

[64] Ibid., II, 170.

[65] John Ruskin, *Unto This Last* [1862], ed. Clive Wilmer (London, 1985), 202.

[66] Ruskin, *Munera Pulveris*, 74.

[67] Lippincott, *Victorian Critics of Democracy*, 91.

[68] Ruskin, *Fors Clavigera*, I, 121.   [69] Ibid., I, 4.   [70] Ibid., I, 277.

which cover his writings about ideal forms of political organization. The truth was that he had an extremely limited view of the competence of government. 'Your prosperity is in your own hands', he told the labourers; 'only in remote degree does it depend upon external matters, and least of all on forms of government'.[71] That had been the message of the Christian Socialists' placard *Workmen of England!* in 1848. Ruskin carried it rather far. 'All systems of government – all efforts of benevolence', he wrote, 'are vain to repress the natural consequences of radical error'.[72] His attitude to parliamentary reform had echoes of the Christian Socialists as well. At the time of the national agitation over the Bill of 1867 he informed the working men that they did not need greater influence in Parliament because the thing they would want, when they had determined what it was – which they had not yet done – 'you will find, not only that you can do it for yourselves, without the intervention of parliament, but that eventually nobody *but* yourselves can do it'.[73] True 'life and liberty', he said, 'no laws, no charters, no charities can secure'.[74] Even the most radical politics would not avail: 'The laws which at present regulate the possession of wealth are unjust, because the motives which provoke to its attainment are impure; but no socialism can effect their abrogation, unless it can abrogate also covetousness and pride, which it is by no means yet in the way of doing'.[75] At the practical level of franchise reform, Ruskin was consistently in favour of universal suffrage, from his first advocacy of it in a letter to *The Times* of 1852, which his father, charged with sending it off, suppressed.[76] As he explained, he held it 'a gratuitous and useless insult to make any man incapable of *giving* an opinion: only let the proper weight be attached to his opinion'.[77] Ruskin was equally consistent, therefore, in upholding the device of plural franchises as a way of protecting enlightenment from mass ignorance. It was a common enough suggestion in the reform debates of the 1850s and 1860s. Ruskin was somewhat frank in putting it on a very refined scale, to secure that government should proceed, 'not by universal *equal* suffrage'.[78]

Though never really spelled out, Ruskin's organization of society implied an organic doctrine of the state: 'The whole nation is, in fact, bound together, as men are by ropes on a glacier'.[79] It was this which led to his opposition to parties, for they were by nature divisive. 'The effect of party government is always to develop hostilities and hypocrisies, and to extinguish ideas', he noted; 'men only associate in parties by sacrificing their opinions'.[80] The organization of political society to achieve the kind of shifts of emphasis that Ruskin envisaged logically required some sort of political association, however. He

[71] Ibid., I, 4.   [72] Ibid., I, 198–9.   [73] Ruskin, *Time and Tide*, vii.
[74] Ruskin, *The Stones of Venice*, II, 'The Nature of Gothic', 163.
[75] Ruskin, *Munera Pulveris*, xxix.   [76] Cook, *Life of Ruskin*, I, 273.
[77] Ibid., I, 276.   [78] Ruskin, *Munera Pulveris*, 161–2.
[79] Ruskin, *A Joy For Ever*, Addenda, 161.   [80] Ruskin, *Fors Clavigera*, I, 5.

wanted a non-political legislature; 'a Parliament into which people might be elected on condition of their never saying anything about politics'.[81] There is, of course, a light touch about this sort of observation, but it is still clear that Ruskin contemplated an arrangement of government with minimal political capacity.

The source of Ruskin's antipathy to popular government lay in his belief in the unalterable nature of some human characteristics and structures. Differences between men were 'eternal and irreconcilable'.[82] His 'continual aim', he remarked in the course of one of his most telling attacks upon Political Economy, 'has been to show the eternal superiority of some men to others, sometimes even of one man to all others'. This was the residue of Carlyle. It was advisable that superior persons should be appointed 'to guide, to lead, or on occasion even to compel and subdue, their inferiors'.[83] One of the troubles with Political Economy, in Ruskin's understanding of it – and it was a common view among Tory paternalists – was that it imposed an insensitive and atomistic science of society in a realm which actually needed the preservation and maintenance of traditional relationships founded upon a sure knowledge of natural human inequalities. Ruskin wanted even work to be hereditary: 'the only proper school for workmen is of the work their fathers bred them to'.[84] Like Kingsley, he supposed it improper for men to seek to remove themselves from the social level in which they were born. 'The healthy sense of progress, which is necessary to the strength and happiness of men', he wrote, 'does not consist in the anxiety of a struggle to attain higher place, or rank, but in gradually perfecting the manner, and accomplishing the ends, of the life which we have chosen, or which circumstances have determined for us'.[85] That most would fall into the category of circumstantial determinism became evident from Ruskin's view of educational opportunity. Education 'should be clearly understood to be no means of getting on in the world, but a means of staying pleasantly in your place there'.[86] Sometimes, indeed, Ruskin seems to be projecting a 'New Feudalism'[87] in which the divisions of rank are very tightly drawn, and where each class has its own peculiar duties in relation to the others.[88] From the earliest age children were to be taught 'the impossibility of equality among men; the good which arises from their inequality', as well as 'the proper relations of rich and poor, governor and governed'.[89] Some men were determined by nature to 'inferior labour' – they were 'fit for nothing better';[90] though Ruskin does suggest that really 'degrading' tasks, such as

[81] Ibid., I, 8.   [82] Ruskin, *The Stones of Venice*, III, 217.
[83] Ruskin, *Unto This Last*, 202.   [84] Ruskin, *Praeterita*, 453.
[85] Ruskin, *Time and Tide*, Letter II, 'Contentment', 8.
[86] Ibid., Letter XVI, 'Education', 96–7.
[87] Hobson, *John Ruskin, Social Reformer*, 158.
[88] Ruskin, *Munera Pulveris*, 173; *Time and Tide*, 10; *Fors Clavigera*, I, 203.
[89] Ruskin, *The Stones of Venice*, III, 215.   [90] Ruskin, *Munera Pulveris*, 135.

'work in mines and at furnaces' should be allocated to criminals.[91] Since wealth, in a properly ordered society, will be derived by legitimate means, and would go to those suited to receive it, a recognition of social inequality based on differences of possession was important in Ruskin's analysis. There were, he argued, just or unjust ways of applying wealth,[92] but money and property imparted a legitimate 'superiority' and a 'fitting reward' for men of 'sagacity'.[93] Working-class men who regarded the rich as their 'natural enemies' were 'dissolute'.[94] Social deference was, for Ruskin, an essential social cohesive. Philanthropists, in their work for the poor, should 'find them some other employment than disturbing governments'.[95] He lamented the decline of the English aristocracy.[96] 'Kings should keep their crowns on their heads, and Bishops their croziers in their hands', he declared.[97] These were not the ideals usually associated with Socialism, and it was hardly surprising, therefore, that, despite the claims later made on Ruskin's behalf by enthusiasts anxious to incorporate him into the English Labour movement, he did not regard himself as a Socialist. Some of his rigid beliefs about the determined inequality of men went very far. He was an opponent of female emancipation;[98] he regarded 'slavery' as 'an inherent, natural, and eternal inheritance of a large portion of the human race';[99] and he supposed that 'both moral and physical qualities are determined by descent, far more than they can be developed by education'.[100]

Though these conclusions may appear less than satisfactory to the modern understanding of social morality, Ruskin's claims to extraordinary insight into the nature of social suffering can be very securely established. They give his thought originality and nobility, and lift him to a quite different intellectual level from the Christian Socialists – Maurice excepted. Ruskin's critique of industrial society, it is true, was romantic and exaggerated: it was not dissimilar to the kinds of reaction found commonly enough among the Tory paternalists, with their vision of a lost world of harmonious social relationships before the dislocation of the 'Steam-Age mentality'. Ruskin's genius lay not in the mere description of a half-mythical social ruin, however, but in the significance he attached to the moral ugliness which was the result for mankind. His lack of personal acquaintance with industrial society led to distortions of its deficiencies: he ignored the raised living-standards of those who moved from rural squalor to the towns. Above all – and it was a symptom of the tragic instability of his later years – he was periodically, and for months on end, afflicted with an illusion of dark clouds extending across the skies of South

[91] Ibid., 133–4.   [92] Ruskin, *Unto This Last*, 112.
[93] Ruskin, *A Joy For Ever*, 147.   [94] Ruskin, *The Crown of Wild Olive*, 29.
[95] John Ruskin, *The Seven Lamps of Architecture* (second edn., London, 1855), Chapter vii, 'The Lamp of Obedience', 194.
[96] Ruskin, *Time and Tide*, 79.   [97] Ruskin, *Fors Clavigera*, I, 5.
[98] Ruskin, *Sesame and Lilies*, 102–5.   [99] Ruskin, *Munera Pulveris*, 166.   [100] Ibid., 6, 130.

London, 'a dry black veil',[101] a veritable 'plague-wind' which was produced by 'phenomena hitherto unrecorded'.[102] At times, he took this to be the consequence of industrial pollution; but in reality the clouds had no external source. Even this disordered vision, however, correctly expresses the depth of Ruskin's rejection of the industrial world, and his language about it is prophetic and apocalyptic. The modern cities of the nineteenth century were 'loathsome centres of fornication and covetousness – the smoke of their sin going up into the face of heaven like the furnace of Sodom, and the pollution of it rotting and raging through the bones and souls of the peasant people round them'.[103] The language deliberately links the physical spoliation with human moral corruption. The 'filth and poverty permitted or ignored in the midst of us are dishonourable to the whole social body'; a mere washing of the face of society would not put things right: 'Christ's way is the only true one: begin at the feet; the face will take care of itself'.[104] The insensitivity of the upper class to the existence of such conditions was simply 'sin'.[105] In the fifth volume of *Modern Painters* there is a famous passage where Ruskin contrasts, almost in the manner of Pugin, the splendours of the Venice of Giorgione's boyhood with the vileness of Turner's boyhood spent in Covent Garden; whereas St Mark's looks down upon the splendid square, St Paul's, in London, is encompassed about with a churchyard, the symbol of death.[106]

Ruskin's main concern, and the core of his originality, was the effect of industrial work itself upon the moral consciousness and human qualities of men. True morality and spiritual discernment, like true art, depends for its truth on a well-ordered society, with proper priorities and, above all, a style of work which enables each person to achieve the satisfaction and fulfilment of his own creative capabilities. In modern society the labourer has become a 'machine' himself, 'an animated tool'.[107] It is not necessary to agree with Ruskin's unrealistic, and unhistorical, solution – the revival of a society based upon craftsmanship, the replacement of machinery where that is possible, and the organization of trade guilds on a distinctly medieval pattern – to appreciate the importance of his actual diagnosis. He even seems to have regarded Gothic architecture and decoration, and the styles of work which produced them in the Middle Ages, as a progressive influence: it promoted 'the love of Change', 'the restlessness of the dreaming mind, that wanders hither and thither among the niches, and flickers feverishly around the pinnacles'.[108] Ruskin's conception of the average medieval workman had, to say the least, some unrealistic dimensions. Yet his essential vision of the degrading and stunting effects of

---

[101] Ruskin, *Fors Clavigera*, I, 146.
[102] John Ruskin, *The Storm Cloud of the Nineteenth Century* (London, 1884), 43.
[103] Ruskin, *The Lord's Prayer*, 28.   [104] Ruskin, *Munera Pulveris*, 133.   [105] Ibid., 132.
[106] John Ruskin, *Modern Painters*, V (London, 1860), Part IX, 'The Two Boyhoods', 297.
[107] Ruskin, *The Stones of Venice*, II, 161.   [108] Ibid., II, 181.

labour in the machine age, while still heavily romantic, has the positive attraction not only of its clear compassion but also of its indictment of unjust economic conditions, themselves producing social imbalances. Ruskin was very emphatic, nonetheless, that discontent was the symptom not of poor social conditions as such, but of the wrong styles of work. His vision was centred in men and their needs, in the genius of their creative potential. It was, he explained, the 'degradation of the operative into a machine' which resulted in the 'vain, incoherent, destructive struggling for a freedom of which they cannot explain the nature'. The 'universal oratory against wealth, and against nobility' – the reform agitations of the nineteenth century, that is to say – was not forced from them 'by the pressure of famine'. Discontent, therefore, was not, in Ruskin's understanding, the fruit of poor social conditions, but of wrong labour: 'It is not that men are ill fed, but that they have no pleasure in the work by which they make their bread'.[109] This was to declare that the reality of social disharmony was interior to men, and was not dependent, as Socialists would have added, on class conflict or growing awareness of social inequality. Ruskin recorded his conviction 'that the peace of God rested on all the dutiful and kindly hearts of the laborious poor; and that the only constant form of pure religion was in useful work, faithful love, and stintless charity'.[110] This religious dimension was not a mere sugaring, however. Like Kingsley's articles in *Politics for the People*, Ruskin's concern was active and Biblical, and associated the message of Scripture with attainable and earthly social justice. 'The Bible hardly ever talks about neglect of the poor', Ruskin observed; 'It always talks of *oppression* of the poor – a very different matter'.[111] Working relationships, both the reward of labour and the style of labour which enabled the fulfilment of human potential, were a matter of justice. Ruskin's critique of Political Economy was anchored to this crucial conclusion.

Although he unquestionably took his detailed and precise criticisms of Political Economy to be absolutely true – whereas in reality some are and some are not – there is no doubt that collectively they disclose the heart of what Ruskin was trying to say about a just social order. They were 'expressions of his passion and his pity; a logical development of his artistic work; a necessary condition of his peace'.[112] In practice he tended to make Political Economy the scapegoat for all the social ills of the England of his day, reserving his most chilling satire for Ricardo, Mill, and Fawcett. 'I cannot tell you of the contempt I feel for the common writers on political economy', he announced.[113] Their entire science was based upon the false elevation of what they had 'stated to be the constant instinct of man – the desire to defraud his neighbour'.[114] 'The

[109] Ibid., II, 163.   [110] Ruskin, *Praeterita*, 447.
[111] John Ruskin, *The Two Paths* (London, 1887 edn.), 226.
[112] Cook, *Life of Ruskin*, II, 129.
[113] Ruskin, *Time and Tide*, 131.   [114] Ruskin, *Fors Clavigera*, I, 100.

modern Liberal politico-economist of the Stuart Mill school', he claimed, 'is essentially the type of a flat-fish – one eyeless side of him always in the mud, and one eye, on the side that *has* eyes, down in the corner of his mouth – not a desirable guide for man or beast'.[115] The most evil feature of the system of thought and practice was its denial of a moral foundation to economic science; Political Economists 'consider men as actuated by no other moral influences than those which affect rats or swine'.[116] The 'let-alone' principle, *laissez-faire*, was 'the principle of death'.[117] A social system established without regard to the 'will or spirit' of men, and which disregarded the 'affections' which bound men together and which could, if recognized, transform working, and therefore social, relationships, was patently evil.[118] In this assumption of ethical resignation, as in the grim consequences of the competitive system, Ruskin was saying what the Christian Socialists had said; and like them he exaggerated the degree of materialism in society. His antipathy towards the practical operations of capitalist economics was unconsciously extended to the false conclusion that the science had no moral foundation whatever. Yet he was not opposed to the idea of a science of society as such – only to the wrong ideas of the Political Economists. His critique, despite the high pitch of his clamorous denunciations, was intended to humanize the science, not to demolish it altogether. His purpose, he wrote in 1863, was not 'an endeavour to put sentiment in the place of science'[119] and Political Economy should be redefined as 'The multiplication of human life at the highest standard'.[120] The work of Political Economy was 'to determine what are in reality useful or life-giving things, and by what degrees and kinds of labour they are attainable and distributable'.[121] The point is an important one. For whereas the Christian Socialists had fired arrows of criticism at the operation of the competitive system, and had found an alternative to it in co-operative enterprise, education, moral education, and moral exhortation to the capitalists, Ruskin's appreciation of the seriousness of economic science meant that he went on to a detailed, highly intelligent, and sometimes truly inventive series of reconstructions. Thus there were, in his major writings on Political Economy – *A Joy For Ever, Unto This Last* and *Munera Pulveris* – some quite extraordinarily acute discussions of wealth, a just wage, competition, the nature of exchange, the division of labour, unemployment, currency and usury. Sometimes, despite the distinction of mind disclosed in these assessments, Ruskin was wrong, either through failure to do the Political Economists justice in his summation of their original positions, or through a misunderstanding of the real nature of society. But the originality and value of his critique ought not to be in doubt. The hostility which he encountered at the time was able to exploit his lack of practical knowledge; he

[115] Ibid., I, 204.
[117] Ruskin, *A Joy For Ever*, 20.
[119] Ruskin, *Munera Pulveris*, xviii.

[116] Ruskin, *Unto This Last*, 169.
[118] Ruskin, *Unto This Last*, 170.
[120] Ibid., 6. [121] Ibid., 10.

was only too easily made to look like 'a man of genius who has travelled out of his province' – as one newspaper declared.[122]

Most important of all, however, were not Ruskin's economic redefinitions, but his prophetic denunciations of a materialist society corrupted by avarice. To the cultured class of his day he said: 'You are a parcel of thieves'.[123] The purchase of cheap goods was 'stealing'.[124] The whole fabric of commercial enterprise was 'gambling with money which is not ours, and stealing from those who trust us'.[125] He hit out at the London bourgeoisie, as their villas engulfed and suburbanized the South London he had once so loved. The 'lodgers in those damp shells of bricks' were guilty of 'cheating in business'.[126] The profit motive elicited widespread 'vulgarity' and 'vice'; it involved 'the degradation of the person involved in it'.[127] If society would put itself in order it must recognize the 'intrinsic value' of things – something independent of opinion and quantity,[128] and the test of the worth of all work.[129] 'Every article of human wealth has certain conditions attached to its merited possession', Ruskin proclaimed; 'when these are unobserved, possession becomes rapine'.[130] Thus his dismissal of the legitimacy of the wealth of the English commercial and industrial classes of his day: it is not surprising that the Labour movement has claimed Ruskin as their own. Wealth, he declared, was justified only when accumulated under certain moral conditions of society. It was also 'the reward of sagacity and industry – not of good luck in a scramble or a lottery'.[131] There was a curious by-product of Ruskin's belief in 'sagacity and industry', and a demonstration of his inherent Protestantism: like a forerunner of Weber, he showed that the Catholic cantons of Switzerland were 'idle and dirty' and the Protestant ones were 'busy and clean'.[132]

As already noticed, there is in Ruskin's consideration of what to do about the evils of his day a problem about determining what is intended to relate to existing society, and what is intended as a series of essays in social and governmental models. Sometimes, like the Marxists, he simply declared that the details could wait upon developments. Even so complex an industrial issue, and one important at the time, as 'the organization of labour' he imagined could be left to 'develop itself without quarrel or difficulty'.[133] Of the well-ordered society of the future he wrote 'what final relations may take place between masters and servants, labourers and employers', only 'experience can conclude'.[134] Since the suggested reforms for existing society and the prescriptions – often very detailed – for the model society occur together in Ruskin's

122 From the *Daily News*, and quoted in Evans, *John Ruskin*, 325.
123 Shaw, *Ruskin's Politics*, 11.   124 Ruskin, *The Two Paths*, 231.
125 Ruskin, *A Joy For Ever*, 208.   126 Ruskin, *Fors Clavigera*, II, 101.
127 Ruskin, *Time and Tide*, 135.   128 Ruskin, *Unto This Last*, 209.
129 Ruskin, *The Crown of Wild Olive*, 11.   130 Ruskin, *Munera Pulveris*, 141.
131 Ibid., 162.   132 Ruskin, *Praeterita*, 227.
133 Ruskin, *Unto This Last*, 163.   134 Ruskin, *Fors Clavigera*, II, 283.

writings, and are more and more confusedly rendered as his mind was dislocated by interludes of partial insanity, the difficulty of separating them is probably unresolvable. But there are some obvious cases where it may be done.

Like the Christian Socialists, and like most within the Victorian intelligentsia, Ruskin was preoccupied with the reform of education, and much of what he has to say about it is clearly intended to have immediate and practical effect. It was, in the first place, to be education for a social purpose. 'The great leading error of modern times', he wrote, 'is the mistaking erudition for education'.[135] Education was to be for all classes, but 'with definite respect to the work each man has to do'.[136] In all classes 'it matters not the least how much or how little they know, provided they know just what will fit them to do their work, and to be happy in it'.[137] It is difficult to imagine a clearer statement of the Victorian conviction that education was a department of social control. Women are to receive education, too, but it must be directed towards helping their husbands – and, above all, must avoid the teaching of theology, a 'dangerous science for women'.[138] Ruskin did not regard education as providing a vehicle for social mobility, either.[139] True education was 'not catechism, but drill'.[140] There are many places in his writings where he sets out the content of the curriculum, and they are on the borderline between the actual and the ideal. Certainly within intended immediate reform, however, was the role Ruskin assigns to the state in education: it was 'the first interference' that government should make for social change.[141]

There are many other extensions of the capacity of the state in Ruskin's writings. There is a well-known passage in *The Stones of Venice* where he contended for a great enlargement of executive political action. 'I hold it for indispensable, that the first duty of a state is to see that every child born therein shall be well housed, clothed, fed, and educated, till it attain years of discretion', Ruskin wrote; 'But in order to the effecting this, the government must have an authority over the people of which we now do not so much as dream'.[142] Elsewhere he advocates state ownership of railways, government retraining for the unemployed, state manufacturing set up alongside private enterprises and in competition with them,[143] and even a government factory to produce artists' colours.[144] All these were within the realm of practical reform. But despite this kind of extension of the area of the state's competence, Ruskin was in the end an anti-collectivist; the regeneration of society must first and foremost derive from the realization and exertions of individual wills. It is individual landowners and

---

[135] Ruskin, *The Stones of Venice*, III, Appendix 7, 'Modern Education', 216.
[136] Ibid., 217.   [137] Ibid., 218.
[138] Ruskin, *Sesame and Lilies*, 104–5.   [139] Ruskin, *Time and Tide*, 96–7.
[140] Ruskin, *The Crown of Wild Olive*, 185.
[141] Ruskin, *A Joy For Ever*, 161. See also, *Time and Tide*, 73, 97.
[142] Ruskin, *The Stones of Venice*, III, 218.
[143] Ruskin, *Unto This Last*, 164.   [144] Ruskin, *A Joy For Ever*, 50.

employers who are charged with the reformation of the existing system. 'Note, finally', Ruskin emphasized, 'that all effectual advancement towards this true felicity of the human race must be by individual, not public effort'. He added: 'Certain general measures may aid, certain revised laws guide, such advancement; but the measure and law which have first to be determined are those of each man's home'.[145]

Some interpreters of Ruskin's thought have supposed that his descriptions of the ideal society are related to the deterioration of his mind during the later depressive illnesses, and that the admittedly rather disjointed and occasional prescriptions in *Fors Clavigera*, in particular, are to be taken as Utopian fantasy.[146] This is probably not the most useful way to see Ruskin's essays in the model state. The details in *Fors* have clear precursors in the writings of his less distracted years, and are anyway not to be regarded as absurd. They are, perhaps, imaginative constructions to set against existing social forms, as a way of showing the scale of their inadequacies; they may be moral paradigms, and underline the truth that Ruskin was not a political thinker but an ethical theorist who used the social imbalances of his time as the data for the assembly, not of blueprints for a real structural transformation, but for new moral foundations.

Many of the descriptions of the ideal society in *Fors* were intended as the title deeds of Ruskin's actual experiment in social engineering: the St George's Company, or Guild of St George, which had its first formal meeting in 1879. There were indeed strangely medieval qualities here; settlements without machinery, subject to rules based upon fourteenth-century Florence, the settlers to pay tithes but to own their land (for Ruskin was an opponent of land nationalization), carefully structured education, and censorship of books. Ruskin himself was in full command, and he set down precise vows and rules for the members.[147] Labour was to be organized by trade guilds, and these guilds, in fact, were to perform functions which in his earlier writings Ruskin had allocated to the state.[148] Even in this plainly impractical experiment in social organization, therefore, Ruskin touches on a theme which was to assume importance in later Guild Socialism. The Guild of St George, which failed after some years to develop into a model society, was not exactly 'Utopian'. It was not communitarian, and it did not promote Socialism but a kind of peasant proprietorship under a hierarchical structure of internal government. It probably represented Ruskin's almost despairing attempt to give some embodiment to the social ideals which the people of England were so patently unprepared to take seriously. The descriptions of the model state which are to be found both in association with the Guild, and generally in his writings – and

[145] Ruskin, *Unto This Last*, 226.
[146] Ruskin's official biographer, for example. See Cook, *Life of Ruskin*, II, 313, 325.
[147] For the eight articles of the St George's vow, see Cook, *Life of Ruskin*, II, 336–7.
[148] Hobson, *John Ruskin, Social Reformer*, 167.

especially in *Time and Tide*, written as early as 1867 – do not really add a great deal in amplification of Ruskin's views, since they are extensions of social values already well established in his critical analyses of the existing order. Some are suggestive of wide state control: government 'regulation of marriage' with state permission to marry as a 'reward' for good citizenship;[149] regular enquiry into the lives of families by 'an overseer, or bishop', who shall send in reports to central authorities;[150] state fixing of prices and wages,[151] and a graded bureaucracy.[152] Everywhere there are strong surviving traces of Ruskin's Tory paternalism, particularly in the directive role assigned to the landed aristocracy and in the ruling that 'there shall be no equality' in the model community.[153] Men, Ruskin contended, can be divided into the 'lordly' and the 'servile', and it was the duty of the wise governor to recognize that 'the whole health of the state depends on the manifest separation of these two elements'.[154] Judgments of that order would have found sympathetic echoes within the Christian Socialism of Maurice and his circle, but they do not anticipate the developments of Socialist thought which were occurring in the England of his day. Ruskin had no sense of social division based on class antipathies, or of class phenomena at all. His contribution was to have charted with precision and imagination the effects of industrial society upon the sensibilities of the individual. His was, characteristically, an individualist response. 'Determine the noblest type of man, and aim simply at maintaining the largest possible number of persons of that class', he declared in 1863, 'and it will be found that the largest possible number of every healthy subordinate class must necessarily be produced also'.[155] Ruskin's contribution to the development of a religious involvement with social criticism was distinctive and original. That his thought still clung to so many features of a doomed social order was in the end a minor feature – when set against the elevated vision of liberated men which lay behind the coded language of his prophetic declarations.

[149] Ruskin, *Time and Tide*, 126.
[150] Ibid., 75–6.
[151] Ibid., 85.
[152] Ibid., 151.
[153] Ruskin, *Fors Clavigera*, I, 163.
[154] Ruskin, *Munera Pulveris*, 136.
[155] Ibid., 6.

8

HUGH PRICE HUGHES

Among the Free Church leaders of Victorian England, two were especially known as exponents of Christian Socialism. They were very dissimilar. John Clifford was a Baptist of provincial working-class origins: he had worked a sixteen-hour day in a lace factory at the age of eleven, and had then become a Chartist. After conversion he took three degrees at London University and entered a ministry which was entirely spent in London. He was overtly political, the author of two Fabian Tracts and the President of the Christian Socialist League in 1894. His passionate resistance to denominational education, and his pacifism, drew him further into party political conflicts, but he never lost the conviction that his ministerial vocation imposed the priority of pastoral over political concerns. He declined an invitation from the North Paddington Liberal Association to be their parliamentary candidate in 1885 precisely because of his spiritual work, yet he wrote at the time, 'My sense of political duty is strong, my sympathy with the people is intense'.[1] Hugh Price Hughes came from the professional class of South Wales, was a markedly conservative Wesleyan Methodist, and though often absorbed with interest in the public issues of the times was never involved with political organizations. His advocacy of social reform was restrained, though it was in some particulars more far-reaching than it at first appeared. 'All law and all policy ought to be shaped in the interests of the poor',[2] he said in 1889, and he meant it. Though of little real acquaintance with working-class society, and not greatly given to social mixing, Hughes was an accomplished publicist for a style of social compassion which was both acceptable to liberal opinion and distinctly religious. As founder and editor of the *Methodist Times* in 1885, as one of the most celebrated preachers in London, and as superintendent of the West London Mission after 1887, he was much more influential than Clifford. It was

[1] C. T. Bateman, *John Clifford* (London, 1902), 144.
[2] Hugh Price Hughes, *The Philanthropy of God: Described and Illustrated in a Series of Sermons* (London, 1890), 'The Problem of London Pauperism', 187.

recorded that 'Members of Parliament, journalists, and others specially interested in public and social questions' attended his Sunday Afternoon Conferences 'in considerable numbers'.[3] His topics covered a wide area, and he was involved in diverse issues as a member of 'many anti-societies',[4] from the Peace Society to the Anti-Vaccination League: but it was for his radicalism in social questions that he was best known. 'The great need of our time is for Christian Socialism',[5] he said in 1884.

Hugh Price Hughes was the grandson of Hugh Hughes, a well-remembered Methodist itinerant preacher whose influence in Wales has been compared, a shade improbably, with that of St Francis in Italy.[6] His father was a physician in Carmarthen, and himself a lay preacher; his mother came from a Jewish family of bankers in Haverfordwest, the Levis. The home was both politically and religiously conservative: they attended the local Anglican Church to receive Holy Communion, as well as the Wesleyan chapel, and this gave Hughes' Methodism an enduringly non-sectarian character. The boy underwent a conversion experience at the age of thirteen and was a preacher at the age of fourteen. At eighteen he left the small boarding school in Swansea where he had been educated alongside the other sons of the local professional class, to attend the Wesleyan Theological College at Richmond. That was in 1865. There he was lively and intellectually quick – a certain fluency rather than distinction of mind – and something of a College character. Beneath the flamboyance, however, were wastelands of depression and self-doubt, a restless inability to reconcile his ministerial vocation with personal qualities which were never disclosed. He burned brightly with enthusiasm for particular things and then relapsed into long periods of apparent somnolence. The truth was that his emotions, his spirituality and his intellect were developing unevenly and at different rates. This became clear in his relationship with the little girl who was to become his wife. He first intended eventual marriage to Mary Katherine, daughter of the Governor of the College, when she was only eleven years old. They had to wait until she left school, at eighteen. The wedding itself did not go smoothly: their carriages got mixed up with those of a funeral procession. Hughes was never particularly at ease in any society, though his courtesy and spiritual depths attracted many. Like Maurice, indeed, he was often in the company of young men, 'who everywhere clustered around him',[7] and to whom he opened up his heart on the pressing social miseries that afflicted his conscience. His was essentially an unoriginal mind, however, and the inspiration that he imparted so forcefully to others derived from practical commitment, from clear summaries of public issues in the light of Christianity,

[3] J. Gregory Mantle, *Hugh Price Hughes* (London, 1901), 117.
[4] D. P. Hughes, *The Life of Hugh Price Hughes* (London, 1904), 370.
[5] Peter d'A. Jones, *The Christian Socialist Revival, 1877–1914* (Princeton, 1968), 406.
[6] D. P. Hughes, *Life*, 6.   [7] Ibid., 82.

and from recognition of an unambiguous path to follow. 'Christianity aims at producing a particular kind of life upon earth', he declared.[8] The way was open for those of earnest religious conviction. Hughes' priorities were always religious, and they were always practical. Having set his hand to the plough he did not look back, and his ministry was confident and his message was simple.

Due to the Methodist three-year Circuit practice (which Hughes regretted, since it did not allow continuity), his early life in the ministry was passed in a number of places: in Dover (1869), Brighton (1872), Tottenham (1875), Dulwich (1878), and Oxford (1881). By the mid-1880s he was the central figure in the 'Forward Movement', a largely Methodist body of social progressivism inspired by the Congregationalist pamphlet *The Bitter Cry of Outcast London*.[9] It was his leadership of the movement which made Hughes 'the chief Methodist of his day'.[10] From 1887 he was Superintendent of the West London Mission, concerned with social and evangelistic work, mostly in Soho and Piccadilly, among the poor and socially despised; the pulpit of the Mission, at St James's Hall, also became one of the most important disseminations of Christian Socialism in England. Missions on the London model were copied in many provincial cities. Hughes served as President of the Methodist Conference in 1898, and was a founder (and in 1896, President) of the National Free Church Council. It was a noble career exemplifying, in fact, Hughes' own contention that 'the heroic energies of the Reformation still survive in the Protestant world'.[11] Those energies, however, were rather differently directed in him than in most of the Christian Socialists of Victorian England. For Hughes had different priorities, and they were characteristic of the Nonconformity of his day. He was concerned essentially with personal and moral rather than with economic conditions. That, in itself, was not greatly at variance with the priorities of Maurice and his circle. But Hughes carried his priority far into the legislative field. Like other Nonconformists of his day, yet with greater cogency and much more publicity, he proclaimed the use of law to secure individual purity, and as a means, collectively, of social regeneration. He was a spearhead of the movement for state intervention in crusades to elevate men and women from the thrall of their own vices.[12] He linked the attack on immorality with the elimination of poverty,[13] and that was why he became so strongly involved with issues like Temperance and the Repeal of the Contagious Diseases Acts. To later generations that kind of vision has seemed restrictive and

[8] Hugh Price Hughes, *Ethical Christianity. A Series of Sermons* (London, 1892), ix.

[9] Published anonymously (but by Andrew Mearns) in 1883.

[10] Jones, *The Christian Socialist Revival*, 406.

[11] Hugh Price Hughes, *Social Christianity: Sermons Delivered in St. James's Hall, London* (second edn., London, 1889), V, 'The Career of the First German Emperor', 72–3.

[12] D. W. Bebbington, *The Nonconformist Conscience. Chapel and Politics, 1870–1914*, 13, 60.

[13] Brian Harrison, *Drink and the Victorians. The Temperance Question in England, 1815–1872* (London, 1971), 207.

puritanical. Hughes was concerned with the whole person, however, and his desire to see men released from the conditioning of vice, imposed by a squalid environment born of poverty, was intended to prepare them for a recognition of their own dignity and worth. His strictures were, in consequence, always much more forceful against the wealthy – whose personal sin could not be attributed to vile circumstances of living. 'The centres of West End pleasure', he said, 'are much more corrupt and degraded than places of amusement in the East End'.[14]

Hughes was indebted to no single writer or thinker for his Christian Socialism. He read widely and almost indiscriminately – 'everything, from serious theological works sent to him to review to the latest novel'.[15] He plunged into the newspapers every day, and his sermons reflected his fascination with current affairs and sensations. There was no depth of learning or sharpness of critical vision here, but an accumulating series of evidences which convinced him that the social suffering of the times was avoidable if society would reorder its priorities. It was during the three years in Dover, his first ministry, between 1869 and 1872, that he first became aware of the problems. While some wandered Dover beach in contemplation of the receding tides of Christian belief, Hughes discovered there a new dimension of Christianity. The source was Alderman Rowland Rees, a fellow Welshman and Methodist, a Radical who dominated local politics, and who became Mayor of Dover, in circumstances of considerable political controversy, in 1883. On hearing of his death many years later, Hughes wrote 'few persons have exerted so much influence over me as he did'.[16] It was the truth. Hughes underwent something like a second conversion experience; but the social radicalism which now settled upon him was essentially practical. Nor was his horizon ever broadened by contact with the influential men of the times. Hughes' circle remained a fairly closed Methodist one. At Oxford, for example, during his ministry there, he never met Ruskin, Max Müller or Jowett – three men whose ideas, for different reasons, he appreciated, and who were all in the city at the time. He did manage to meet T. H. Green, through attending a course of his lectures, but it cannot be said that his interpretation of them – 'the philosophical expression of the good old Methodist doctrine of entire sanctification'[17] – inspires the conviction that he fully understood what he heard. He was much more attracted to J. R. Green: 'the first English historian who had a proper conception of the true object of history'.[18] He thought this because Green wrote about the common people

---

[14] Hugh Price Hughes, *Essential Christianity, A Series of Explanatory Sermons* (London, 1894), 121.   [15] D. P. Hughes, *Life*, 212.

[16] Ibid., 79. For details of Rees's life, see Hilary Spurling, *Ivy When Young. The Early Years of I. Compton-Burnett* (London, 1974), 36–43 (Rees was the grandfather of Ivy Compton-Burnett).

[17] D. P. Hughes, *Life*, 134.

[18] Hughes, *Social Christianity*, 'The Career of the First German Emperor', 68.

instead of dynastic ambitions; he left the impression, important for Hughes' Christian Socialism, that 'we cannot attain our own highest ethical level except in an ethicised society'.[19] If asked to name his favourite thinker, Hughes would have said Mazzini. In 1900 he visited his grave in Genoa as 'a tribute of affectionate admiration'.[20] He regretted Mazzini's failure to arrive at a pure understanding of Christianity – he had not become a Methodist, that is to say – but contended 'that everything that is best in Mazzini himself is due to Christ'.[21] He especially took to the essential Mazzinian doctrine that rights presuppose duties; what he constructed from him was a Christianized democratic creed. He was 'the most philosophic of religious statesmen'.[22] The basis of Hughes' attitude to industrial society was provided by Carlyle, with his 'grim, vivid way'.[23] He supposed that Carlyle was 'right when he said that man is born not to command, but to obey', but wrong 'in the kind of authority he wanted to set up'.[24] Liberal criticism of authority came from the school of John Bright, the man who he believed, with some justification, had stamped the reformist politics of the nineteenth century with religious moralism. 'We have entered upon a perfectly New Era of English history', Hughes said, 'and the human agent of this unparalleled revolution is John Bright'.[25] Hughes' writings were spattered with references to Ruskin, but he seems to have appreciated him more as art critic than as Socialist. Where he does show himself aware of 'the impassioned prophetic teaching' of Ruskin,[26] it is generally in order to endorse some aspect of Ruskin's traditionalism – and especially of the idea of giving a new social rôle to the old aristocratic order.[27] Of the more immediately religious luminaries of English thought in the nineteenth century Hughes was most attracted to Arnold (after whom he named his eldest son), because of his liberal Anglicanism, and Westcott, because of his social reformism. He particularly took to Westcott's critique of individualism,[28] and regarded Westcott's equation of the Christian virtues of 'Righteousness, Peace, and Joy' with 'Equality, Liberty, Fraternity' as 'the most important social truth that has been uttered in our time'.[29] For the leaders of the Christian Socialism of the mid-century he had scant regard. Kingsley he never forgave for supporting the Crimean War, for joining the Defence Committee of Governor Eyre of Jamaica, and for his vilification of Dissent in *Alton Locke*. Of Maurice he hardly seemed aware at all, even though Hughes' daughter, in her *Life*, suggests that Maurice 'had a great influence upon his theology'.[30] There are few indications

[19] Hughes, *Essential Christianity*, 40.
[20] Hugh Price Hughes, *The Morning Lands of History* (London, 1901), 328.
[21] Hughes, *Social Christianity*, 'The Supremacy of the Law of Christ', 22.
[22] Hughes, *Ethical Christianity*, 171.
[23] Hughes, *Social Christianity*, 'Jesus Christ and the Masses', 6.
[24] Ibid., 201. [25] Hughes, *Philanthropy of God*, 46. [26] Ibid., 230.
[27] Hughes, *Social Christianity*, 'The Career of the First German Emperor', 69.
[28] Ibid., xii. [29] Hughes, *Philanthropy of God*, 268.
[30] D. P. Hughes, *Life*, 476.

of this in Hughes' sermons and writings. An entire published sermon on the Maurician theme of the Kingdom of Christ does not mention Maurice once.[31]

When it came to personal experience of social conditions, Hughes' middle-class background imposed the same kind of limitations as inhibited most of the other Christian Socialists. At Dover, it was true, his Chapel was in the middle of the poor quarter of the town, and this doubtless contributed to Hughes' heightened sense of social compassion; but in his farewell sermon, on leaving, 'he referred with sorrow to the fact that he had not been able to visit the poor more in their own homes'. He had not, he said, had 'the leisure to do much of this himself, though he inspired others to do it'.[32] At the West London Mission, after 1887, he was an administrator and publicist, only very infrequently in personal contact with the poor. Although his enthusiasm for the working classes was utterly genuine, and felt in the innermost parts of his soul, Hughes found actual relations difficult. He was by temperament – in his daughter's euphemism – 'socially fastidious'.[33] Conscious of the problem, and in an agonized attempt to put it right, Hughes made a point of talking to strangers he chanced to encounter in a not entirely successful attempt to acquire some social data: 'omnibus drivers, navvies, shop assistants, railway men, all manner of persons in railway carriages, were to him fields of endless inquiry'.[34] Like so many who attempted social enlightenment in nineteenth-century England, he was often unaware of how much preceding generations had tried to achieve the same goals. In 1889 he wrote 'the real facts of the lives of the poor have never yet been made the subject of a careful, patient, exhaustive, scientific study'.[35] This was not a sophisticated critique of the Blue Books, or Mayhew or Marx: it merely disclosed gaps allowed by his haphazard selectivity in reading. In 1894 he was able to describe the horrifying conditions in the clothing sweatshops, the subject of *Alton Locke* forty years before, as 'recently come to light'.[36] But where he was well informed, Hughes was impressive in his determination to link knowledge and activity. His whole sense of Christianity moved him: when he first met Josephine Butler, in the house of Alderman Rees in Dover – the 'brave woman, full of the Holy Ghost'[37] – he broke down in tears. He became one of the leading campaigners for the repeal of the Contagious Diseases Acts, and from this work he gained some knowledge of the life-styles of some of the classes he had not before encountered. It was from another woman, Octavia Hill, that he learned about slum housing, and came to believe in collectivist solutions for housing reform.[38] Hughes' general conclusion about working-class information was correct, as applied to himself, as doubtless it was to most

[31] Hughes, *Essential Christianity*, 'The Everlasting Kingdom of Christ', 58.
[32] D. P. Hughes, *Life*, 87.   [33] Ibid., 281.   [34] Ibid., 166–7.
[35] Hughes, *Philanthropy of God*, XIII, 'The Problem of London Pauperism', 188.
[36] Hughes, *Essential Christianity*, 38.
[37] Hughes, *Social Christianity*, 'The Hopefulness of Jesus Christ', 233.
[38] Hughes, *Philanthropy of God*, 278.

of the people he addressed in West London: 'We know very little of them, and they know very little of us'.[39]

For all that, Hughes was remarkable for the energy with which he took up the work of inspiring social reform, in calls from his London pulpit, which not only revitalized Methodism but reached far beyond into the developing conscience of English Christianity. The labour was the more impressive for being against the grain of his temperament. 'Of one thing I am profoundly convinced', he declared in his most well-known collection of published sermons, *Social Christianity*, 'it will be impossible for us to evangelize the starving poor so long as they continue in a starving condition'.[40] Social reform must precede all attempts at the infusion of morality. He linked moral behaviour with the conditioning of environments; 'the Christian citizen whose imagination is inspired of God dreams of social changes which would make it as easy for his fellow-citizens to do right as it is now for them to do wrong'.[41] A society, he believed, 'largely founded upon fear and distrust' was bound to become 'a mere police regime' because it forced people into criminality.[42] Society itself 'must take a big share of the blame for the sin and folly of those who break the law'.[43] Hughes used to recommend Samuel Barnett's *Practical Socialism* as showing the clear relationship between poverty and crime.

Yet despite this conviction that social conditions had to be improved before men could behave morally, Hughes in practice taught that only moral men could improve social conditions. There were anti-democratic implications, at least for the earlier stages in the process of social regeneration. He condemned the movement of the rising middle classes to the suburbs, thus leaving the inner cities to the socially deprived – who were 'growing poorer and poorer'.[44] Those who beheld London could judge the evil, for there 'tens of thousands of people are obliged to live in tenements that are not fit for animals'.[45] With an apocalypticism not unlike Kingsley's, Hughes declared that poverty was 'menacing social order and the stability of the state'.[46] Unlike the earlier Christian Socialists, he rejected emigration as a solution for poverty.[47] The wider solution, he contended, must involve nothing less than the transformation of society by state provision and moral regeneration. In the meantime, at the West London Mission, he took up the organization of rather traditional works of charitable social relief. There were Temperance works, penny-banks, clothing and provident clubs, a thrift society, soup kitchen, two Dispensaries for the sick, a Labour Bureau for the unemployed, a servants' registry, a crèche,

---

[39] Hughes, *Social Christianity*, 'Jesus Christ and the Masses', 6.
[40] Ibid., 'Jesus Christ and Social Distress', 31.
[41] Hughes, *Ethical Christianity*, 40.   [42] Ibid., 122.
[43] Hughes, *Social Christianity*, 'Jesus Christ and the Masses', 14.
[44] Ibid., 6.   [45] Ibid., 'The Hopefulness of Jesus Christ', 223.
[46] Hughes, *Philanthropy of God*, 197.
[47] Hughes, *Social Christianity*, 'Jesus Christ and Social Distress', 30.

university extension lectures, and a 'Poor Man's Lawyer' for free legal advice. The three thousand services and meetings a year were mostly evangelistic, but Hughes himself made weekly presentations of the need for home missionary work to be associated with social reform. Like the other Christian Socialists, Hughes and his wife were attracted to the revival of sisterhoods, and the result was that some of this work was undertaken by the 'Sisters of the People', a Methodist order inspired by Catholic and Anglican sisterhoods, and by the Salvation Army, but free from 'objectionable vows and iron regulations'. The term 'Sister', it was explained, was 'used in its human and democratic sense, and not with an ecclesiastical signification'.[48] Thus sanitized, the Sisters began their work in 1894, and were soon copied in some other cities. They were intended to afford 'a sphere for refined, educated women, who, with their superior privileges and wider outlook, can accomplish work and exert an influence impossible to those who have had no such advantages'.[49] Hughes said that their lives were an illustration of 'Ethical Christianity'.[50]

The social principles which Hughes enunciated from the platform of the Mission, in St James's Hall, were a blend of collectivism and moral exhortation. He used political language and spoke of things which were at the time exciting political activists; but he was always himself scrupulous in avoiding partisan identification. The very marked political Conservatism of his home, which he had persisted in advertising during his years as a student, left no traces at all. The tutelage of Alderman Rees in Dover had made him into a Gladstonian Liberal, and he made no secret of it in his private life. Each turn of Gladstone's political wheel moved Hughes in the same direction, from the Bulgarian Atrocities in 1876 to Home Rule in 1885. 'Who is Mr. Gladstone, father?' his daughter asked when very young. 'A man who says his prayers every morning' was the reply.[51] But Hughes never went to political meetings, never preached party politics from the pulpit, nor openly supported a Liberal platform: to have done so would, he supposed, have been to have acted in a manner which could only be regarded as divisive by those to whom he was sent as a minister of religion. The rules did not apply to Mrs Hughes, who sat on the Executive Committee of the Women's Liberal Federation. Hughes always questioned her closely about the meetings she attended, to gain a kind of vicarious political involvement for himself.[52] The detachment from party politics must have been exceedingly difficult for one who was not only personally interested in them but who also espoused a view of Christianity which impelled political action. 'A profound instinct has taught the masses of the people that if Christianity is not applicable to politics', he said, 'Christianity is an antiquated delusion'.[53] Hughes made many pronouncements which his Conservative co-religionists found con-

[48] D. P. Hughes, *Life*, 201.
[49] Mantle, *Hugh Price Hughes*, 125.
[50] Hughes, *Ethical Christianity*, dedication.
[51] D. P. Hughes, *Life*, 119.
[52] Ibid., 266.
[53] Hughes, *Ethical Christianity*, 29.

troversial because of their obvious political content, but he was consistent in his denial of a party affiliation.

It was not unusual, of course, for those who claimed a Christian Socialist identity to operate within the generous boundaries of Gladstonian Liberalism. Clifford certainly did, and so did Thomas Hughes. Where Clifford and Hugh Price Hughes differed from the others, however, was in their gravitation towards those Radical sections of the Party which advocated collectivist solutions to social evils. Hughes' actual 'Socialism' was always a bit vague; usually he seemed to imply collectivism when he used the word – as, indeed, it was common enough in the 1880s and 1890s for men to mistake Radicalism for Socialism, just as their predecessors in the mid-century had called Chartists 'Socialists'. Hughes had been marginally influenced by the writings of Louis Blanc: they were 'a factor in his political development'.[54] Yet it is difficult to find much trace of Blanc's ideas in Hughes' writings and sermons. He was not especially attracted to the co-operative ideal, and shared some of the scepticism about democracy which was almost a hall-mark of Christian Socialism. He opposed the Second Reform Bill in 1867, believing that the working classes were unfit for the franchise,[55] and approved of Bright's 'lofty moral grounds' for supporting a reform which left out the residuum of dependent citizens. He lamented 'the low and selfish and antagonistic lines' on which 'democratic movements are too frequently advocated'.[56] Christ, on the other hand, he believed had founded true democracy, and it was 'only in our own time', that they were 'beginning to realise the democratic doctrine of Jesus Christ'.[57] It was a teaching which required 'equality of opportunity' for every person; the substitution of 'Character for Cash, and Brains for Birth'. It was 'the most radical revolution the human race has ever experienced and it is absolutely irresistible'.[58]

With time, he came to expand his definition of those he was prepared to allow with safety to enter political society, and by 1892 felt able to declare that 'the very extension of the franchise which has taken place in our own time' was 'a direct result of the doctrine of Jesus Christ that personal rights are more sacred and precious than property rights'.[59] This shift of view was not remarkable, and it followed general trends within educated opinion; Hughes was unusual only in the pedigree he gave to the acceptance of more liberal ideas. In another area that had worried the Christian Socialists Hughes also demonstrated the movement of opinion. His critique of Political Economy was less prominent than in the thought of most others; educated opinion, again, had already indicated that the days of Political Economy as the ruling ideology of economic and social thought were nearing their end. His observations on Political

[54] D. P. Hughes, *Life*, 82.   [55] Ibid., 135.
[36] Hughes, *Philanthropy of God*, 54.   [57] Hughes, *Essential Christianity*, 280.
[58] Ibid., 281.   [59] Hughes, *Ethical Christianity*, 110.

Economy were, anyway, not very subtle. The system was 'heartless folly',[60] inspired by 'the devil', and 'the example and influence of Jesus Christ' was now 'undermining the very foundations upon which the Satanic doctrine rests'.[61] The whole notion of 'enlightened self-interest' as the basis of human association was the service of 'mammon'.[62] All business and all economic activity had to come under the rule of Christ. 'It is one of the fundamental ethical axioms of Christianity that all business which takes advantage of the ignorance or weakness of our fellow-men is anti-Christian'.[63] Happily, however, he noted that Political Economy was 'greatly discredited and despised'.[64] Here was a battle almost won.

The main points of Hughes' social message were collected together in four published volumes of sermons: *Social Christianity* (1889), *The Philanthropy of God* (1890), *Ethical Christianity* (1892), and *Essential Christianity* (1894). They represent the substance of his West London Mission platform, and are internally very consistent. His view of Christ was like Stewart Headlam's: he was 'essentially a man of the people – a working man'.[65] The educated and the cultured had not supported him, and those, indeed, who had called for his death were 'hirelings and hangers-on of the wealthy and titled'.[66] In opposition to the arbitrary rule and imperial despotisms of the ancient world, Christ had declared 'rights' and 'freedoms'.[67] These rights attached to 'man as man', and they illuminated the lives of the poor with new hope, so that, as being brought to fulfilment in the nineteenth century, the 'voices of humanity' were expressing Christian truth whether they were aware of it or not. 'The last are already first', Hughes declared, 'and the "common people" are climbing the thrones of power'.[68] Christ had also preached the unity of the human race: 'Humanity is a living organism, and every influence passes through the whole of it'.[69] Hughes emphatically did not believe, however, that the development of humanity was equal in all parts of the world, and there were political implications in a wide, global context, which went well with his leanings towards Imperialism. 'The vast majority of the human race are as yet unfit for representative or even constitutional government', he said, with particular reference to Asia, Africa, and South America.[70] Even southern Europe was in an unsound position – 'European races which rejected the Reformation and its higher ethical standard'; since 'the morality of the Middle Ages is not sufficiently exalted to fit men for political freedom'.[71] The British Empire, by contrast, was 'essentially

---

[60] Hughes, *Social Christianity*, 'Jesus Christ and the Masses', 13.
[61] Hughes, *Ethical Christianity*, 170.
[62] Ibid., 172.   [63] Hughes, *Essential Christianity*, 36.   [64] Ibid., 123.
[65] Hughes, *Social Christianity*, 'Jesus Christ and the Masses', 3.
[66] Hughes, *Ethical Christianity*, 107.
[67] Hughes, *Social Christianity*, 'Christ the Greatest of Social Reformers', 53.
[68] Hughes, *Ethical Christianity*, 75.
[69] Hughes, *Essential Christianity*, 38.   [70] Ibid., 281.   [71] Ibid., 282.

an empire of peace', held together by feelings of 'Humanity', 'compassion', and 'Fraternal Solidarity', and, above all, by Christianity. 'It is not Lord Wolseley and his glittering host, but the Missionary Societies, that have created and will preserve the British Empire', Hughes believed.[72] The real enemies of Imperialism were 'the politicians and journalists who favour a military spirit'.[73] Not surprisingly – though in the face of the Peace movement and of influential sections of Nonconformity – he supported the government over the South African War. His reasons were characteristic of his general medley of opinions: Kruger was a reactionary opponent of true political liberalism; the Boers were not particularly interested in Temperance reform; and they oppressed the blacks.[74] Hughes' support of British Imperialism reflected his belief in the practical application of what he took to be the righteousness of the Christian gospel. It was about basic human conditions, for 'Christ was literally a radical', who said 'that the thoughts of men must be changed, then everything will be changed'.[75] Regenerated men had then the obligation of social reconstruction: 'Christ came to save the Nation as well as the Individual'.[76] There was a clear political consequence of a most fundamental sort. 'The highest conceptions of Christian statesmanship cannot be carried out until society is leavened with Christian ideas', Hughes thought.[77] No Christian country had yet existed;[78] despite centuries of Christian government the people were not elevated. Like Headlam, again, Hughes believed that the Kingdom of Heaven could be constructed with the materials of the world. 'We are strangers and travellers here', he said: 'That is no reason why we should neglect our duty here, or why we should fail to put forth strenuous efforts to extend the kingdom of God on earth, and to make earth as like heaven as possible'.[79] Hughes' optimism sometimes touched almost millenarian frontiers of expectation. 'When Personal and Social Christianity are preached with equal earnestness', he declared, 'the kings of the earth will bring their glory into the City of God, and the days of her mourning will be ended'.[80] And again: 'The day is coming when justice and love and peace will reign with unchallenged supremacy in every land; and when men will literally do the will of God on earth as angels do it in heaven'.[81]

Yet Hughes was sceptical of Socialism as the means of this blessed vision, despite his acclamation of its positive qualities. Certainly 'the deeply religious side of Socialism' – by which he meant social reform – was, he thought, 'slowly revolutionizing European society'.[82] But 'many of the Social and Political ideals which now fill the air are impracticable and positively mischievous simply because unregenerate human nature is incapable of rising to them'. Too many

72 Hughes, *Philanthropy of God*, 97.
73 Ibid., 117.
74 D. P. Hughes, *Life*, 557.
75 Hughes, *Philanthropy of God*, 239.
76 Hughes, *Social Christianity*, viii.
77 Hughes, *Philanthropy of God*, 241.
78 Hughes, *Social Christianity*, 'National Character Determined by National Laws', 139.
79 Hughes, *Essential Christianity*, 10.
80 Hughes, *Philanthropy of God*, 270.
81 Hughes, *Ethical Christianity*, 76.
82 Hughes, *Essential Christianity*, 39.

reformers were trying 'to construct a noble city in the absence of noble citizens'.[83] This was the point reached by other Christian Socialists, and like them Hughes fell back on the long-term hope of educational and moral advancement as the preliminary to social righteousness. In the meantime his strictures against Socialism for attempting to move forward in unfavourable moral circumstances were at times very sharp. Socialists, he declared in *Social Christianity* were 'illogical' and 'mischievous' in Germany, but there the state had been foolish to attempt to suppress them by force.[84] In England, as in Germany, social reform in the interests of the masses was the right way to prevent them from accepting 'the socialist creed', for 'all subversive political parties thrive upon social misery'.[85] It is clear that Hughes was attempting, in such passages, to distinguish between the secularized Socialism of Europe and the 'Socialism' which, for him, resided in the radical wings of English Liberalism. The distinction was a fair one. Hughes persisted, however, in condemning even English Socialism for what he understood to be its crude materialism – and it was a view which must confine, to some extent, the nature of his Christian Socialism. 'The fatal delusion' of materialist Socialism, he said, was the notion that if men achieve good standards of living, and sufficient 'mental and physical enjoyment', their needs will have been accomplished: 'Why that is the ideal of a mere animal!' He added 'I hesitate to say this because I so deeply sympathise with the desire of working men for a much larger share of the treasure, the leisure, and the pleasure of life'.[86] It would be tempting to categorize Hughes as a social reformer, on the Chamberlain side of Liberalism, who merely used the rhetoric of 'Socialism' as the means of demonstrating a well-meant desire to help the socially deprived. There is, indeed, something of that about Hughes; but there was also something else. In his advocacy of law and state action to achieve a just society he entered an area of public debate which, whilst not exclusively or even typically Socialist, had several overlaps with Socialism as understood in his day.

Hughes cited the abolition of prize-fighting as evidence that law could legitimately exist ahead of opinion, as a means both of moral enforcement and of social education.[87] It has been pointed out that Nonconformists at the time were beginning to abandon *laissez-faire* attitudes in order to legislate against particular social ills,[88] and this was only to formalize the practical exceptions which had been made throughout the nineteenth century to the general principle of non-state interventions in such questions as factory reform and public health. Hughes reinforced it with the doctrine that persons were more

[83] Ibid., 174.
[84] Hughes, *Social Christianity*, 'The Career of the First German Emperor', 77.
[85] Ibid., 78.   [86] Hughes, *Essential Christianity*, 6.
[87] Hughes, *Social Christianity*, 'National Character Determined by National Laws', 142.
[88] Bebbington, *The Nonconformist Conscience*, 13.

important than property, and that laws should now be framed which recognized it: 'We must see that such changes are effected in our English law as will extend to human beings the same protection that is now given to their property'.[89] Consistent with his other ideas, Hughes also taught that only regenerate, Christian men could make 'Christian laws and Christian policies and Christian institutions'.[90] There was a touch, or perhaps more than a touch, of moral élitism in this: the law which was in advance of opinion was to be the work of Christian activists. He had an unflinching respect for authority, provided it was exercised by those of 'noble principles', and explicitly approved Ruskin's justification of the view 'that the privileged classes are the natural leaders of men'.[91] He lamented the decline in respect for authority in contemporary society, and believed that, for social advance, 'authority will have to be built up on a new foundation', since 'men really crave to be under authority'.[92] Hughes conceded the difficulty in getting the balance between authority and freedom right, but supposed that in his own times the danger came from an excess of libertarianism. 'Freedom', he said, was 'counfounded with lawless licence'.[93] Social evils would scatter 'like chaff before the wind' if society was possessed of 'the necessary self-suppression and disciplined obedience to reasonable authority'.[94] He was alarmed by the 'widespread insubordination' of children in Victorian society: evidence, he imagined – surely a little overdrawn – of the approaching collapse of all social discipline.[95] Although, in good Dissenting style, he denounced the doctrine of passive obedience to governors as 'odious' and 'detestable' and 'anti-Scriptural', he nevertheless insisted on the Christian duty of obedience to the state. With less than sound prophetic insight (in view of the totalitarianism to come) he predicted that the twentieth century would not be 'in much danger of an extravagant and superstitious submission to authority'. The problem was the abuse of freedom,[96] and the threat to the progress of the nation lay in 'vulgar irreverence'; for 'in the extreme reaction from the tyranny and servility of the past, men are now in danger of cultivating the most foolish and mischievous excesses of self-assertion'.[97] It is never quite clear whether the authority he defended was in the hands of the traditional classes, purged of social selfishness, in the Ruskin sense, or a structured emanation from emergent democracy. Certainly he seems to have favoured the wealthy doing their duty to the poor, rather than the abolition of private wealth as such. Their duty was envisaged not as an old-fashioned, paternalistic essay in charitable enterprise, however, but as a

[89] Hughes, *Social Christianity*, 'National Character', 148.
[90] Hughes, *Philanthropy of God*, 242.
[91] Hughes, *Social Christianity*, 'The Career of the First German Emperor', 69.
[92] Ibid., 'The Authority of Christ', 201.
[93] Hughes, *Ethical Christianity*, 84–5.
[94] Ibid., 86.   [95] Ibid., 88   [96] Ibid., 90.
[97] Hughes, *Essential Christianity*, 234.

kind of enlightened class response to consciousness of social suffering. The rich were urged to implement the Parable of the Talents. 'Money, both inherited and accumulated', was to be used to clean up the condition of the cities, and for works of evangelization, so that 'hatred of the wealthy', the 'most dangerous social symptom of modern Europe', could be eliminated.[98] The choice was stark: 'Christianity or revolution'.[99] Wealth and 'rank', Hughes argued, were legitimate, but needed to be freed from selfish abuse, for the privileged were 'the trustees of the bounty of Heaven, in order that they may joyously and effectually serve the unprivileged and the outcast'.[100] It was, to say the least, an old-fashioned view. Those who used their wealth for social improvement were 'the true aristocracy of the country'[101] – a formal dignity for the heirs of Manchester Radicalism, the respectable urban bourgeoisie who were the staple of the Nonconformity which Hughes knew. He even had a future promise for the poor which was almost a classic of the philanthropic caricature: 'You may receive no homage on earth, but when you die angels will salute you as one of a royal race, and you will wear a crown in heaven'.[102]

Despite all this, Hughes did advocate collectivist solutions to the evils of poverty, one of the few Christian Socialists who did, and this must give some content to the Socialist aspect of his idealism. Legislation, he believed, was not 'mere force'. It was 'educational'. Hughes was advanced within Nonconformity for his espousal of a positive attitude to the state. Law could always be used for immoral purposes, and Hughes instanced the Liquor laws and the Contagious Diseases Acts to show that law could make men bad. But by the same evidence it could moralize men. The Mosaic code had done that, and so had the Factory Acts.[103] 'The statute-book', he declared, 'is the national conscience'.[104] Moral persuasion was not enough to achieve reform. The force of law, the power of the state, was essential. It was necessary for slum clearance: 'a part of true religion consists in securing laws which will absolutely prohibit such buildings'.[105] Moral evils were next. 'Heavy fines, and if they fail, imprisonment ought to be the swift punishment of all editors, printers and newspaper proprietors who publish betting intelligence'.[106] State action for poverty itself was required by the sheer scale of the problem. The work transcended private charity and 'must be undertaken in some way by the state'.[107] Hughes never gave actual programmes, or precise plans. 'Practical and effective methods of grappling with the problems will soon be discovered', he insisted, 'when we have realized that it is both legitimate and necessary for the

[98] Ibid., 49–50.   [99] Hughes, *Social Christianity*, 'Jesus Christ and the Masses', 15.
[100] Hughes, *Ethical Christianity*, 103.
[101] Hughes, *Essential Christianity*, 121.   [102] Hughes, *Ethical Christianity*, 102.
[103] Hughes, *Social Christianity*, 'National Character Determined by the National Laws', 140.
[104] Ibid., 141.   [105] Hughes, *Social Christianity*, 'Jesus Christ and the Masses', 15.
[106] Ibid., 'Gambling', 268.   [107] Hughes, *Philanthropy of God*, 196.

state to use all the resources of civilization to abolish pauperism'.[108] He did hint at a redistribution of wealth by state compulsion: 'I am in favour of all legislative and social changes by which the fruits of human industry may be more widely distributed among the industrious'.[109] But there was, again, no clue as to what he actually intended, and since Hughes elsewhere propagated a limited view of state competence[110] it would be hazardous to see such an utterance as an anticipation of a Socialist planned economy. Although he disagreed with W. T. Stead's notion of a 'civic Church',[111] he encouraged his social workers in London to get involved with local politics. One of the Sisters of the People stood for election to the St Pancras Borough Council, and two others became Poor Law Guardians.[112] It was clear that Hughes associated this kind of involvement with a Christian need to activate civic reform. He urged the London County Council to build houses for the poor, public baths were to be provided 'in all directions', monopolies in the food trade were to be broken by local government action, but, he added rather disappointingly, 'with respect to warm clothes, the poor must help themselves'.[113]

Like most of the other Christian Socialists, Hughes was critical of the Churches of his day for past failings in their social duties, and for their poor record at interpreting the essential message of Christianity in social terms. He had no structural ecclesiastical alterations to propose in order to change this – as the Anglicans, in the tradition of Arnold, sometimes did. He regretted Christian disunity as a hindrance to effective social work – the Church was 'a mob rather than an army'[114] – yet recognized some modern strengths. The Church, in all classes, was better respected than in the past, showed healthy signs of growth (particularly seen in the Salvation Army), and had good prospects.[115] Attacks upon the Christian message came from those who misunderstood it,[116] and the Church was itself usually to blame for this. The 'social failure of Christianity' was 'not the fault of Christianity or of Christ, but of us Christians who have been selfishly individualistic'.[117] Hughes had impatience with ecclesiastical history and tradition: what mattered was personal acquaintance with Christ.[118] The history of the Churches was full of errors; like Headlam, he considered it 'a very startling fact that Atheists and Agnostics often realise the social aspirations and ideals of Jesus Christ immeasurably better than Christians'.[119] He also made the familiar point that Christians had often behaved as if their faith had 'nothing to do with business, with pleasure, and with politics'; as if it was only concerned

[108] Ibid., 198.
[109] Hughes, *Essential Christianity*, 6.
[110] Hughes, *Philanthropy of God*, 244–9, for example; or *Social Christianity*, 62.
[111] D. P. Hughes, *Life*, 399.
[112] Ibid., 235.
[113] Hughes, *Philanthropy of God*, 278–9.
[114] Hughes, *Ethical Christianity*, 86.
[115] Hughes, *Essential Christianity*, xii.
[116] Hughes, *Ethical Christianity*, vii.
[117] Hughes, *Social Christianity*, xii.
[118] Ibid., 'The Authority of Christ', 200.
[119] Hughes, *Essential Christianity*, 173.

with interior spirituality.[120] Christ had, on the contrary, come into the world to establish a real Kingdom, 'to reconstruct human society'.[121] The disciples had seen this, and they were 'the greatest revolutionists the world has ever seen'.[122] The modern Church had not seen it at all, not even in the texts of Scripture: 'we have deadened our consciences and paralyzed our energies by explaining away passages that refer to this present life, and by comfortably assuming that they describe what is and not what earth ought to be'.[123] The aim of all Christianity, Hughes declared, was the 'holy city'. Because they had not really sought that aim 'the Socialist movement, which is the great peril of modern society, is often fiercely anti-Christian'.[124] The moderation of Hughes' own Socialism was always visible.

The centre of Hughes' work for humanity never shifted from personal rather than industrial or economic issues. He was the archetypal Nonconformist crusader for evangelistic and moral purposes, more concerned with the elimination of wrong conduct than of wrong structures. He did, of course, associate the two, but his priorities were always clear. It was not that he was an opponent of pleasure, or even – given his early resort to law to accomplish his programme – a moral authoritarian. He was filled with horror at wasted lives: his motive was the achievement of human dignity, the recognition of human potential. That was very evident in his support for women's rights. He believed that it was Christianity which had led to the improvements in the social position of women, that had begun to emancipate them 'from the tyranny of masculine selfishness'.[125] He argued for an equal distribution of material benefits and labours between the sexes. 'Whatever it is right for man to do, it is right for woman to do', he said – although he added that no woman should ever be 'a navvy'.[126] The statute-book must be purged of discriminatory legislation.[127] The education of women had been 'grossly neglected'; the Universities of Oxford and Cambridge, in their attitudes to women, were 'still in mediaeval darkness'.[128] He favoured votes for women even though he feared they would vote for the Conservatives.[129] Hughes' own freedom from received mores was not entirely complete. At the West London Mission the recipients of aid and counsel were divided between the sexes.[130] In general, however, he was energetic in all areas where the exploitation of women prevailed. It was 'the mainspring of his work',[131] beginning in his first decision to campaign for the

[120] Hughes, *Social Christianity*, 'Jesus Christ and Social Distress', 21.
[121] Hughes, *Essential Christianity*, 172.
[122] Hughes, *Social Christianity*, 'Christ the Greatest of Social Reformers', 56.
[123] Hughes, *Ethical Christianity*, 28.
[124] Hughes, *Essential Christianity*, 169.
[125] Hughes, *Philanthropy of God*, 145.   [126] Ibid., 146.
[127] Ibid., 149.   [128] Ibid., 165–6.   [129] Ibid., 170.
[130] D. P. Hughes, *Life*, 225.
[131] Bebbington, *The Nonconformist Conscience*, 41.

abolition of the Contagious Diseases Acts at the start of his ministry, in that encounter with Josephine Butler in Dover.[132] The work also drew him into co-operation with W. T. Stead and his campaign against juvenile prostitution.[133] His first resort, again, was to law: 'Christians shall use the Criminal Law Amendment Act to close down brothels'.[134] The same was true for the elimination of gambling, and the link to social conditions was important here, too. 'It is impossible to exaggerate the evils of gambling', he said, for they elicited 'an overpowering appetite'.[135] The wrong was social as well as moral: 'it promotes gain through another's loss' and was therefore 'anti-social and anti-Christian'.[136] He suggested the setting up of a national 'Anti-Gambling Society', to educate public opinion on the question, to agitate for the exclusion of gamblers from sitting in Parliament and from public office, and to frame laws for the prosecution of gamblers.[137] Hughes once visited Monte Carlo, to see for himself the centre of corruption, as he regarded it, and was duly appalled. The Casino itself was like 'the chapel at Dartmoor Convict prison' – a curious comparison – and the transactions within, 'the pleasures of sin', were 'the very essence of stealing'.[138] Hughes was also a vociferous opponent of drink. At Richmond College, as a youth, he had quarrelled with some of his more puritanical contemporaries by insisting on having a barrel of beer at cricket matches,[139] but that, also, changed at Dover. There he signed the Temperance Pledge, and gave himself to the humanitarian aspects of the movement. Drinking ruined domestic budgets and broke up family life; the Liquor Trade was 'the greatest of all existing hindrances to the progress of the Gospel in England'.[140] So consistently did he emphasize the point that to his fellow workers in the Mission it sometimes 'seemed the only question'.[141] In the Sunday Afternoon Conferences, in 1889, he listed eight social evils 'against which we must wage ceaseless war'. They were mostly to do with this sort of moral crusading: 'Pauperism, Ignorance, Drunkenness, Lust, Gambling, Slavery, Mammonism, and War'. He added a ninth, 'Disease'.[142] With these kinds of issues he was at ease. With the more overtly economic or political he was less concerned, and although he joined in the general clerical mêlée of sympathy over the Dock Strike in 1889, and was in principle favourable to trade unions (yet 'grieving indeed over some of their tendencies'[143]) he kept clear of involvement. Despite insisting on the necessary relationships between social conditions and low morality he always placed his emphasis on the personal aspects of regeneration. That way, he believed, 'the sacredness of every human

---

[132] Mantle, *Hugh Price Hughes*, 43.   [133] Ibid., 85.
[134] Hughes, *Social Christianity*, 'Jesus Christ and Social Distress', 24.
[135] Ibid., 'Gambling', 260.   [136] Ibid., 264.   [137] Ibid., 266–8.
[138] Hughes, *Morning Lands of History*, 331–2, 337.   [139] D. P. Hughes, *Life*, 44.
[140] Hughes, *Social Christianity*, 'Our Duty in Relation to the Licensing Clauses of the Local Government Bill' (1888), 168.   [141] D. P. Hughes, *Life*, 235.
[142] Hughes, *Philanthropy of God*, 275.   [143] D. P. Hughes, *Life*, 363.

being, however poor, however ignorant, however degraded' remained the Christian priority.[144] 'Both the Bible and History', he said, 'teach me that the human race is not going to be evangelized either by Politicians or by Schoolmasters'.[145] The way forward was to appeal to the best in man, to the Christian principle 'of overcoming evil by good'.[146] A 'low estimate of human nature chills the soul and blights all our hopes'.[147] Hughes was far too respectable to be directly influenced by Headlam, but he echoed another of Headlam's themes: 'the distinction which is so commonly made between the secular and the sacred is a deadly anti-Christian delusion'.[148] The lines he sometimes drew with such apparent precision between social and personal issues were thus in practice often indistinct.

Over some of the other questions which excited Nonconformity Hughes was cautious. His Wesleyan inheritance drew him back from divisive matters within the churches; his dislike of sectarianism made him cautious of extremism. He therefore kept out of the Disestablishment campaign, although he disapproved of the Establishment of religion in principle.[149] He tried to avoid embroilment with the Education question, distrusting the political emphasis it required, and only gave reluctant and rather tardy support to Clifford's assault upon the 1902 Education Act.[150] He was more active in the Peace movement, regarding the Crimean War as 'the most wicked event in English history',[151] and arbitration in the *Alabama* claims, 'the most glorious event'.[152] Past religious support for warfare was 'the darkest and most scandalous page in the lamentable history of ecclesiastical Christianity'.[153] These opinions, however, were later modified by his endorsement of colonial wars and his advocacy of Imperial Federation.

There were, in Hugh Price Hughes, no peaks of sublime spirituality; he was burdened with no great intellectual insights and no original arrangements of knowledge. He was a propagandist of righteousness who sought much for others and very little for himself. 'Christ will not', he said, 'give you wealth or position, or troops of friends, or what the world calls happiness, but peace'.[154] Confronted early in his life with the facts of social misery he responded with decency and thorough dedication. The English Free Church tradition was enriched by the example he gave.

[144] Hughes, *Social Christianity*, 'Christ the Greatest of Social Reformers', 62.
[145] Hughes, *Philanthropy of God*, 254.
[146] Hughes, *Ethical Christianity*, 124.
[147] Hughes, *Essential Christianity*, 283.
[148] Hughes, *Ethical Christianity*, 30.
[149] D. P. Hughes, *Life*, 483.
[150] Ibid., 502–3.
[151] Hughes, *Philanthropy of God*, 58.
[152] Ibid., 108.
[153] Ibid., 66.
[154] Quoted in D. P. Hughes, *Life*, 213.

9

BROOKE FOSS WESTCOTT

Perhaps more than any other it was Westcott who gave Christian Socialism respectability, who legitimized its existence within the Church, and who, in the process, diluted it. There was nothing discreditable about that: after the prophetic forerunners and the preoccupied zealots, it is always necessary for popularizers to get to work if new ideas are to take hold. Westcott was suited by temperament for the task. His moral seriousness had shown an early development. A schoolboy contemporary later recorded that his conversation was about things 'which very few schoolboys talk about – points of theology, problems of morality, and the ethics of politics'.[1] Forty years later he told the undergraduates of Peterhouse, where he was preaching, to 'dare to commit yourselves to the pursuit of a lofty ideal'.[2] It was a persistent theme of his life; a constant recommendation to others.[3] What Westcott did was to employ the available rhetoric of Socialism in a declaration of the need for social reform. It was an extension of his moral seriousness, derived much more from a rather traditionalist religious position than it was from any political source. The declaration also rather noticeably lacked content. Scott Holland, one of the founders of the Christian Social Union in 1889, remarked that no one could afterwards remember what Westcott had actually said at the inaugural meeting in Sion College – 'only we knew that we were lifted, kindled, transformed'.[4] That is no small thing to have achieved, and Westcott's service to the cause of Christian Socialism was in the end an enormously important one precisely because he inspired men who would otherwise have been antagonistic to take it seriously. Many were said to have joined the Christian Social Union because they 'felt that under his presidency it could not become an instrument of

[1] Arthur Westcott, *Life and Letters of Brooke Foss Westcott* (London, 1903), I, 6.
[2] Brooke Foss Westcott, *Waiting for Power from On High. A Sermon Preached in the Chapel of Peterhouse* (Cambridge, 1883), 8.
[3] David Newsome, *Bishop Westcott and the Platonic Tradition* (Cambridge, 1968), 33.
[4] A. Westcott, *Life*, II, 16.

Liberals or Radicals, and that, though good Conservatives, they were safe in joining it'.[5] It was largely due to him that by the first decade of the twentieth century the ideals of the Union 'had thoroughly permeated the Church of England, especially the hierarchy'.[6] Westcott's religious emphases were attractive to his contemporaries as well. Here was no priest ranging beyond his conventional territory, taking draughts from alien pools. He was known for a kind of mysticism, though Westcott was himself unhappy about admitting to it. 'The Vision of God', he said, 'justifies man's invincible instinct that there is a progress in the course of nature and history, which cannot be determined by things themselves, and gives fresh energy to the social feelings through which society moves forward towards that final harmony of man with man, and of class with class, and of nation with nation'.[7] For him, Christian Socialism was an impulse in the flow of long historical development, and, if viewed from a correct perspective, a familiar application of the teaching of Christ in the context of later Victorian England. For Westcott, it was the times which were at variance with experience, not the ideals of 'Socialism'. The existing relations of capital and labour, he observed in his famous speech at the Hull Church Congress in 1890, 'are modern and transitional'. Wage labour, he continued 'though it appears to be an inevitable step in the evolution of society, is as little fitted to represent finally or adequately the connection of man with man in the production of wealth as at earlier times slavery or serfdom'.[8] In presenting an acceptable critique of social and economic conditions, Westcott became an influential figure within the Church, and through chance involvement in the settlement of the Durham coalminers' strike in 1892, when he was Bishop of Durham, he acquired a wider reputation for social compassion – an Anglican Manning.[9]

Westcott's life was largely given to education and scholarly work. He once turned down an offer of the Archdeaconry of Northampton because he was unprepared to undertake an ecclesiastical rather than an educational office.[10] He was born in Birmingham in 1825, son of a quiet man of leisured pursuits and independent means. At King Edward VI School, in the city, he came under one of the great influences of his life – the headmaster, James Prince Lee. The School too, produced other boys who were later to form the group of distinguished theologians in Cambridge: Lightfoot and Benson. Westcott went up to Trinity in 1844. He was ordained in 1851, and the following year started teaching at Harrow School. There, during an eighteen-year period of service, he began the

[5] Joseph Clayton, *Bishop Westcott* (London, 1906), 159.
[6] Peter d'A. Jones, *The Christian Socialist Revival, 1877–1914* (Princeton 1968), 217.
[7] Brooke Foss Westcott, *Christian Aspects of Life* (London, 1897), 'Via Hominis Visio Dei', 399.
[8] Brooke Foss Westcott, *Socialism* (London, 1890), 8.
[9] Geoffrey Best, *Bishop Westcott and the Miners* (Cambridge, 1966), 21.
[10] A. Westcott, *Life*, I, 304.

theological writing which, until he was raised to the episcopate, was the main work of his life. He was rather a conservative Biblical scholar, perhaps less impressive than his pupils at Cambridge, Hort, Lightfoot and Benson.[11] Judgments on such matters are relative, however, and Westcott was, by any standards, still a scholar of distinction and influence. From 1870 he was Regius Professor of Divinity in Cambridge. His lectures, like those of Maurice, were ill-attended by undergraduates, who found him difficult to understand,[12] and after twenty years he was released into the bishopric of Durham. He had, together with these posts, occupied canonries at Peterborough (from 1869) and Westminster (from 1883), and in 1875 he became a Chaplain to the Queen. It was a very straightforward Anglican career; a deserved and steady advance to leadership by one known for moderation, good judgment, and sound scholarship. The Durham years, from 1890 until his death in 1901, were a natural continuation of the application of those qualities, and yet Westcott is remembered almost entirely for the social interests which Durham brought into public prominence. They were not born of those years, however; Westcott's preceding development had disclosed signs of what was to come.

Just as his doctrine of humanity, and the presence of Christ in all men, had inspired Maurice with a concern for society, so Westcott's 'Incarnational' theology directed him towards social concern. It provided 'if not the immediate stimulus, at least the ultimate rationale of his Christian Socialism'.[13] Christ's presence in the world had consecrated the material, and the structures of social life which men created out of their existence in the world contained within themselves the intimations of eternal realities. The divine was mediated through particular material circumstance, and Christian men should therefore direct themselves to discerning its patterns and to elevating human experience to recognize its true purposes. In *The Gospel of Life*, based upon his twenty years of lecturing in Cambridge, Westcott wrote: 'The Incarnation binds all action, all experience, all creation to God; and supplies at once the motive and power of service'.[14] The Incarnation also seemed to demonstrate the utility of Westcott's Platonic method. It 'reconciles the partial truths which give power to the conflicting theories of Individualism and Socialism'.[15] It gave 'a distinct force, which nothing else could give, to the responsibilities of brotherhood'.[16] Westcott's Incarnational theology was thus inherently optimistic about the progress of human society. He accepted the world of the nineteenth century, and modern learning, and liberal reform, as all revealing new aspects of the

[11] Bernard M. G. Reardon, *From Coleridge to Gore. A Century of Religious Thought in Britain* (London, 1971), 351.

[12] Owen Chadwick, *Westcott and the University* (Cambridge, 1962), 15.

[13] Reardon, *From Coleridge to Gore*, 354.

[14] Brooke Foss Westcott, *The Gospel of Life* (London, 1892), xxi.

[15] Brooke Foss Westcott, *Christian Social Union Addresses* (London, 1903), 5.

[16] Westcott, *Christian Aspects of Life*, 80.

ancient truths of God. He was an enthusiast for humanity. Men could not be separated from their context, and the Gospel truths had first to be expressed within the expectations of that context before they could begin to transform humanity and so improve society. 'Every human deed and word and thought has in it an eternal element', he told the Durham miners in 1901. Yet there was no chance 'of creating humanity afresh'.[17] The transformation was to be within social realities – once again the emphasis centred upon society and its needs. 'Our part', Westcott said of society, 'is to learn its capacities, its tendencies, its position, its destiny, and, in the strength and by the light of the Incarnation, to strive unrestingly to bring it a little nearer to its goal'.[18] He denied the power of material or intellectual improvements to reform society, pointing out how such expectation had always been frustrated. The problem was a moral one. 'Good conditions of life, however needful for other reasons, do not make men good', Westcott contended; 'social improvement is bound up with individual improvement'.[19] But as the lives of individual men were conditioned by their social circumstance so there was necessarily, as the other Christian Socialists had noticed, a relationship between social and personal regeneration. There were tensions in this distinction of the individual and the social which Westcott never succeeded in resolving. As an advocate of social change he was nevertheless conscious of the dangers to individuality resident in most of the available methods to bring it about. There were, he remarked, 'two opposite lines of movement in social change', the one towards 'uniformity of conditions', and the other towards the 'development of personal differences'. A choice had to be made between 'these rival views of the aims and methods of life'.[20] His own choice, between collectivism and individualism, was in the end heavily weighted towards individualism – the very principle, identified as the ideology of Political Economy, which he nevertheless spent so much time attacking. Yet he came nearer than some others within the Christian Socialist tradition to recognizing the problems and attempting a reconciliation of the forces at issue. 'It remains to show', he said in 1890, 'how the richest variety of individual differences can be made to fulfil the noblest ideal of the State'.[21] But he never really did show how, within his terms of reference, it was possible.

Whatever the potential for social reformism implicit in Westcott's Incarnational theology, over the long period of its development, he did not in fact make the link between religious and social ideas until comparatively late in his life. It was in the sermons at Westminster, in his years as a canon after 1883, that his social interests first became apparent.[22] Westcott himself, however, traced his social concern back to his earliest years. 'From my boyhood I have also been

[17] Brooke Foss Westcott, *An Address at the Annual Service for Miners* (London, 1901), 6.
[18] Brooke Foss Westcott, *Social Aspects of Christianity* (London, 1887), 114–15.
[19] Westcott, *Christian Aspects of Life*, 15.
[20] Ibid., 260.   [21] Westcott, *Socialism*, 8.   [22] Clayton, *Bishop Westcott*, 156.

familiar with the life of the poor', he claimed in the 1890s, 'I knew something of their trials and of their desires'.[23] He remembered the Chartist demonstration in the Bull Ring at Birmingham as a formative event in his social consciousness;[24] he recalled the speeches of Feargus O'Connor with a kind of sympathy.[25] When Kingsley, as a schoolboy, had seen the Reform Bill riots in Bristol it had turned him into a conservative, but in Westcott's memory the Chartist disturbances had made him a partisan of change. He felt no indignation at the behaviour of the mob in the 1848 Revolution in Paris – 'they had doubtless great grievances to complain of, and perhaps no obvious remedy but to be gained by force'.[26] The picture of 'the Two Nations' drawn in Disraeli's *Sybil* – 'which haunted me in my College days'[27] – also inspired a compassionate desire to be open to the aspirations of the poor. There is no reason to suppose that Westcott's recollection of these influences was imaginative, but he probably, in the perspective of his later interests, invested them with a heightened teleology. His real knowledge of working-class society was very slight, and on arrival at Durham, in 1890, he needed to be equipped with practical information about social conditions by the Vicar of Gateshead.[28] Outside of his Biblical scholarship Westcott read very little. Among the earliest influences, through discussions in his student days in Cambridge, were Llewelyn Davies, the Christian Socialist, and Alfred Marshall, the economist.[29] It was the latter who apparently taught him to concentrate on 'paths that strengthen the consumer and call forth the best qualities of those who provide for consumption'.[30] Westcott's understanding of social and economic facts and theories was always patchy, however, and Scott Holland, who used to complain about the repetitive nature of Westcott's social declamations, doubted if he ever really knew about social evils at all.[31] This was an extreme assessment; what Westcott actually emphasized, as intellectuals do, was the pursuit of social principles and ideas rather than a serious study of social fact. 'A recognized social ideal is one of our sorest needs', he said.[32] He had few guides; no particular intellectual debts in the social field. His Platonic method, indeed, suggested the partial nature of all insights, and the need for a synthesis. 'No one line of study, no one school of thought', he declared, 'can secure that mastery of the facts which we require in order to take the next step in social reform rightly'.[33] Yet his conviction that religious and social truth came from the union of contradictions was probably not derived from Maurice, since it occurred too early in his life.[34] The influence of Maurice

[23] Westcott, *Christian Aspects of Life*, 276.
[24] A. Westcott, *Life*, II, 261.   [25] Ibid., I, 7; Westcott, *Christian Aspects*, 285.
[26] A. Westcott, *Life*, I, 101.   [27] Westcott, *Christian Aspects*, 79.
[28] David L. Edwards, *Leaders of the Church of England, 1828–1944* (London, 1971), 216.
[29] D. O. Wagner, *The Church of England and Social Reform since 1854* (New York, 1930), 204.
[30] Brooke Foss Westcott, *Lessons from Work* (London, 1901), 260.
[31] Wagner, *The Church of England and Social Reform*, 215.
[32] Westcott, *Christian Aspects of Life*, 251.
[33] Ibid., 233.   [34] Newsome, *Bishop Westcott and the Platonic Tradition*, 14.

on his Christian Socialism was anyway rather peripheral, at least in the sense of direct inspiration. Westcott himself claimed that he owed much to Maurice[35] – but he meant the Maurice of *Social Morality*, the furthest removed of all the Master's works from his Christian Socialist writing. There was a section on the Quakers in Westcott's *Social Aspects of Christianity* (1887) which is remarkable for not once mentioning Maurice's essential critique of the Quakers in *The Kingdom of Christ*.[36] The two men did not get on particularly well at Cambridge early in the 1870s when they were professors together – Maurice refusing to co-operate over lecturing arrangements.[37] When, later, Westcott read the biography of Maurice he was surprised at 'how deep my sympathy is with his most characteristic thoughts'.[38] Even if, as at least one scholar has concluded,[39] Westcott had read more of Maurice than he admitted, it is clear that the influence was fairly indirect. Westcott claimed some affinity with Comte, but the essentials of his intellectual outlook, and his liberal attitude to social institutions, can be much more easily traced to Prince Lee and to Arnold. Prince Lee, he rightly declared, was the greatest 'among the great teachers of his time',[40] and despite his later rather sharp observations about Prince Lee's conduct over *Essays and Reviews* in 1860, and his career as a bishop ('one series of disasters'[41]), the print made upon his mind by the great educator was enduring. Westcott was among that large number who knew Arnold and were influenced by his ideas through reading Stanley's *Life* of 1844. Twenty years later he recorded returning to it 'for the hundredth time' with 'wonder and profit'.[42] Like Ludlow, Westcott had enormous respect for Vinet – 'the one man I would have liked to meet'.[43] He occasionally cited Ruskin, but not with any great insight into Ruskin's complicated mind, and almost none into his social critique, finding, indeed, J. A. Hobson's criticisms 'substantially just'.[44] There were far more quotations in his writings from the poet Browning. Carlyle he positively disliked, with his 'crabbed sentences and coarse metaphors';[45] but he sometimes read him none the less, on the generous ground that it is always possible 'to learn even from a foe'.[46]

Despite Westcott's openness to modern and liberal intellectual influences he was always very insistent on the importance of past tradition, and though he nowhere spoke systematically about the organic nature of society and the state it was implicit in his view of things. He loathed material and mechanistic interpretations of social relationships, whether they presented themselves in the

---

[35] Westcott, *Social Aspects of Christianity*, xii.
[36] Ibid., 119–34.　　　　[37] A. Westcott, *Life*, I, 369.
[38] Edwards, *Leaders of the Church of England*, 214; Reardon, *From Coleridge to Gore*, 354n.
[39] Newsome, *Bishop Westcott and the Platonic Tradition*, 14.
[40] Westcott, *Christian Aspects of Life*, 188.
[41] A. Westcott, *Life*, I, 212, 279.　　　　[42] Ibid., I, 332.
[43] A. G. B. West, *Memories of Brooke Foss Westcott* (Cambridge, 1936), 28.
[44] A. Westcott, *Life*, II, 317.　　　　[45] Ibid., I, 44.　　　　[46] Ibid., I, 158.

forms of Political Economy or in classical contractual theories of government. The latter, indeed, were 'idle fictions', since 'the sustaining force of states is not material but spiritual'.[47] His Incarnational theology, of course, projected that the spiritual would be represented in the shifting material circumstances of worldly existence, and his Platonic method insisted upon the fragmentary nature of particular perceptions of truth: the link of the past and the present through continuing organic relationships provided a bond of cohesion which helped men to recognize the spiritual realities otherwise seemingly disparate in the conditions of the earthly life. God himself, Westcott taught in traditional fashion, was the source of all authority in the world, and governments were to be seen as divine institutions, the reflection 'however incomplete of an eternal order'.[48] The state 'embodies in the temporal order the principles which belong to the spiritual order so far as they have been recognized in the common life'.[49] The stages of recognition were sketched in three tiers. The family, first (and not the individual), was 'the unit of mankind'; it was an expression not only of the divine law but of the divine nature. In their experience of family association men would see 'a revelation of God in which they can find the principles at least of the right answers to many of the most urgent problems of society'.[50] Next, the nation, like the family, was 'involved in the very constitution of man'.[51] In his various descriptions of the nation, Westcott's resort to organic images was immediate – 'the Nation is a greater Man, a living, a divine whole'.[52] Nations are not naturally, furthermore, in a condition of competition and conflict; their interests are identical since they represent the same divine law for mankind.[53] The third tier of human social organization was Humanity itself – 'the Race', the essential 'kinsmanship' of peoples.[54] It is easy to discern, in these categorizations, an affinity to Maurice's understanding of society. The tiers each have their own integrity and purposes, and none must exclude or override the other for the fulness of human life to be experienced and for human organization to develop. But it is unlikely that Westcott borrowed from Maurice; it was their shared philosophical method which they had in common and it produced similar conclusions. At this level, too, Westcott maintained the traditional Christian teaching about the structures of government. 'Christianity is not allied to any form of government', he declared, but Christians 'are bound to secure, if they may, that form which, as they believe, will best enable their country to fulfil its service to the race'.[55] Westcott rarely descended to detailed consideration of government. Even when he came to consider franchise reform, of which he approved, it was in order to point to its service in eliciting a sense of

[47] Westcott, *Social Aspects of Christianity*, 37.   [48] Ibid., 44.
[49] Westcott, *Christian Aspects of Life*, 231.   [50] Westcott, *Social Aspects of Christianity*, 31.
[51] Ibid., 37.   [52] Westcott, *Christian Aspects of Life*, 60.
[53] B. F. Westcott, *Christian Union for the Promotion of Simultaneous Disarmament* (London, 1889), 7.
[54] Westcott, *Social Aspects of Christianity*, 57.   [55] Westcott, *Christian Aspects*, 250.

organic unity throughout society: 'men cannot stand alone: we gain freedom that we may advance to union'.[56] Yet like Maurice, again, he seems to have implied that in the end men are most truly free when they are rightly adjusted in their own minds to their position in society. 'Each in his proper sphere – workman, capitalist, teacher – is equally servant of the state, feeding in his measure that common life by which he lives'.[57] Ruskin would not have disagreed.

Because the material forms of human association embodied and disclosed the divine scheme, it followed, for Westcott, that Christian concern for the fate of society must be paramount. He found 'three social lessons' in the person of Christ himself. They showed that men are brothers, that their shared and universal sin is forgiven, and that their endeavours in the world have lasting significance – 'how we are shaping slowly out of things transitory that which will abide for ever'.[58] This gave a very elevated status to men's concern for social action. Christ came into the world to 'deal with the whole of life', with 'life in every phase of its progressive activity'.[59] The Kingdom was collective and not individual. As Westcott said in his Hull speech on Socialism in 1890: 'They must show that Christianity, which has dealt hitherto with the individual, deals also with the State, with classes, with social conditions, and not only with personal character'.[60] Here was the more familiar stuff of Christian Socialism. The Kingdom, he contended, was 'not simply the deliverance of individual souls' but 'the establishment of a Divine Society'.[61] It was the immanence of the eternal in the material nature of things; 'For the Kingdom of God is at once spiritual and historical: eternal and temporal: outward and inward: visible and invisible: a system and an energy'.[62] There was urgency for action now, in the fearful deprivations of existing society, for 'eternal life is present and not future only'.[63] Nor was this a mere sideshow of Christianity: 'social work is indeed of the essence of the Gospel'.[64] In the words which so impressed Hugh Price Hughes – '"Righteousness, peace, joy": these are', Westcott declared, 'the Christian translation of Equality, Liberty, Fraternity'.[65] The task of the day was to persuade Christians themselves that 'behind every social question there lies not only a moral but also a religious question'.[66] He was in fact heartened by signs that the Church was already responding, correctly discerning the social interests in those who were working for the growth of ecclesiastical machinery through such bodies as the Church Congresses and the new diocesan conferences.[67] He also believed he saw a growth of religious feeling in all classes – a conclusion which may not be so

[56] Ibid., 264.
[57] Westcott, *Social Aspects*, 45.
[58] Ibid., 9, 14.
[59] Ibid., 89.
[60] Westcott, *Socialism*, 10.
[61] Westcott, *Social Aspects*, 86.
[62] Ibid., 88.
[63] Westcott, *Lessons from Work*, 178.
[64] Ibid., 35.
[65] Westcott, *Social Aspects*, 91.
[66] Ibid., 141.
[67] Westcott, *Christian Aspects*, 12.

easily established – and 'on all sides a frank recognition, such as never was before, of social evils, of overcrowding, of intemperance, of profligacy, and an unwearied search for the means of dealing with them effectually'.[68] Thus the task and the springs of consciousness; like the other Christian Socialists Westcott turned next to consider the suitability of the Church for service as the agent of social regeneration.

Westcott took a more kindly view of the Church of England's social capabilities than some others. His career had been uncontroversial, and his smooth path to preferment and his sound Anglican manners left him with few reservations about the nature of the institution he served so faithfully. Its failings were due to a reluctance to appreciate its potential; it 'stands before us rich with unused resources of power'.[69] There was indeed optimism in Westcott's belief that the Church of England was already 'striving to use great possessions and great place so as to bind all classes together more closely in the unity of one life, and to offer in all its freedom and grace a Gospel to the poor',[70] and that it had already 'united all classes by sympathetic contact'.[71] Westcott never really understood either the nature or the depth of class attrition, and his view of the Church as a social mediator was accordingly in some things unrealistic. Although he acknowledged past failures of the Church, particularly its failure to emphasize the corporate against the individual,[72] there was, in Westcott, little of that breast-beating to which some others of his tradition gave themselves. Indeed, he thought 'the history of the Church is a series of ethical victories'.[73] He saw the clergy as a body of men well placed 'for moderating with wise faith discussions which will open the way' for solutions to social questions.[74] He advocated Church reform, but not directly in relation to future social functions. Westcott's concern was with reform as a means of safeguarding the spiritual claims of the Church against the increasingly anomalous erastian controls of the State.[75] He was not an opponent of Establishment, however, although he confessed to having once disliked the connexion of Church and State. Despite his organic view of the state, and his corporate image of the Church, Westcott was devoid of Coleridgean idealism in his endorsement of the establishment of religion. He was converted to the idea of a National Church in 1848, by 'observance of the wretched spirit of its opposers'.[76] Having decided upon the utility of an Establishment, however, he quickly advanced to recognizing its thematic compatibility with his general position on the organization of society, and this did encompass the language of Coleridge and of Maurice. 'If the nation is a living whole', he observed in 1886, 'its constitution

[68] Westcott, *Christian Union Addresses*, 73.
[69] Westcott, *Social Aspects*, 78. [70] Westcott, *Christian Aspects*, 67.
[71] Ibid., 273. [72] Ibid., 39.
[73] Ibid., 243. [74] Westcott, *Socialism*, 11.
[75] A. Westcott, *Life*, II, 249. [76] Ibid., I, 142.

will be incomplete if it has no organ for the development and for the expression of its spiritual powers: if it has not, in other words, a national Church'.[77] An Establishment of religion could 'consecrate the whole life of a people';[78] it could inspire men with 'devotion to public service'.[79] Westcott's reservations about Nonconformity derived from his sense of its 'isolating narrowness'.[80] It held men back from full participation in the life of society. The Church of England, too, would be better for broadening the basis of its operations, and this was to be achieved by the admission of a larger lay voice to its administration and ministry, by a recognition of 'the prophetic call of laymen'.[81] Westcott took a vigorous part in opposing the parliamentary attempts of 1893 to disestablish the Welsh Church.

Since Westcott's Christian Socialism was centred in his ideal of human brotherhood, it was not surprising that he saw the Church itself as 'the realisation of the brotherhood of man'.[82] Socialism was accorded a comparable broad and elevated definition. It was 'a theory of life', to be contrasted with 'Individualism'. Socialism regarded humanity 'as an organic whole, a vital unity formed by the combination of contributory members mutually independent'. Its aim was 'the fulfilment of service', whereas the aim of Individualism was 'the attainment of some personal advantage'. The scheme was a simple one: 'the method of Socialism is co-operation, the method of Individualism is competition'. This was the central thesis of his celebrated lecture on Socialism at the Church Congress of 1890;[83] a lecture 'gravely rebuked' by the Conservative press.[84] Together with the collected sermons from Westminster, *Social Aspects of Christianity* (1887), a selection of largely social sermons of the 1890s, drawn from his Durham years, *Christian Aspects of Life* (1897), and, to a lesser extent, *The Incarnation and the Common Life* (1893), this constitutes the major source for Westcott's Christian Socialism. It is clear that he wished to dissociate his own Socialism from *Socialism*, a word 'discredited by its connection with many extravagant and revolutionary schemes', but which deserved to be 'claimed for nobler uses'. He dismissed discussion of current forms of Socialism – 'the paternal Socialism of Owen, or the State Socialism of Bismarck, the international Socialism of Marx, or the Christian Socialism of Maurice, or the evolutionary Socialism of the *Fabian Essays*' – in order to consider, instead, 'the essential idea' behind each system, the unifying whole of which they were partial representations.[85] The intention was to raise the whole matter outside the squalid divisions of politics and party, and

---

[77] Westcott, *Social Aspects*, 75.   [78] Ibid., 76.
[79] Westcott, *Christian Aspects*, 79.   [80] Westcott, *Social Aspects*, 145.
[81] Westcott, *Lessons from Work*, 233ff. See also *Social Aspects*, 79, 115.   [82] Ibid., 68.
[83] Westcott, *Socialism*, 4. The Lecture was published as a pamphlet by the Guild of St Matthew. For the original text, see *The Official Report of the Church Congress Held at Hull* (London, 1890), 320
[84] Clayton, *Bishop Westcott*, 164.   [85] Westcott, *Socialism*, 3.

the result was to give Socialism a very general interpretation indeed. 'Socialism, as I have defined it', Westcott said, 'is not, I repeat, committed to any one line of action, but every one who accepts its central thought will recognize certain objects for immediate effort'. These, too, were rendered in large terms: 'that labour shall be acknowledged in its proper dignity as the test of manhood, and that its reward shall be measured, not by the necessities of the indigent, but by its actual value as contributing to the wealth of the community'.[86] A few years later he was still more incorporative in his discussion of Socialism – 'under which term I include all the obligations which are seen to follow from the sense of the solidarity of mankind, from the application, that is, of the Incarnation to life'.[87] It was hardly surprising that his contemporaries found Westcott's Socialism 'something of an enigma'.[88] Like most of the other Christian Socialists, he was very anxious to distance himself from actual politics. Socialism was a moral response to social misery; it did not involve party activity, and Westcott never in his life appeared on a political platform.[89] He confessed to being 'carried absolutely away' by Gladstone's speeches, but had no sense of political agreement with him. Disraeli left him unmoved: 'How can you possibly admire a man who maintained that "there is no gambling like politics?"'.[90] Westcott insisted on moral seriousness in politicians.

The great embodiment of Westcott's social principles was the Christian Social Union of 1889. Though he was the first President of the Union, the new organization was not his own work. Its formation grew originally more upon Oxford than upon Cambridge foundations – at meetings of the 'Holy Party' from 1875, convened by J. R. Illingworth.[91] The organizing spirits of the Union were Gore and Scott Holland, who were concerned with the creation of a more broadly based, and less doctrinally divided, body than the Guild of St Matthew to attract Church opinion to social principles. In this they were successful, and Westcott's adhesion was a major seal of respectability. The Union was exclusively Anglican, and soon attained a membership of six thousand – none of whom came from the working classes. It was perfectly suited to Westcott's views. It avoided party politics, or politics of any sort. It drew up large principles. It was, above all, an extremely effective propagandist body – not in general educated society, which remained largely unaware of its existence, but within the leadership of the Church. By the end of the century nearly a third of episcopal appointments within the Church of England came from its membership. The political detachment of the Union became apparent in 1893, when the Independent Labour Party was founded. Very few members,

[86] Ibid., 5.   [87] Westcott, *Lessons from Work*, 34.
[88] Edwards, *Leaders of the Church of England*, 218.
[89] Clayton, *Bishop Westcott*, 172.
[90] West, *Memories of Brooke Foss Westcott*, 15–16.
[91] See Jones, *The Christian Socialist Revival*, 166–7; E. R. Norman, *Church and Society in England, 1770–1970* (Oxford, 1976), 181.

and none of the leaders, joined it. The Christian Social Union, in fact, was never committed to Socialism at all: the price of respectability was a lower threshold of social reformism. It did not even endorse *Christian* Socialism, and Westcott actually criticized 'what is called Christian Socialism' for being 'a most vague phrase'.[92] The platform of the Union, however, faithfully reflected the broadness of Westcott's own social principles. It had three points: 'to claim for the Christian Law the ultimate authority to rule social practice'; to 'study in common how to apply the moral truths and principles of Christianity to the social and economic difficulties of the present time'; and to 'present Christ in practical life' as 'the enemy of wrong and selfishness'.[93] Westcott later observed that although the essential object of the Union was to study ways of embodying 'the Christian Law' in society it had to recognize that 'the embodiment takes place slowly, and it can never be complete'.[94] Nor was the Union to step outside its self-defined rôle as an educative and propagandist body. 'It has no programme of immediate reform', Westcott insisted; 'members reserve their freedom of opinion, and use it; but it would be disastrous if the Union itself were to be identified with a party or with a class'.[95] In practice local branches did undertake some limited action: in Oxford members organized a boycott of trades which paid low wages to their employees, and in London a delegation waited upon Parliament to call for a revision of the Factory Acts. As a force making for social awareness within the leadership of the Church, on the other hand, the Union was quite extraordinarily successful; and it is in some large measure to the credit of Westcott that in removing fears about the radical nature of 'Socialist' critiques of society he had succeeded, with Gore and Scott Holland, in preparing the English Christianity of the early twentieth century for a new appreciation of the need for social change.

For all that, as already pointed out, Westcott's contribution was only achieved by generalizing the content of Christian Socialism to the level at which imprecise objectives and commonly held human principles enabled acceptance. In 1887 one journal observed: 'with every word almost of Canon Westcott's general propositions partisans of all schools will agree'. The difficulty 'is in the application'.[96] Westcott was very clear that the application was not within his province. 'I do not venture to suggest the rules of the fellowship which I forsee', he said.[97] In his great speech on Socialism in 1890 he declared: 'I do not enter now on any questions of detail'. His purpose was 'simply to direct attention to questions which go to the very heart of the Gospel'.[98] When once he came near to a discussion of the distribution of wealth

[92] A. Westcott, *Life*, II, 261.
[93] See Westcott, *Christian Aspects*, 'The Christian Social Union', 220.
[94] Ibid., 242. [95] Ibid., 252.
[96] Quoted in K. S. Inglis, *Churches and the Working Classes in Victorian England* (London, 1963), 280.
[97] Westcott, *Social Aspects*, 146. [98] Westcott, *Socialism*, 12.

he drew back in order to notice the problems 'and then to set them aside'. The question, he said, 'is not "How do we get our incomes?" but, "How do we use them?"'.[99] This was, in effect, a declaration for old-style social paternalism rather than for even the most elementary stage of Socialism. The corporate work of Christians, Westcott believed, 'is not action, but preparation for action';[100] their duty to the world was 'to form opinion'. Applications of the grand principle of human brotherhood would proceed according to 'different ways'. They would receive 'not one answer, but many'.[101] When he spoke, as he did to the Durham diocesan conference, about 'speculative' criticism being 'wholly subsidiary to action',[102] he did not mean to descend from the general to the particular, but to preach up the virtue of acting to cultivate a consciousness of fellowship and social service. He did not mean to incite actual political or economic activism. 'As citizens we are all bound to be workers', he told a Christian Social Union meeting at Macclesfield in 1898, knit together by 'the master-thoughts of corporate obligations and corporate interdependence'.[103] That was how he understood 'action'. It was a matter of raising consciousness. The purpose was to stimulate men to see that in a Christian society 'the thought of personal gain is subordinated to the thought of public service';[104] and the result of this sort of thinking would elicit 'a revelation of life'.[105] Westcott was again not far removed, here, from Maurice's key notion that men find their reconciliation through thinking differently about the social state rather than through changing it. In practice it led, in Westcott, to the advocacy of simplicity of living by the rich, 'adopted by choice and not of necessity',[106] for 'it is in personal expenditure that we all find some scope for the continuous daily application of Christian principles'.[107] Socialists, however, believed in doing something about the large majority who had no opportunity, through sheer want, for moral calculation about the discharge of their resources. The industrial device that corresponded to Westcott's idealism was the voluntary council, or 'Joint Board', at which the various sides of a particular industry could meet together. Such a body existed in the Durham coal trade between 1894 and 1896, and it was Westcott's knowledge of its operation which made him favour a universal application. 'For Westcott', Professor Best has written, in his examination of Westcott's industrial experience, the conciliation board was 'a means of reconciling working-men to a subordinate industrial role which would sometimes require of them self-sacrifice, and always self-discipline'.[108] Although his actual proposals were never really concrete, Westcott was forever fearful that men would think him 'visionary'. His reply

[99] Westcott, *Lessons from Work*, 342.
[100] Westcott, *Christian Aspects*, 234.
[101] Westcott, *Socialism*, 13.
[102] Edwards, *Leaders of the Church of England*, 217.
[103] A. Westcott, *Life*, II, 259.
[104] Westcott, *Christian Aspects*, 266.
[105] Ibid., 268.
[106] Westcott, *Social Aspects*, 148.
[107] Westcott, *Lessons from Work*, 347.
[108] Best, *Bishop Westcott and the Miners*, 28.

was itself tinged with reference to the Utopian: 'I can only say that I have suggested nothing which has not been realised on a large scale, under harder circumstances and with scantier knowledge than our own, by Franciscans, by Moravians, by Quakers'.[109] In another place he conceded that some of his objectives were 'an unattainable ideal', but that 'unattainable ideals are the guiding stars of life'; they were 'a test for existing industrial organizations'.[110]

Westcott's conservatism about applications ought not to detract from an appreciation of how seriously he himself believed that his ideals of brotherhood and harmony would transform society. The priority for industrial change, he said, was moral: 'we shall not think simply of higher wages, or of cheaper production, or of the advancement of one class, but rather of reconciling interests'. They had yet, however – he added in characteristic vein – to determine how 'the ideal may be realized'.[111] Certainly the evils of class needed to be recognized and overcome. But not *all* class consciousness was regrettable: 'the feeling of class is healthy, like the narrower affections of home, till it claims to be predominant'.[112] The real problem, Westcott supposed, was class ignorance; 'the rich know little of the temptations and feelings of the poor: the poor know little of the burdens and anxieties of the rich'.[113] There was also a dread, in Westcott, of popular movements based on class feeling, since they operated to break down the organic basis of society. 'To take part in class movements on class grounds', he declared, 'will be impossible for those who believe that the highest welfare of the body is the highest welfare of all the members'.[114] And again, consistent with his general attitude, he added, 'I do not presume to say how the antagonism of classes can be finally removed'. What he looked to was 'the victory of larger human sympathies over the narrowness of class'.[115] It is clear that he did not regard social class as a condition of economic or cultural or status consciousness, but as a simple social arrangement from which there followed the unhappy consequence of sectional interests. He believed that every 'true nation' had 'wide differences in power, in fortune, in duty', and that the aim of the Christian was 'not to obliterate these differences but to harmonize them' by showing 'that they can minister to the vigour of one life'. He will not, furthermore, strive 'to confound class with class, but to bind all classes together in their characteristic distinctness by the consciousness of mutual service'.[116] This kind of observation, particularly when related to Westcott's growing emphasis on the imperial destiny of the nation, seems more calculated to lead to the aggrandisement of a national ideal than to the attainment of social justice as commonly understood within evolving English Socialism. Westcott's innocence of any desire to move in directions which had

[109] Westcott, *Social Aspects*, 149–50.
[110] Westcott, *Lessons from Work*, 308, 310.
[111] Westcott, *Christian Aspects*, 262.
[112] Westcott, *Social Aspects*, 45.
[113] Westcott, *Christian Aspects*, 80.
[114] Ibid., 232.
[115] Ibid., 247.
[116] Westcott, *Social Aspects*, 42–3.

political, and therefore, as he supposed, narrowing implications, probably heightened his unconscious espousal of potentially corporatist doctrines of the state. The ideals of 'brotherhood' and 'equality' were interchangeable for him; they amounted to 'social fellowship'.[117] The fruits, and even applications, were for the future. 'I will even dare to say', he once said, 'that the next century will witness serious endeavours to apply the principle of fellowship, of co-operation in the largest sense, to political social and industrial problems'.[118] Westcott's terms of reference were too broad, and his concepts too vague, to enable this to be reckoned an utterance of prophetic genius, however.

The essentially non-collective nature of his aspirations to social improvement were well shown in his extraordinary and life-long hankering for the monastic life. This was not 'monastic' in the Catholic sense, but a kind of small-scale exercise in moral seriousness with wider social implications. It was in his later years at Harrow School that Westcott's distaste for luxury led him to a preoccupation with small unit material renunciation, although he had experienced earlier promptings, when his undergraduate imagination had been fired by chance visits to Ambrose Phillips de Lisle's Cistercian revival, Grace Dieu, whose buildings, by Pugin, had recently been completed amidst some publicity. 'Not that I believe in the Romish creed', Westcott was anxious to point out, 'but their practice allures me'.[119] What he came to envisage, in the 1860s, was 'an association of families, bound together by common principles of living', with a common income but not common property. The purpose was 'the conquest of luxury, the disciplining of intellectual labour, the consecration of every fragment of life'.[120] There was more than a slight touch of Westcott's later Christian Socialism in the scheme. It was, in fact, a sort of early representation on a small and imaginative scale of the ideas of brotherhood, harmony, and simplicity, which his Christian Socialism attempted to translate into national existence. Charles Gore, who was impressed by a Westcott sermon about monasticism when he was a pupil at Harrow in 1868,[121] later became his successor as president of the Christian Social Union, and later still founded the Community of the Resurrection in at least partial fulfilment, surely, of Westcott's original vision.

Westcott, as Professor Owen Chadwick has noticed, 'hid vast conservatisms beneath revolutionary-sounding language'.[122] In the sphere of public policy this was most obviously disclosed in his conviction, echoing the teachings of Carlyle and Ruskin, that great men are destined to lead and the generality to follow: 'great men stir the enthusiasm, and direct the movements, and administer the resources of the multitude which, for the most part, is inclined to

---

[117] Ibid., 44, 45.   [118] Westcott, *Lessons from Work*, 295.
[119] A. Westcott, *Life*, I, 40.   [120] Ibid., I, 264.
[121] G. L. Prestige, *The Life of Charles Gore* (London, 1935), 10.
[122] Chadwick, *Westcott and the University*, 26.

acquiesce in things as they are'.[123] Unhappily, he supposed, modern capitalism had inherited the social ascendancy of the old feudal order without its sense of social obligation. What was needed, to restore a balanced society, was 'some industrial organization corresponding to the old military organization'; for 'privilege, if rightly interpreted, is a call to special devotion'.[124] Despite his rejection of competitive economic practices, Westcott actually had no intention of dismantling the capitalist order; he wished, instead, to see it assume the neglected duties of the past. He was always insistent on the organic continuity of the national life – it was one of the things which gave England's historical development unique qualities of stability[125] – and this living inheritance transcended class and made it impossible to 'start afresh' in national experience.[126] The people were a single people; there could be no breaks in national development, and certainly no elimination of any particular section, without mortal injury to the body politic. It was a deeply conservative doctrine. Allied to it was Westcott's insistence on the priority of duties over rights. To allow men to cultivate 'a theory of rights' would result in 'fierce conflicts'.[127] There had, in the past, been a need to urge certain rights because of then existing injustices, but these had now been corrected and the elevation of rights, in the world of the late nineteenth century, would destroy 'the unity of life'.[128] Notions of equality, also, 'may be so presented as to destroy the richness and beauty of life' and issue in a 'sterile monotony' which 'obliterates the past'.[129] The powers of men are different and 'equal development does not involve equality'.[130] Westcott did not conceal these views. One of his bluntest declarations was made to an audience of miners in 1894: 'Some men should have a high place and large means' he told the poor men assembled to hear him.[131] Liberty, he taught, could rapidly pass into license, and 'then the calm strength of the whole is lost in innumerable fragments'.[132] Fraternity was sometimes the pretext 'for arresting the growth of the more advanced'.[133] It was a bleak message for the socially deprived, and there was more. The relationship of masters and servants, he said, was like that of fathers and families, and so was the relationship of employers and workmen.[134] Property was sacred: 'it reveals to us how the concentration of riches, material or spiritual, becomes a social good, fruitful beyond any equality of possession'.[135] When he heard about a Papal Encyclical (presumably Leo XIII's Rerum Novarum of 1891) which appeared to base property rights upon labour he was extremely shocked at such 'revolutionary and socialistic' teaching.[136]

[123] Westcott, *Christian Social Union Addresses*, 71.
[124] Westcott, *Christian Aspects*, 265.
[125] Ibid., 273; *Social Aspects*, 146.
[126] Ibid., 39.
[127] Ibid., 139.
[128] Westcott, *Christian Aspects*, 38.
[129] Westcott, *Social Aspects*, 91.
[130] Westcott, *Socialism*, 5.
[131] A. Westcott, *Life*, II, 388.
[132] Westcott, *Social Aspects*, 92.
[133] Ibid., 93.   [134] Ibid., 28.
[135] Ibid., 31.
[136] West, *Memories of Brooke Foss Westcott*, 29–30.

Intimations of the need for change and realizations of social injustice affect people in different ways and in different dimensions of a single person. Westcott's persistent conservatism, for all its strength, is not to be read as surviving traditionalist paternalism. It was more approximate to the cultural conservatism of the Liberal intelligentsia. Westcott, in fact, endorsed the first steps of a very moderate advance to collectivist solutions to social evils. The functions of the state, he said, could not be restricted to the administration of justice, the preservation of order, or the furtherance of prosperity; 'it must deal in some way with the circumstances of social life, with pauperism, with the unemployed, with intemperance', and also with the promotion of personal moral purity.[137] He spoke of 'stages' in the growth of the state.[138] On the other hand, he also declared that collectivism 'would impoverish life', and was 'essentially selfish, sacrificing the future to the present'.[139] He had two conflicting views about law as well. For the fulfilment of the Christian social law, he said, 'we do not trust to legislation'.[140] There were perils, for 'legislation is often a mere appeal to force under the influence of some season of excitement' and should be 'the last and not the first thing in social reform'. Their first duty should be 'to reform the unwritten laws of social intercourse' rather than 'to alter the statute book'.[141] Until the conscience is 'enlightened and aroused', he said, 'legislation must be ineffective'.[142] Law rests upon force, and cannot 'work a moral revolution'.[143] Yet he also maintained that legislation was educative: 'it serves as a schoolmaster for the immature and the undisciplined'.[144] This aspect of things became especially clear in his advocacy of temperance reform. Laws to curtail drunkenness were 'an impressive declaration of the popular will'. They still depended, he noted, on public opinion for their effectiveness.[145] Westcott was a very long way from Maurice's horror of public opinion.

There were a number of areas in which Westcott showed himself willing to promote changes which must, of their nature, produce political consequences. He came to see the need for a redistribution of wealth, but he discussed it in very general terms and warned that any action should involve no more than 'careful adjustment' in order 'to obtain a result which shall be adequately remunerative to capital and just to labour'.[146] Elsewhere, when he touched on this issue, it was to consider the distribution of wealth within the working classes themselves.[147] Other declarations are very broad – all wealth was 'to be administered for the common good'.[148] Westcott was simultaneously progressive and conservative on the question of women's rights. He had a general disposition to see advances in the education and social position of women, and yet he was opposed to their

137 Westcott, *Christian Aspects*, 231.
138 Westcott, *Socialism*, 8.
139 Westcott, *Christian Aspects*, 274.
140 Ibid., 254.
141 Ibid., 234.
142 Westcott, *Lessons from Work*, 257.
143 Ibid., 274.
144 Westcott, *Christian Aspects*, 254.
145 Westcott, *Lessons from Work*, 274.
146 Westcott, *Christian Aspects*, 230.
147 Ibid., 269.
148 Westcott, *Christian Social Union Addresses*, 4.

admission first to the ancient universities and then to degrees.[149] He actually believed that women should not aspire 'to do all that men do', for 'home' was the 'woman's kingdom'.[150] He supported the co-operative movement but did not take any part in its organization. The co-operative ideal, he claimed, was 'a master principle of life', and as embodied in the co-operative societies it expressed 'the right organization of labour',[151] and 'advance towards industrial concord'. Its moral value was 'greater than its economic value'.[152] Co-operative production was 'a discipline for a larger fellowship'.[153] These assessments are very much within the older Christian Socialist tradition, and Westcott himself traced his adhesion to the co-operative principle to his undergraduate enthusiasm for the movement begun by Maurice, Kingsley and Hughes.[154] Westcott approved of trade unions: workers banded together for mutual service.[155] 'They provide', he said, 'an education in self-government' for their members. He regarded the 'economic effects' of trade union activity as 'more chequered', however. They tended to limit enterprise, 'to check vigorous ability', and encouraged a (to him) unwholesome preference for class interests. But these disadvantages, he supposed, could be overcome.[156] Westcott's most well-known involvement with labour was his successful conciliation in the Durham coalminers' strike of 1892. Very shortly after his arrival in Durham, two years before, he had convened a series of private conferences on social questions at Auckland Castle, and his involvement in the coal dispute followed naturally enough from them.[157] The episode gave him a national reputation as the friend of labour, but Westcott himself was not tempted by it to enlarge his involvement, and shortly afterwards declined an invitation to speak at a rally on behalf of the unemployed in Trafalgar Square. This was characteristic of his careful assessment of the division between spiritual and temporal functions, between moral and economic issues. All legitimate reforms, he believed, 'must develop and strengthen character',[158] and the service of the Church was to point the way and cultivate the opinion – all else was outside its proper sphere. Even in the question of education, to which Westcott had devoted so large a slice of his life, and where he fully accepted the involvement of the Church through its system of schools, his main preoccupation was with the moral consequences. The 'object of education', he argued, was 'to train for life, and not for a special occupation'; it was a great force, also, for cultivating and directing instincts of social service and social harmony. The 'noblest fruit of education is character, and not acquirements', and religion was its basis.[159] The great evil of the day, he

[149] A. Westcott, *Life*, I, 413.
[150] Westcott, *Christian Aspects*, 198, 201.
[151] Ibid., 258.
[152] Ibid., 263.
[153] Westcott, *Socialism*, 9.
[154] A. Westcott, *Life*, II, 109.
[155] Clayton, *Bishop Westcott*, 167.
[156] Westcott, *Lessons from Work*, 311–12.
[157] See Best, *Bishop Westcott and the Miners*, 21ff.; A. Westcott, *Life*, II, 115ff.
[158] Westcott, *Christian Aspects*, 236.
[159] Ibid., 204, 208.

thought, was that 'education is coming to be regarded as a provision for the acquisition of material riches',[160] as a preparation for some particular work, or as an intellectual training for its own sake.

Westcott's development, then, disclosed a personal blend of old and new, of traditionalist and progressive tendencies. Towards the end of his life he adhered to that large section of opinion which promoted Imperialism, and he translated his ideals to a wider sphere. 'An Empire', he said at Tufnell Park in November 1900, 'is the embodiment on a large scale of two ideas characteristic of our generation – association and service.' An empire, he insisted, 'is a step towards the attainment of the earthly destiny of men', and in the furtherance of this advance 'the conditions of political and spiritual progress are seen to be identical'.[161] An empire, moreover, promoted 'the brotherhood of men', and the incorporation of 'many nations as organs in one body' was 'essential for the hallowing of our national work'.[162] These were very large and very ultimate claims for Imperialism, and Westcott, who always spoke with great precision, fully saw the implications. 'A world-wide Empire is a faint earthly image of the Kingdom of God', he insisted.[163] The Anglo-Boer War heightened existing divisions within educated opinion about the purposes of empire, and Westcott's public utterances helped to precipitate a split in the Christian Social Union over the issue. 'We have to show', Westcott said of the war in South Africa, 'that we are still worthy to hold, both by might and by counsel, the Empire which has been entrusted to us'.[164] In the 1880s Westcott had been active in promoting disarmament and in upholding the ideal of arbitration as the only moral way of resolving international disputes; he believed that the morality of this was so simple that 'it does not involve any abstract theories'.[165] By 1900, however, he had come to believe that it was impossible 'for us to submit to arbitration the fulfilment of our imperial obligations'.[166]

In many things Westcott had demonstrated a detachment from the received opinions of his contemporaries; towards the end of his life, however, he had shown, on a particularly sensitive issue, a remarkable proximity to the mixture of shifting values around him. So it had been, in reality, with most of those whose understandings of Christian involvement with the world have been discussed here. Those others, too, sensed the spiritual gravity of their causes just as Westcott did, and responded, often at great cost to their worldly prospects,

---

160 Westcott, *Lessons from Work*, 47.
161 Ibid., 370, 383.
162 Westcott, *Social Aspects*, 57.
163 Westcott, *Lessons from Work*, 227.
164 *The Obligations of Empire*, by the Bishop of Durham (London, 1900), 6.
165 Westcott, *Christian Union for the Promotion of Simultaneous Disarmament*, 6.
166 Quoted in Wagner, *The Church of England and Social Reform*, 283.

with compassion and altruism. 'The issue of our brief earthly work is greater than we feel at once', Westcott told the Durham miners in the last year of his life; 'we, all of us, are not only fashioning the generation which will follow us here, but are hastening or hindering the coming of the Kingdom of God'.[167] It is this impression of the eternal dimension of their labours which most persists.

[167] Brooke Foss Westcott, *An Address at the Annual Service for Miners* (London, 1901), 12.

IO

THE CONTRIBUTION

It is misleading to regard the Christian Socialists of the nineteenth century as precursors of the modern advocacy of Church involvement with social politics. They were prophets of their times, not men who anticipated later developments – prophets, that is, in the correct sense: they discerned ultimate meanings and moral lessons in the conditions of their day. They were hardly political at all. Maurice's original belief that the existing society of contemporaneous England already embodied the institutional apparatus of the universal and spiritual society was plainly conservative, as was his conclusion that social regeneration would follow when all men recognized their integration with society. Westcott's expression of the same basic scheme of things, though with some variations of language and detail, showed that the Maurician inheritance continued to promote a non-political attitude to social reform. Those who followed Maurice's elevated doctrine of humanity, but who nevertheless departed from it by seeking some actual alternative to the structure of society – men like Ludlow, Neale, and Headlam – were still, in the end, extremely cautious of political action. Even Headlam, the most activist of them all, who had clear links with Fabian Socialism, finally declined to espouse a rigorously political version of the Social Gospel.

Most of the Christian Socialists were also very wary of ideology, except as deposited within rather orthodox theology. They allowed themselves a range of ecclesiastical preferences, from Maurice's and Kingsley's Broad Churchmanship to Headlam's Sacramentalism; but the general tone of their theological outlook was conservative. Maurice courted disaster with the religious authorities because of his liberal views on eternal punishment – which carried the whiff of universalism; his conception of Biblical criticism, and his acceptance of traditionalist defence of the ecclesiastical Establishment, however, identified him as belonging very much to the old world. The same could be said, with appropriate adjustments for intervening developments of thought, for Westcott or for Hugh Price Hughes. In their social beliefs the Christian Socialists were equally reticent about ideological expression. Where they spoke at all in general terms about the nature of society (rather than its condition in their day) they were usually careful to avoid resort to novelties. Indeed, most of them accepted the conventional social beliefs of their day, and their opposition to democracy or to equalitarianism depended upon very familiar repetitions of the formulae of social authoritarianism drawn from traditional society. The few who escaped from this, like Headlam, were regarded as extremists or eccentrics by the others. It is arguable that their very conservatism in these important matters gave the Christian Socialists a chance to be influential – that this non-ideological approach to the problems of society coincided with the conventional pragmatism of the English political tradition.

The general refusal of the Christian Socialists to recognize the need for political solutions obviously made them enemies of the growth of collectivism. In that sense they were enemies, too, of modern collectivist Socialism. But most of the Socialism current at the time that Maurice and his circle adopted, rather uneasily, the title 'Socialist' had no positive doctrine of the state, and it would be a grave anachronism to suppose that the Christian Socialists could have foreseen – as almost no one else was able to foresee – the rise of the modern collectivist state. Socialism, in the 1840s, meant opposition to the competitive effects of classical Political Economy, it meant highly localized experiments either in communitarianism or in co-operative production, it implied some sense that the labouring masses were entitled to education, and it demanded the admission of 'the people' to political management. The very vagueness and incoherence of much 'Socialist' rhetoric left the Christian Socialists with no precise models. In fact they did not really need them, for their understanding of 'Socialism' did not reach the threshold of social experiment – the authentic hallmark of mid-nineteenth century Socialism. They certainly agreed with the first three points in the early Socialist agenda, but their solutions were to be highly in-dividualistic. Men were to be raised from the thrall of ignorance and social misery; the method, however, was to be educative and moral, not through experiments of social engineering or through the legislative powers of politicians. Small-scale co-operative enterprise seemed the perfect solution: it fostered self-help among the working men, it encouraged moral responsibility, and if combined with a programme of adult education (as Maurice came to believe) it elicited that human dignity which existing competitive society denied. Maurice's economic ethicism, like his organic traditionalist doctrines about the state were, and were intended to be, a substitute for political action. He was opposed to collective action because it was insensitive to the unitary nature of social truth: men developed their different insights into reality through separate and authentic experience, but it was through the reconcili-ation of their opposites, not through the imposition of one view upon another, that truth was advanced. Politics was linear and blunt – the insensitivity of partisan men to the fact that their own conception of the truth was partial. Political action therefore destroyed the organic basis of society by obliterating the continuing life of its varied components. Legislation, that is to say, was for Maurice the last way of achieving the harmonious relationships of the Kingdom of Christ. The fall-out of his Idealism extended across the Christian Socialism of the century. It matched the anti-collectivist and anti-centralization rural prejudices of men like Thomas Hughes, and the social paternalism of men like Kingsley and Ruskin, to produce an unevenly hostile attitude to the involvement of organized Christianity with political processes. The strength of surviving popular erastianism in England, with its suspicions about the rôle of the clergy in public life, was anyway ready to suppress any impulses to political action the Christian Socialists might have felt.

With so many apparent limitations, and with so much of their social vision still blinkered by the practices of traditional society, how then may it be supposed – as it should be – that the contribution of the Christian Socialists was of lasting value? The answer lies in the success of their real objectives. What they sought was not a collective way of restructuring society but a means of transforming its interior relationships through the recognition of common human elements more fundamental and durable than the accidents of shifting circumstances. They were, that is to say, true prophets in seeing, in the course of their social criticism, some permanent truths about men. They had no grasp upon the facts of class attrition in their day, but saw, instead, the basic injustices of a society which allowed mutual exploitation for individualist economic gain. They were largely ignorant of the mechanics of class phenomena, yet appreciated, as few in their generations did, the crippling effects of mass ignorance on the developments for which society was materially ready. They understood the latent dignity in the poor men and women whose actual lives were depressed by their conditions of housing and of work into permanent squalor. They perceived that brutalization was not the natural lot of a large part of society but that the selfishness of the few made it so. They thought, in fact, the way the modern world thinks about these kinds of matters, and it is only too easy, from the perspectives of the twentieth century, to fail to see how great was their achievement in releasing themselves from the common prejudices of their contemporaries.

The contribution of the Christian Socialists is therefore to be sought in a long projection. They were not alone, of course, in helping to remould received social attitudes, and it was part of the prophetic abilities of a man like Headlam to have perceived the moral importance of the secular forces of social improvement – even though they, too, were small in numbers and suffused with unpopularity. The Christian Socialists were intellectuals: this, also, gave their social preoccupations a kind of vicarious quality. What is remarkable, however, is their break with convention. In the face of every disadvantage they placed their resources, intellectual and spiritual, in the service of the cause they had discovered. Their contribution merged into the general body of influences making for social reform, and cannot easily be judged on its own. The co-operative movement, for example, developed independently in the nineteenth century, with very little indebtedness to the involvement, for a time, of the Christian Socialists. A general consciousness of the wrong conditions of working-class life was emerging quite autonomously, and Christian Socialism may even be seen as a symptom of it, rather than a contributory cause of unambiguous originality. The modern collectivist state, of course, grew out of the congruence of the various repositories of this consciousness, through empirical adaptation and pragmatic action. But it was the Christian Socialists who helped to impress Christian opinion with the validity of social criticism, who allied the Church with some of the most dynamic social forces of the modern era. Reform was a gradual process, and the early influence of Maurice and his circle was negligible. By the end of the nineteenth century, however, the Christian Socialists' critique was lodging itself effectively enough in the mind of the Church.

BIBLIOGRAPHICAL NOTES

General

The two most useful works, which together cover all the various stages of Victorian Christian Socialism, are Torben Christensen, *Origin and History of Christian Socialism, 1848–54* (Aarhus, 1962) and Peter d'A. Jones, *The Christian Socialist Revival, 1877–1914* (Princeton, 1968). Charles Raven's *Christian Socialism, 1848–1854* (London, 1920) has been almost entirely superseded by Christensen. Among other general studies are G. C. Binyon, *The Christian Socialist Movement in England* (London, 1931); Armand Cuvillier, *Buchez et les Origines du Socialisme Chrétien* (Paris, 1948); D. O. Wagner, *The Church of England and Social Reform since 1854* (New York, 1930); and P. N. Backstrom, *Christian Socialism and Co-operation in Victorian England. Edward Vansittart Neale and the Co-operative Movement* (London, 1974). Some general works on the nineteenth-century church have sections on Christian Socialism: W. O. Chadwick, *The Victorian Church* (London, 1966, 1970); G. Kitson Clark, *Churchmen and the Condition of England* (London, 1973); K. S. Inglis, *Churches and the Working Classes in Victorian England* (London, 1963); Stephen Mayor, *The Churches and the Labour Movement* (London, 1967); G. I. T. Machin, *Politics and the Churches in Great Britain, 1832 to 1868* (Oxford, 1977); E. R. Norman, *Church and Society in England, 1774–1970* (Oxford, 1976); and, for the theological background of particular writers, B. M. G. Reardon, *From Coleridge to Gore. A Century of Religious Thought in Britain* (London, 1971). For assessments of the leaders, see John Ludlow, 'Some of the Christian Socialists of 1848', in *Economic Review*, III and IV (1893–4); Thomas Hughes, 'Prefatory Memoir' to the 1881 edition of Charles Kingsley's *Alton Locke*; and P. R. Allen, 'F. D. Maurice and J. M. Ludlow', in *Victorian Studies*, XI (1968). Of the many, and ephemeral papers and journals produced by the Christian Socialists, the most well-known were: *Politics for the People* (1848); *Christian Socialist* (1850); *Journal of Association* (1852); *Tracts on Christian Socialism* (1850); *Tracts by Christian Socialists* (1850); *Tracts for Priests and People* (1861); *Christian Socialist* (1883); *Church Reformer* (1885); *Church Socialist Quarterly* (1909); and *Church Socialist* (1912). Some specialist studies illustrate aspects of the work or background of Christian Socialism: W. G. Roe, *Lamennais and England. The Reception of Lamennais's Religious Ideas in the Nineteenth Century* (Oxford, 1966); J. F. C. Harrison, *A History of the Working Men's College, 1854–1954* (London, 1954), and *The Early Victorians, 1832–51* (London,

1971); Geoffrey Rowell, *Hell and the Victorians. A study of the nineteenth century theological controversies concerning eternal punishment and the future life* (Oxford, 1974). For contemporary observations on the social conditions which the Christian Socialists criticized, and for occasional references to the position of religion in working-class society, see Frederick Engels, *The Condition of the Working Class in England*, ed. W. O. Henderson and W. H. Chaloner (Oxford, 1958); F. C. Mather (ed.), *Chartism and Society. An Anthology of Documents* (London, 1980); *An Anthology of Chartist Literature* (Foreign Publishing House: Moscow, 1956); Henry Mayhew, *London Labour and the London Poor* (2 vols., 1851; 4 vols., 1861–2), and an abridgment, ed. Peter Quennell (London, 1969); Andrew Mearns, *Bitter Cry of Outcast London* (pub. anonymously, London, 1883); William Booth, *In Darkest England and the Way Out* (London, 1890).

F. D. Maurice

The standard biography of Maurice, by his son, like so many other Victorian productions of its sort, is most useful for the letters it reproduces: Frederick Maurice, *The Life of Frederick Denison Maurice* (second edn., London, 1884). Alec Vidler has written the most about Maurice's life and works, and his assessments are both acute and balanced: *The Theology of F. D. Maurice* (London, 1948), *Witness to the Light. F. D. Maurice's Message for Today* (New York, 1948), and *F. D. Maurice and Company. Nineteenth Century Studies* (London, 1966). The most recent historical study, by Frank McClain, *Maurice. Man and Moralist* (London, 1972), is excellent. A rather dated work is Claude Jenkins, *Frederick Denison Maurice and the New Reformation* (London, 1938). Of Maurice's rather large output of writings, the most important – from the perspective of the present study – is *The Kingdom of Christ or Hints to a Quaker Respecting the Principles, Constitution and Ordinances of the Catholic Church*. Originally published in 1838, it is most accessible in the edition of 1958 (London, ed. A. R. Vidler) which is itself based on the second edition of 1842. Of Maurice's social writings, or works which had implications for his social attitudes, see: *Eustace Conway: or, The Brother and Sister. A Novel* (London, 1834); *Subscription No Bondage* (Oxford, 1835); *Reasons for Not Joining a Party in the Church* (London, 1841); the Introduction to William Law, *Remarks on the Fable of the Bees* (Cambridge, 1844); *The Epistle to the Hebrews* (Preface, with a review of Newman's *Theory of Development*) (London, 1846); *The Religions of the World and their Relations to Christianity* (London, 1847); *The Lord's Prayer* (London, 1848); *The Prayer Book Considered Especially in Reference to the Romish System* (London, 1849); *Reasons for Co-operation. A Lecture Delivered at the Office for Promoting Working Men's Associations* (London, 1851); *The Reformation of Society and How all Classes may contribute to it* (London, 1851); *Sermons on the Sabbath Day, on the Character of the Warrior, and on the Interpretation of History* (London, 1853); *National Education* (London, 1853); *Learning and Working* (Cambridge, 1855); *Administrative Reform and its connexion with Working Men's Colleges* (Cambridge, 1855); *The Indian Crisis* (Cambridge, 1857); *The Epistle of St. John. A Series of Lectures on Christian Ethics* (Cambridge, 1857); *The Suffrage, Considered in Reference to the Working Class, and to the Professional Class*, in *Macmillans Magazine*, II, No. 8 (June 1860); *The Workman and the Franchise, Chapters from English History on the Representation and Education of the People* (London, 1866); 'Do Kings reign by the Grace of God?', in *Tracts for Priests and People*, II (1860–1); *The Commandments, Considered as*

Instruments of National Reformation (London, 1866); *The Conflict of Good and Evil in our Day* (London, 1865); *The Conscience. Lectures on Casuistry* (London, 1868); *The Ground and Object of Hope for Mankind* (London, 1868); and *Social Morality* (London, 1869).

Charles Kingsley

Due to the ideological preferences in his wife's editing of his letters, the official biography of Kingsley gives a very imperfect impression of his life and ideas: *Charles Kingsley: His Letters and Memories of his Life* (London, 1876). The deficiencies, however, can in some areas be corrected through reference to some good modern works. The most perceptive are Susan Chitty, *The Beast and the Monk. A Life of Charles Kingsley* (London, 1974); Una Pope-Hennessy, *Canon Charles Kingsley, A Biography* (London, 1948); and Brenda Colloms, *Charles Kingsley. The Lion of Eversley* (London, 1975). It is also helpful to consult Margaret F. Thorp, *Charles Kingsley, 1819–1875* (Princeton, 1937); Stanley E. Baldwin, *Charles Kingsley* (Ithaca, 1934); Guy Kendall, *Charles Kingsley and his Ideas* (London, 1947); A. J. Hartley, *The Novels of Charles Kingsley. A Christian Social Interpretation* (Folkestone, 1977); C. W. Stubbs, *Charles Kingsley and the Christian Social Movement* (London, 1899); Elspeth Huxley, *The Kingsleys. A Biographical Anthology* (London, 1973); Colwyn E. Vulliamy, *Charles Kingsley and Christian Socialism* (Fabian Tract No. 174, London, 1914); and R. B. Martin, *The Dust of Combat. A Life of Charles Kingsley* (London, 1959). Of Kingsley's novels, those with the largest and most informative social content are *Yeast. A Problem* (1848); *Alton Locke* (1850); *Hypatia* (1853); *Westward Ho!* (1855); and *Two Years Ago* (1857). The most important of his social writings is *Cheap Clothes and Nasty* (by 'Parson Lot', London, 1850). Other works with social themes include: *The Saint's Tragedy; or, The True Story of Elizabeth of Hungary* (London, 1848); *Three Lectures on the Ancien Régime* (London, 1867); *The Limits of Exact Science as Applied to History* (Cambridge, 1860); *Health and Education* (London, 1874); *Who are the Friends of Order? A Reply to certain observations in a late number of 'Fraser's Magazine' on the so-called 'Christian Socialists'* (London, 1852); *Village Sermons* (London, 1849); *Sermons on National Subjects* (London, 1852, 1854); and *Sermons for the Times* (London, 1855).

J. M. Ludlow

Ludlow wrote a very lengthy and unpublished autobiography, and it has recently been well edited and shortened by A. D. Murray: *John Ludlow. The Autobiography of a Christian Socialist* (London, 1981). This must be the starting-point for any enquiry into Ludlow's ideas. There is also a very useful modern biography: N. C. Masterman, *John Malcolm Ludlow. The Builder of Christian Socialism* (Cambridge, 1963). The most important of Ludlow's writings are 'Labour and the Poor' (by 'John Townsend'), in *Fraser's Magazine*, XLI (January 1850); and *Progress of the Working Class, 1832–1867* (London, 1867). This book was written in collaboration with Lloyd Jones; all but the first twenty-five pages are by Ludlow, however. Other aspects of Ludlow's social interests can be seen in *British India, Its Races and Its History* (Cambridge, 1858); *Thoughts on the Policy of the Crown towards India* (London, 1859); and *Woman's Work in the Church. Historical Notes on Deaconesses and Sisterhoods* (London, 1865). Some of Ludlow's most influential contributions were made in Christian Socialist serial publications: see 'The Suffrage', I–VI, in *Politics for the People* (6 May to 10 June 1848); 'The People', in *Politics* (13 May 1848); 'Politics', in *Politics* (20 May 1848); 'Party Portraits', I–IV, in *Politics* (27 May to 15 July 1848); 'Rights and Duties', in *Politics* (3 June 1848); 'Government', in *Politics* (10 June 1848); 'The Ballot', I–II, in *Politics* (17 June, 1 July 1848); 'Qualification and Payment of Members, and Duration of Parliament', in *Politics* (8 July 1848); 'Electoral Districts and the Representation of Minorities', in *Politics* (15 July 1848); 'The Principle of the Poor Laws', in *Politics* (15 July 1848); and 'The Great Partnership', in *Politics* (July Supplement, 1848). *Working Associations of Paris,* and *Prevailing Idolatries – Political Economy* are Nos. IV and VI in *Tracts on Christian Socialism* (1850). See also 'A Dialogue on Doubt', in *Tracts for Priests and People,* VI (Cambridge, 1861).

Thomas Hughes

There is a good life of Hughes by Edward C. Mack and W. H. G. Armytage: *Thomas Hughes* (London, 1952). Interesting references to him can be found in David Newsome, *Godliness and Good Learning. Four Studies on a Victorian Ideal* (London, 1961); Norman Vance, *The Sinews of the Spirit. The Ideal of Christian Manliness in Victorian Literature and Religious Thought* (Cambridge, 1985); and J. A. Mangan, *Athleticism in the Victorian and Edwardian Public School* (Cambridge, 1981). Hughes' religious thought is best explained in his *Religio Laici,* in *Tracts for Priests and People,* I (Cambridge, 1861). His values and moral seriousness emerged with great clarity in the judgments made of others in the biographical studies of his later years: see *David Livingstone* (London, 1889); *James Fraser, Second Bishop of Manchester. A Memoir* (London, 1887); and *Memoir of Daniel Macmillan* (London, 1882). The two Tom Brown novels, and especially the second, are full of social comment: *Tom Brown's School Days, (by An Old Boy)* (London, 1857), and *Tom Brown at Oxford* (Cambridge, 1861). Hughes' advocacy of rural society and its pursuits is best seen in *The Scouring of the White Horse; or The Long Vacation Ramble of a London Clerk* (Cambridge, 1859). Hughes' chief social studies are *The Old Church; What shall we do with it?* (London, 1878); *The Manliness of Christ* (London, 1879); *Rugby, Tennessee, being some Account of the Settlement founded on the Cumberland Plateau by the Board of Aid to Land Ownership, Limited* (London, 1881); and *Memoir of a Brother* (second edn., London 1873). Hughes also wrote the preface to Edward Neale's *Manual for Co-operators, Prepared at the Request of the Co-operative Congress Held at Gloucester in April, 1879; and Revised 1888* (Manchester, 1888). Reference should also be made to Hughes' 'Prefatory Memoir' to Charles Kingsley's *Alton Locke* (London, 1881 edition): it is a history of the Christian Socialism of the mid-century.

Stewart Headlam

F. G. Bettany's *Stewart Headlam: A Biography* (London, 1926) is a fair account, but it is unhappily rather allusive in places, and sometimes very imprecise about references. There is a good essay by Kenneth Leech in *For Christ and the People. Studies of four Socialist Priests and Prophets of the Church of England between 1870 and 1930,* ed. Maurice Reckitt (London, 1968), which repairs some of the gaps. Headlam's chief social and moral writings were: *The Church Catechism and the Emancipation of Labour* (London, 1875); *The*

Sure Foundation. An Address Given before the Guild of St. Matthew (London, 1883); *The Doubts of the Faithful Sceptic the Confirmation of True Theology* (London, 1875); *Christian Socialism* (Fabian Tract No. 42, 1892); *The Service of Humanity and Other Sermons* (London, 1882); *The Meaning of the Mass. Five Lectures with other Sermons and Addresses* (London, 1905); *The Place of the Bible in Secular Education. An Open Letter to the Teachers under the London School Board* (London, 1903); and *Priestcraft and Progress* (London, 1878). For Headlam's principal speeches at Church Congresses, see *The Official Report of the Church Congress held at Leicester, 1880* (London, 1881), p. 650; *The Official Report of the Church Congress held at Reading, 1883* (London, 1883, 428); and *The Official Report of the Church Congress held at Wolverhampton, 1887* (London, 1887), p. 174.

John Ruskin

So much has been written about Ruskin – and even about Ruskin solely as a social critic – that selection is difficult. Ruskin's own works comprise an edition of thirty-nine volumes (ed. E. T. Cook and A. Wedderburn (London, 1903–12)). There have been numerous biographical and critical studies. It may perhaps be best to start with the two latest: the introduction by Clive Wilmer to his edition of *Unto this Last and Other Writings of John Ruskin* (London, 1985), and the first volume (the second has yet to appear) of Tim Hilton's *John Ruskin, The Early Years, 1819–1859* (Yale, 1985). Both are excellent. Reference should be made to Sir E. T. Cook's *The Life of John Ruskin* (second edn., London, 1912), which is still the standard biography, and to Derrick Leon, *Ruskin. The Great Victorian* (London, 1949); Robert Hewison, *John Ruskin. The Argument of the Eye* (London, 1976); and Joan Evans, *John Ruskin* (London, 1954). For specialist studies of Ruskin's social and political beliefs, see Bernard Shaw, *Ruskin's Politics* (London, 1921); J. A. Hobson, *John Ruskin, Social Reformer* (London, 1898); F. W. Roe, *The Social Philosophy of Carlyle and Ruskin* (Port Washington, 1921); B. E. Lippincott, *Victorian Critics of Democracy* (Minneapolis, 1938); and Peter Quennell, *John Ruskin. The Portrait of a Prophet* (London, 1949). Ruskin's own autobiography, *Praeterita*, published between 1885 and 1889, was re-issued by Oxford in 1978 with an introduction by Kenneth Clark. It is remarkable for its exclusions. Of Ruskin's works, those which contain the most social criticism are: *The Seven Lamps of Architecture* (1849); *Notes on the Construction of Sheepfolds* (1851); *The Stones of Venice*, II and III (1853); 'The Political Economy of Art' (1857) – published as *A Joy for Ever; Modern Painters*, V (1860); *Unto this Last* (1862); *Munera Pulveris* (1863); *Sesame and Lilies* (1865); *The Crown of Wild Olive* (1866); *Time and Tide by Weare and Tyne. Twenty-five letters to a Working Man of Sunderland on the Laws of Work* (1867); *Fors Clavigera* (1871–84); *The Lord's Prayer and the Church. Letters to the Clergy* (1880); *The Storm Cloud of the Nineteenth Century* (1884); and *On the Old Road. A Collection of Miscellaneous Essays, Pamphlets etc.* (1885).

Hugh Price Hughes

The main biography is by his daughter: D. P. Hughes, *The Life of Hugh Price Hughes* (London, 1904). It is very imprecise and uncritical. J. Gregory Mantle, *Hugh Price Hughes* (London, 1901), is similar. Both books, however, give a sound enough account of the outline of events of Price Hughes' life. The best source for detailed observations on the social movements of his years at the West London Mission is the *Methodist Times* (from 1885). His classic works on social and moral theory are: *Social Christianity: Sermons Delivered in St. James's Hall, London* (London, 1889); *The Philanthropy of God: Described and Illustrated in a Series of Sermons* (London, 1890); *Ethical Christianity. A Series of Sermons* (London, 1892); and *Essential Christianity. A Series of Explanatory Sermons* (London, 1894). There are occasional references to English social issues in his published travel notes of a visit to the eastern Mediterranean, *The Morning Lands of History* (London, 1901).

[handwritten notes]

Brooke Foss Westcott

The official biography, by Westcott's son, is rather selective and relates little, for example, about the early life; but it remains valuable for the reproduction of letters: Arthur Westcott, *Life and Letters of Brooke Foss Westcott* (London, 1903). It can be supplemented with Joseph Clayton, *Bishop Westcott* (London, 1906), and A. G. B. West, *Memories of Brooke Foss Westcott* (Cambridge, 1936), which in some ways offers the most telling, if unconscious, insights. There is a good section on Westcott in David L. Edwards, *Leaders of the Church of England, 1828–1944* (London, 1971). There are also some excellent contributions to the Westcott Memorial Lectures series: Owen Chadwick, *Westcott and the University* (Cambridge, 1962); Geoffrey Best, *Bishop Westcott and the Miners* (Cambridge, 1966); and David Newsome, *Bishop Westcott and the Platonic Tradition* (Cambridge, 1968). Westcott's main social writings are: *Social Aspects of Christianity* (London, 1887); *Christian Union for the Promotion of Simultaneous Disarmament* (London, 1889); *Socialism* (London, 1890) – also in *The Official Report of the Church Congress held at Hull* (London, 1890), p. 320; *The Gospel of Life* (London, 1892); *The Incarnation and the Common Life* (London, 1893); *Christian Aspects of Life* (London, 1897); *Lessons From Work* (London, 1901); *An Address at the Annual Service for Miners* (London, 1901); and *Christian Social Union Addresses* (London, 1903). This last work reproduces addresses given between 1894 and 1900, and was published after Westcott's death; many are also to be found in his earlier collections of sermons and addresses – *Christian Aspects of Life*, for example.

INDEX